Modern Luck

Radium luck

Modern Luck

Narratives of fortune in the long twentieth century

Robert S. C. Gordon

First published in 2023 by
UCL Press
University College London
Gower Street
London WC1E 6BT

Available to download free: www.uclpress.co.uk

Text © Author, 2023

The author has asserted his rights under the Copyright, Designs and Patents Act 1988 to be identified as the author of this work.

A CIP catalogue record for this book is available from The British Library.

Any third-party material in this book is not covered by the book's Creative Commons licence. Details of the copyright ownership and permitted use of third-party material is given in the image (or extract) credit lines. If you would like to reuse any third-party material not covered by the book's Creative Commons licence, you will need to obtain permission directly from the copyright owner.

This book is published under a Creative Commons Attribution-Non-Commercial 4.0 International licence (CC BY-NC 4.0), https://creativecommons.org/licenses/by-nc/4.0/. This licence allows you to share and adapt the work for non-commercial use providing attribution is made to the author and publisher (but not in any way that suggests that they endorse you or your use of the work) and any changes are indicated. Attribution should include the following information:

Gordon, R.S.C. 2023. *Modern Luck: Narratives of fortune in the long twentieth century*. London: UCL Press. https://doi.org/10.14324/111.9781800083592

Further details about Creative Commons licences are available at
https://creativecommons.org/licenses/

ISBN: 978-1-80008-361-5 (Hbk)
ISBN: 978-1-80008-360-8 (Pbk)
ISBN: 978-1-80008-359-2 (PDF)
ISBN: 978-1-80008-362-2 (epub)
DOI: https://doi.org/10.14324.111.9781800083592

Printed and bound by CPI Group (UK) Ltd, Croydon, CR0 4YY

To Jill and Lionel

Contents

Preface		ix
Part I		**1**
1	Something old, something new	3
2	Word trees and etymologies	17
Part II		**37**
3	Lucky numbers	39
4	Lucky places, lucky lines	58
5	The luckiest man	77
6	Moral luck and the survivor	97
7	Luck and the low life	120
8	Early style and child's play	136
Afterword		153
References		159
Index		169

Preface

This book has taken shape over a number of years – too many years – and it began in a dark place. As I was working in the early 2000s on the remarkable Holocaust writer and survivor Primo Levi, I noticed how often he turned to an idea of luck or good fortune as part of his 'explanation' for the awful suffering that had befallen him at Auschwitz and for the impossibly improbable fact of his survival. Levi was a marvellously articulate and sensitive thinker about so many aspects of his own history and that of millions like him, and his probing of the role of luck was no exception. But my second realization was that he was far from alone: every Holocaust survivor I read or heard seemed to return to the theme, insistently, anxiously. Every story of survival was a story of good luck. I began to wonder about the implications of this beyond the concentration camps and hiding places of the Second World War. If, as many have posited, the Holocaust encapsulated some dark essence of modernity, and if luck was such a persistent trope in stories told about it, was there some underlying tie that bound luck, or stories told about luck, to modernity? This is the question that lies at the heart of this book. Although it turns to the Holocaust more than once, in particular in Chapter 6, it deliberately goes out of its way to step beyond it, to explore over the course of its eight chapters the role of luck and luck stories across as broad a canvas as I could paint of the literary, cinematic and cultural field from the late nineteenth century to the early twenty-first, the 'long twentieth century' of my subtitle. I also took the decision to step outside the narrow confines of my own specialist field, Italian literature and cinema (although I draw regularly on this too), in order to tap into the wider (indeed universal) resonances and affective pull of this short simple word, luck, which pervades so much of our self-perception and underpins so many of the stories we tell about our own lives, the fictions that accompany it. This has made the work on the book challenging, for sure, but also consistently enriching and pleasurable, a genuine journey of discovery as I tapped into the energy that this concept seems to transmit to all those who have tackled it, myself included. The shadow of the dark place where I started, however, never quite went away. Luck stories are not only stories with happy endings, after all; they are also reminders of the fragility and danger that always lie only a moment away. Just as I was finishing the book, war broke out over the very same area of Eastern Europe that Levi and his few companions travelled across in 1945, on their long and unlikely journey home.

All the time spent on this book has left me with too many people to thank properly for their help, advice and patience. I have presented work-in-progress and received precious feedback in various forums: a public lecture hosted by the Centro studi internazionale Primo Levi, Turin (thanks to Fabio Levi and Domenico Scarpa), followed by lectures at the Stockholm Italian Cultural Institute (thanks to Paolo Grossi), the University of Notre Dame (thanks to Zyg Baranski) and Edge Hill University (thanks to George Talbot); a public lecture at the National Library of New Zealand, jointly hosted by the departments of History and Italian at Victoria University, Wellington (thanks to Giacomo Lichtner); a keynote lecture at the Society of Italian Studies Biennial Conference in Oxford (thanks to Martin McLaughlin); the Bickley Memorial Lecture at St Hugh's College, Oxford (thanks to Giuseppe Stellardi); a conference on 'Literature and Contingency', at Warwick University in Venice (thanks to Tina Lupton); a talk at home to the Cambridge University Italian department research seminar. I was lucky indeed, finally, to be able to finish the book manuscript and present its findings during my time as Visiting Scholar at Ca' Foscari, University of Venice (thanks to Alessandro Cinquegrani and Simon Levis Sullam). Early versions of some of the approaches and readings in the book, all thoroughly revised and reshaped here, were published as: *'Sfacciata fortuna': La Shoah e il caso* (Turin: Einaudi, 2010); 'Turns of chance: Modern luck and Italian modernism', in Guido Bonsaver, Brian Richardson and Giuseppe Stellardi, eds, *Cultural Reception, Translation and Transformation from Medieval to Modern Italy* (Oxford: Legenda, 2017), pp. 257–71; and 'Luck stories: Stress-testing contingency and agency in post-war American literature', *Textual Practice*, 32.4 (2018): 509–27.

My warm thanks are also due to Florian Mussgnug, one of the UCL Press 'Comparative Literature and Culture' series editors, and to Chris Penfold, Sue Leigh, Glynis Baguley, Martin Hargreaves and others at UCL Press, as well as to two anonymous readers; to all my colleagues in the Italian department at Cambridge, especially Abi Brundin and J. D. Rhodes for their friendship during a very fruitful period of leave spent in Rome in 2021; to Rachel Plunkett, April McIntyre and Geoffrey Kantaris, for keeping me sane when all thoughts of luck were forgotten during two crazy Covid years as co-chair of my faculty in Cambridge; and to Pierpaolo Antonello, Ann Caesar, Julian Ferraro, Simone Ghelli, the late Norman Geras, Vittorio Montemaggi, David Porter, Guido Vitiello, Heather Webb and others for conversations and suggestions.

Although they may be surprised to hear it, the book would not have been possible without my family, B, B and L, who must have wondered what I'd been up to. The book is dedicated to Jill and Lionel, for a lifetime of love and support.

Un coup de dés jamais n'abolira le hasard
('A throw of the dice can never cancel chance')
                    (Stéphane Mallarmé, 'Un coup de dés', 1897)

Of all the gin joints in all the towns in all the world, she walks into mine
                                        (*Casablanca*, 1942)

I'm feeling lucky
                              (www.google.com, 1998–)

Part I

1
Something old, something new

Luck is all around us.[1] There is a certain school of cultural anthropology that is intent on tracking the structures, categories and beliefs that recur across all human societies, transcending the profound differences in history and culture that separate them. This school of ambitious universalists – which is by no mean uncontroversial, both within the field of anthropology and beyond – seems to be looking for something like the cultural core of what it is to be human, perhaps even for hints of a deep genetic matrix for human consciousness itself. One of the most influential among them, Donald Brown, produced a compendium of these phenomena in a book of 1991, and in among his four hundred or so instances of what he calls these 'human universals', we find 'beliefs about fortune and misfortune'.[2] In other words, beliefs about luck.

I have little doubt that that every single reader of this book has an instant, intuitive and relatively untroubled sense of knowing what I mean when I talk about luck, a notion so familiar, so pervasive and so usefully loose and plural in its meanings as to constitute no less than the very stuff of (almost) everything that happens to us in our lives.[3] Luck can be good or bad, can be mapped onto anything and everything that befalls us ('falling' is a motif knottily tangled up with our cultural conceptions and lexicon of luck, as we shall see), without our knowing quite why. Luck is a relatively free hit, too: we can evoke it on any number of occasions and for any number of reasons, as a consolation, as a celebration, as a declaration of (false?) modesty, as an explanation of how things we have not understood have come to pass, and of how we feel about them: 'just my luck!', 'it was a lucky break', 'hard luck', 'my luck was in'. It designates an event in our lives and an affect attached to the event. It is malleable, meaningful, touching, accessible and, as Brown tells us, ubiquitous.

But luck is also nowhere and nothing at all. At some level, just beyond the easy everyday recourse to it and our shared intuitive sense that it shapes everything that happens to us, we know that luck is a shorthand for nothing very much, a nonsense or a fantasy, an empty vessel or at best a placeholder for and a deflection away from more troubling and more complex matters about human lives. If luck comes to mean more or less everything that happens to us, it is hard to say that it means anything at all. Its contours are *too* loose. Science, mathematics and philosophy, among other things, can come to our aid to a degree by defining and conceptualizing many of luck's sister terms or cognate concepts – such as chance, contingency, randomness, probability and others – but those disciplines and their epistemologies tend to tread much more gingerly around our baggy notion of luck. After all, we know, most of us, at least in our more rational moments – not, say, when we are about to throw the dice or lay a bet at a roulette table – that there is in fact no agency nor substance to luck, no feature of the (non-fantastical) phenomenal world that we can label luck, no hard concept that constitutes it as such, and no attribute of luckiness that is anything other than imaginary. And yet we are tempted again and again, against our better judgement, to act as it if were so. The energy of its attraction, its fantastical pull, is perhaps better probed by psychoanalysts and psychologists than by mathematicians or philosophers. It is at best a belief (Brown's universal is carefully couched in this regard, as belonging to a category of *beliefs*), a tenuous but powerful fantasy that the world is somehow biased, influenced in its outcomes regarding myself and others, in a way that is beyond the purely random, either in general as a state of being or personhood, or at any given moment and in any given action (e.g. the dice throw). Worse, perhaps it is something less even than a belief; it is often no more than an intuition, that feeling of a moment. This was well captured by 'Dirty' Harry Callahan, eponymous hero of *Dirty Harry* (dir. Don Siegel, 1971) and one of the more iconic and violent deities in the modern luck pantheon, as he pointed his Magnum in the face of an unfortunate (unlucky) hoodlum: 'You've got to ask yourself a question: "Do I feel lucky?" … Well, do you, punk?' Philosophers have debated the extent to which Harry or the hoodlum in that moment *knows* how many bullets are left in the chamber of the gun and so how clean the call-out to luck is in this stand-off, and what it means for the film's politics and morals and more.[4] But what is not in doubt is the sheer material force of the question. In the barrel of his gun, Callahan has materialized an idea of luck out of nothing at all into a brutal and fatal reality.

The human universal of belief in luck can be tracked not only with an anthropologist's eye on the rich variety and underlying affinities of human cultures in our world today, but also across the whole of human history and prehistory. There are vast bodies of ancient traditions of beliefs, talismans, religious and magical practices (religion and magic feature multiply in Brown's list, and in all talk of luck) focussed obsessively on turning the violent uncertainties of the world towards propitious outcomes, harnessing contingency towards a lucky end and keeping bad luck at bay. These practices are elemental and primal, a matter of life and death, since warding off bad luck most often and immediately means warding off illness, starvation, violence or death; and attempting to attract the blessings of good luck most likely means dreaming of the birth of a child, the acquisition of wealth or simply enough food to survive, or perhaps even love and happiness. Luck practices look and have always looked to the essence of the good life, the life lived well or badly, not so much in the moral sense as in the material sense. Indeed, luck has a particularly awkward and thus fertile relationship with both morality and economy, as we will see repeatedly in this book.

All these practices and traditions have produced a remarkably rich iconography and material culture of luck, and these have left traces in the archaeological and historical record across the world, as well as in residual everyday beliefs. And they have also, crucially for our purposes here, bequeathed us their stories, legends and myths. The best-known stories of luck, in the Western tradition at least, centre on the deities of classical and ancient religion – 'Tyche' for the Greeks, 'Fortuna' for the Romans – and their associated visual culture.[5] It would be an impossible, or an impossibly lengthy, task to attempt to survey these classical traditions in full, but we can turn for an illuminating synthesis, literally a visual snapshot, to the great German collector and iconologist Aby Warburg and his extraordinary unfinished project of the late 1920s, the *Mnemosyne Atlas*.[6] In his *Atlas*, Warburg attempted to collate and collect in a series of multiple-image panels the deep iconography of Western imagination and myth from the classical world to the Renaissance. A key panel in his project, panel 48, was on 'Fortuna', for Warburg the very image of man's early modern self-liberation. Panel 48 is made up of 32 images containing motifs, talismans and archetypes from this millennial tradition, and also, as its interpreters have noted, an evolving picture of Fortuna's field of operation, its shifting sites, dynamics and defining ground as the 'pagan' evolved into the 'Christian' and from there, as Warburg and his contemporaries saw it, into the autonomous subject and cultural forms of the Renaissance.[7] Present among the cluster are Fortuna as a goddess turning the wheel of fate, from high to low, low to high, blind and indifferent, but all-powerful; Fortuna holding a two-headed staff, or a horn of plenty, the cornucopia, or showering coins onto her subjects;

Fortuna with a protruding forelock of hair, representing an opportunity to be seized, grabbed at, boldly and violently (associated with the Greek *kairos* or Latin *occasio*); or Fortuna as a ship on the sea in the storm of events (Romance languages retain this association in terms such as *fortune de mer*, French for a sea disaster, and the Italian *fortunale*, a tempest), or at the tiller or prow, holding a sail against the wind, turning the very fate of the world. Coming out of these latter multiple maritime motifs, Warburg saw signals of a new agency for modern (here, Renaissance) man alongside the all-powerful goddess, man as merchant navigating at sea, trading and conquering lands and peoples, searching for 'fortune'. Shakespeare too tapped into the force of the maritime imagery, not least in these famous lines from *Julius Caesar*:

> There is a tide in the affairs of men
> Which, taken at the flood, leads on to fortune;
> Omitted, all the voyage of their life
> Is bound in shallows and in miseries.
> On such a full sea are we now afloat,
> And we must take the current when it serves,
> Or lose our ventures.[8]

All these figures and icons from ancient myth and religion are matched in variety and force by any number of ancient superstitions and magical beliefs centred on luck, many of which survive in some form into the present day, in the form of culture or folklore. Take the examples of the curse of bad luck brought by the *malocchio* or *iettatura*, the evil-eye curse, in southern Italian folklore, or the many propitious talismans of good luck, from horseshoes to four-leaved clovers in Northern European and Celtic traditions, to Japanese *maneki-neko* cat figurines, or indeed the comic figure in Yiddish tales of the fool, the *schlemiel* or the *schlimazel*, the person whose luck has bent out of shape ('mazel' is both a Hebrew and a Yiddish term for luck).[9] No less than Tyche or Fortuna, these figures and objects embody or materialize luck good or bad and drive the energy of stories, tales, legends – or rather cycles of stories, tales or legends – that are elaborated around them. In this light, we can refine the loose link that was posited above between luck and all the various stuff that happens in human lives into something a little tighter: luck is a happenstance that invites a story to be told, about you, me or us, a story to be shared, to be told once and then again and again. This point about the bond between luck and storytelling, and the seriality of luck stories, is a crucial one, since it points to how luck establishes its easy familiarity, creates types that spill over beyond the boundaries of any single event or tale, or any single one of us. And it also draws a direct and powerful link between older forms of storytelling, such as the folktale and myth, and newer forms of storytelling, in particular the novel, which in its modern form was born in serial sequence.[10] The hero of the modern novel is far detached from the types who populate folktale traditions, but they share a shape of seriality, an episodic pattern of events than run on from other events, which resonates strongly with the luck stories of old. (We will see in Chapter 8 how richly this shape also persists into the modern offspring of the folktale, the children's story.) To turn again to words, the semantic field shared by words such as adventure, venture, even simply event itself, which drives so much of narrative as a universal force, as well as the historically contingent birth of the modern novel, comes close to and at times intersects precisely with the field of luck and chance and happenstance (cf. Latin *venire*, to come, to happen).

'High' and 'low', then, both among the gods of ancient myth and among the humble folk of popular tales; across this spectrum the luck of what the world throws at us as human beings has been processed variously and richly into figures, beliefs and, crucially, stories. High and low stories represent equally powerfully figures of a *Weltanschauung*, a philosophy and a vision of the world, inherent in the stories of what happens in that world, the luck of the world, as Antonio Gramsci argued with force in his *Prison Notebooks,* when he reclaimed folklore as a form of popular philosophical thinking, as a sedimented 'conception of the world and of life'.[11]

Gramsci, for sure, would want nothing to do with the conservatism of the transversal and the transhistorical, with the static fixity of the universal, if being universal necessarily means permanence and immunity to change. The high and low forms of luck, their icons, traditions and stories, are not the same across time and place, nor indeed is any one culture's manifestation of its beliefs in luck identical to any other's. Luck may be universal, but it does not stand still. We might argue along with the evolutionists about whether or not cultural change takes place in smooth and infinitesimal gradual steps or whether there is a kind of 'punctuated equilibrium', which means that sudden external changes in prevailing conditions dramatically shift the ground beneath the feet of any given cultural category or idea.[12] But it seems plausible to suggest that paradigm shifts in societies and cultures bring with them, or at least open breaches that allow, paradigm shifts in their constituent, transversally universal elements, and that these two shifting plates are mutually impactful. It is a core working hypothesis of this book that our modernity represents one of those shifts, and that, whatever we may mean by that slippery term 'modernity', it has brought with it, along with many other profound changes, new paradigms of luck and of modern luck stories.

To capture this fluidity in cultural change, as it flows over and remoulds apparently permanent strata of human intuition and belief, we can go back to Aby Warburg and his *Mnemosyne Atlas*. Several of the icons in panel 48 were, as we saw, precisely intent on capturing a striking transformation or moment of modernization as, in Warburg's conception, a maritime Fortuna encapsulated the geography and worldview of a newly dominant, mercantile Renaissance ethos. This adapted iconography was consonant with a new imaginary and a new capitalist (and, we might add, colonialist) economy. It might not be too far-fetched to suggest that Warburg himself, working in the 1920s in Hamburg, recalling his studies in Italy, was also tapping into new, looming shifts in his own twentieth-century modernity, a dark modernity that would in due course threaten his legacy, his Jewish family and, until its removal to London in 1933, four years after Warburg's death, his library, as well as displace once again the paradigm of fortune in the world. (We will see in Chapter 6 how the Holocaust marked a point of fracture in the modern mythology of luck.)

Modern luck stories, then, spill over into and evolve alongside figures of modernity and its storytelling forms. Indeed, they help tell us what modernity, and perhaps particularly the human experience of modernity, have been in imagination and affect. Modern luck stories are open (possibly even democratic) and pliable tools for stress-testing the modern, just as they have been, throughout human history and prehistory, tools for navigating all our ancestors' older worlds and older beliefs. In practice, however, this distinction between old and new is a little too neat; rather, just as they can be vessels for both local and universal beliefs, luck stories are more plausibly to be read as tools for tracing the borderline between the old and the new, for stress-testing the viability of older, inherited forms of knowledge of ourselves as individuals, as communities, as a species, in the face of the new. It is an archaeology of luck stories that we need, then, as well as a narratology, if we are to probe the nature of modern luck, since few of the motifs and icons from the ancient traditions seem to disappear entirely. Indeed, as we will see along the way in this book, the recurring presence of ships, coins, blindfolds, lucky and unlucky fools, women (or 'ladies'), in even the most modern of modern luck stories, confirms their persistent 'afterlives' (a crucial concept for Warburg, often cited in his original German, *Nachleben*) in the modern.[13]

What remains of these old luck talismans and tales, these stories ask – and we can ask in turn of these stories – when luck puts on its modern guise?

It might be objected with some validity that all belief systems and their related cultural forms undergo shifts, recalibrations and hybridizations over time as they evolve into new versions of themselves, so why lay particular emphasis on our experience of the current modernity, whether that is conceived of as a post-Enlightenment arc or a long-twentieth-century phenomenon? But there is a particular reason why questions about luck and luck stories bear telling weight in relation to *this* modernity: it is in this period that the forces of capitalism, secularization, democracy and the rise of positivistic and probabilistic sciences combine, in large parts of Europe and the West at least, to dismantle systematically – at least apparently and on the surface – the paradigmatic force of life's fortune as understood through religion, belief in God, fate or destiny on the one hand, and the magical power of everyday superstition and ritual to influence it, on the other. This is the shift captured in Max Weber's influential notion of the 'disenchantment' of the world in the wake of Protestant modernity, or in another compelling phrase, this time from historian and philosopher of science Ian Hacking, in 'the taming of chance', by way of the emergence of the scientific method, rationalism and the numerical determinism of statistics as an instrument of state and civil society in the nineteenth century.[14] But if we look across the long twentieth century and around us in the early twenty-first, it is certain that we do not live in a cool, dry world of hyper-rational calculation, particularly not when it comes to individual lives and human choices, hence Mr Spock's recurrent disappointment with the messy emotions and half-baked decision-making of his space-travelling human companions in the narrative cycle of *Star Trek*. The *universal* survival of old luck beliefs, their afterlives, the persistence deep into the modern age of a fascination with the unknowable mysteries of pure happenstance, and the occult forces that lie behind it, is one of those abiding irritants, a fly in the ointment that reminds us that modernity is rather more complex, 'enchanted' and old than we might have thought. The shock of the new and the shock of the old co-exist – or rather, the shock of the old in the face of the new – and they merge across a varicoloured spectrum.[15] Modern luck stories are brilliant prisms that allow us to demerge, refract and recreate these constituent elements.

Something old, something new, then; and we might gloss further, something fast, something slow. 'Thinking, fast and slow' was an influential formulation coined by psychologist Daniel Kahneman to summarize his work with Amos Tversky on the array of intuitive ('fast') cognitive biases and 'heuristics' in the human mind that clash with slower, more deliberative and more systematic processes.[16] Assumptions about luck come to us fast and first, we might say with Kahneman, but co-exist with our slower calculations of cause and effect, probability and morality, and many luck stories delve into the awkward clash this two-speed co-existence throws up.

This dual dynamic also taps into a further aspect of the high–low spectrum noted above (something high, something low, perhaps), where luck was seen in relation to scales and registers of literature or storytelling. Here, instead, the high–low polarity can be filtered through social scale or class. The tradition of luck mythology, starting from its founding iconography, was inherently bound up with luck as a rising up on high or a falling off down low: the wheel turned by the goddess Fortuna was a vision of great men or kings laid low by a simple twist of fate; and conversely, the original hero of the modern novel was the young man (invariably a man) from humble stock thrust into the modern arena to make his mark, climb the ladder, make his fortune. He does so through a mixture of talent and circumstance, an echo of Machiavelli in *The Prince*, who argued for the need to train the prince's 'virtue', meaning his talents and skills as a leader, as a force to resist and tame 'fortune', or to take arms against it, in order to remain in power and keep his people subject.[17] But the modern hero is no prince, and therein lies his specific mythical power: the chance of luck and low cunning to propel him from low to high. He is paradigmatically poor, downtrodden, racially, sexually or socially excluded; and this low–high dynamic remains at the core of many modern luck stories and suggests how they are also necessarily, deeply, political, even democratic. They dream of an equality of opportunity, of a chance, a chance to take 'my shot', as Lin-Manuel Miranda's Alexander Hamilton and his fellows put it in his 2015 musical *Hamilton*, a twenty-first-century work that revels in its construction of a new variant of the origin story of America and the myth of the American dream, through the triumph of a poor Caribbean immigrant who becomes a founding father of the revolution and thus also of modernity, as captured in Miranda's rolling lyrics: 'How does a bastard, orphan, son of a whore and a Scotsman, dropped in the middle of a forgotten spot in the Caribbean by providence, impoverished, in squalor, grow up to be a hero and a scholar?'[18] All this, even as the system of the modern state, its economy, its disciplines, institutions and structuring inequalities work relentlessly to preserve power and hierarchy and to keep the American dream of the rise of the humble hero as just that.[19] Modern luck stories are thus in their way exquisitely, perhaps essentially, but also illusorily, bound up with democracy, with this modern myth of making of the ordinary citizen of the world (or of America, which as a myth-space of the modern comes to the same thing for many in the twentieth century). They are open, pluralist, undetermined and thus in a sense free. Here is E. B. White on New York, one capturing of the euphoria of ordinary modern Western man (White refers below to 'person', 'residents', 'strangers', 'individuals', but also to 'he' and 'him'), monadic and self-sufficient, in exile and searching, encountering the extraordinary modern, urban myth-space of New York, armed with nothing but an openness to the sheer life force, the risks and the rewards of luck:

> On any person who desires such queer prizes, New York will bestow the gift of loneliness and the gift of privacy. It is this largess that accounts for the presence within the city's walls of a considerable section of the population; for the residents of Manhattan are to a large extent strangers who have pulled up stakes somewhere and come to town, seeking sanctuary or fulfillment or some greater or lesser grail. The capacity to make such dubious gifts is a mysterious quality of New York. It can destroy an individual, or it can fulfill him, depending a good deal on luck. No one should come to New York to live unless he is willing to be lucky.[20]

This dynamic openness to luck, to newness and loss of control, need not, finally, be limited to New York, nor to the American dream, nor indeed to young men on the make, for all their power as archetypes and drivers of modernity. It is a mode of thinking and a position in relation to the world that is fully translatable and transferable into quite different environments and ecologies, or gender- and subject-positions, for example into realms of the natural and the animal, as captured with compelling force in Helen Macdonald's mournful but euphoric account of her training of an untameable goshawk, *H is for Hawk*:

> You pour your heart, your skill, your very soul, into a thing – into training a hawk, learning the form in racing or the numbers in cards – then relinquish control over it. That is the hook. Once the dice rolls, the horse runs, the hawk leaves the fist, you open yourself to luck.

Hers too is a modern luck story.[21]

*

This book sets out to chart the defining patterns and motifs of modern luck and of modern luck stories. It argues in its very method and structure that stories, and the representations and images embedded within them, are constitutive elements of our shared modern notion of luck, far more than their being merely illustrative appendages to some free-floating idea of luck. This argument is made in part on a general point of principle, which says that stories of varying kinds constitute our very being in the world, give shape to our consciousness of it. But there is also something tighter and narrower at stake, a more specific facet of the figure of luck as we have been laying it out here. Luck, that is, attaches itself to and is born out of sequences of events of human experience, as perceived by the human subject, as felt experience. It is not a pure concept with attendant real-world features; it is more the other way round, a phenomenon more akin to an adjectival projection by us onto the world – this or that event or experience perceived as 'lucky' or 'unlucky' – which can then be abstracted out, reverse-engineered into a shared but inevitably evanescent, shaky entity called luck. All of this means that luck exists only through and in human action, perception and experience, and therefore – since experiences and perceptions are invariably strung out into (narrative) sequences of before and after, of cause and effect – through stories, with their attendant patterns and emblems. All of this means also that luck is an engine for the *production* of stories. Modern luck produces modern luck stories, for sure, but to some significant degree modern luck stories also produce modern luck, and both produce modern stories *tout court*, forging elements of modern narrative and often modernity itself.

Through tracing luck as narrative, then, we will see the shape it takes in our modernity, or the shape of that modernity over the long twentieth century. Of course, we need to be alert to the specificities of particular contexts, to historical moments, periods and places within that long phase of modernity, as well as to the politics of narrative during this time, in other words to exclusions, voices unheard for reasons of gender, race, education or social hierarchy. But there is enough overarching consistency to see patterns between the specifics, to read the symptoms and trace the arc of a modern iteration of luck. The chapters in Part II thus follow deliberately unpredictable and eclectic pathways through bricolages of storytelling cultural objects, from late nineteenth-century staging posts (Fyodor Dostoevsky, Thomas Hardy, Carlo Collodi), through the modernist canon and popular fiction of the early to mid-twentieth century (Luigi Pirandello, Damon Runyon, Jorge Luis Borges, Tom Stoppard), from the genre literature of the mid- to late century (Philip K. Dick, Shirley Jackson) to the literature of trauma (Alice Sebold), slavery

(Harriet Jacobs) and the Holocaust (Imre Kertesz, Primo Levi), to the mass cultural media of superhero comics and television (Stan Lee, David Milch), to the cinema of European auteurism and genre (Vittorio De Sica, Michael Haneke, Gérard Depardieu), Hollywood comedy and action films (Michael Curtiz, Woody Allen, Clint Eastwood), up to contemporary fiction (Alice Munro, Angela Carter) and children's literature (J. K. Rowling, Pseudonymous Bosch). The book aims to embrace as pertinent and to the point a certain rough and ready quality in the terminology of luck, a certain embarrassment when set alongside those apparently more rigorous and clear-cut sister concepts (contingency, probability, randomness and so on), convinced that the permeability and shared intuitive sense of luck makes it more than worthy of a serious attempt to tease out its defining features, for all its fuzziness. The book therefore tries – and fails, repeatedly and knowingly – to stick to luck *as such*, to distinguish where possible the vocabulary of luck from that of chance, fortune, risk and all those many other possible near-synonyms. But even as this list of possible alternatives floats into view, it is clear that the lexical and semantic field of 'luck-ness' is extremely rich and disconcertingly fluid, especially if we open our perspective, as we surely must, outwards, onto languages and cultures beyond English. Indeed, this fluidity must be part of the very object of study in itself, one part of an explanation of how it is that luck can slip and merge and fade in and out of view so readily. Its slipperiness, its messiness and its multidimensionality, in language and idea, is part of what makes it so compelling, so familiar and yet so strangely ungraspable. The prolific lexicon of luck will be the subject of the next chapter.

Notes

1 Luck's ubiquity has produced a proliferation of books and other studies across a remarkable array of genres and disciplines, from mathematics to philosophy, from economics to psychology, from anthropology to history, from astronomy to quantum physics, and more; at various levels of marketing and pitch, from impenetrable academic tracts to management guru studies, from pop self-help manuals to (as we will see in Chapter 8) children's literature. This book's primary focus is on storytelling, in media such as literature and film (as well as occasionally in drama, song and visual art); but all those other fields and their large bibliographies are nevertheless highly pertinent interlocutors. In any case, invariably – even if without necessarily interrogating themselves on why they are doing so – such works almost all illustrate their arguments and explications with anecdotes, news stories, art and literature, biographies and autobiography, in short with stories. The luck stories studied in this book are, in other words, shared primary matter for all this vital flow of reflections on luck. Some of the key works in these contiguous fields that I have consulted are: Barbara Blatchley, *What Are the Chances? Why we believe in luck* (New York: Columbia University Press, 2021); Reuven Brenner, Gabrielle Brenner and Aaron Brown, *A World of Chance: Betting on religion, games, Wall Street* (Cambridge: Cambridge University Press, 2008); Brian Clegg, *Dice World: Science and life in a random universe* (London:

Icon Books, 2013); New Scientist, *Chance: The science and secrets of luck, randomness and probability* (London: John Murray, 2016); E. J. Coffman, *Luck: Its nature and significance for human knowledge and agency* (New York: Palgrave Macmillan, 2015); Steven D. Hales, *The Myth of Luck: Philosophy, fate, and fortune* (London: Bloomsbury Academic, 2020); Thomas M. Kavanagh, ed., *Chance, Culture and the Literary Text* (Ann Arbor: University of Michigan Press, 1994); Nicholas Rescher, *Luck: The brilliant randomness of everyday life* (Pittsburgh, PA: University of Pittsburgh Press, 2001); Tina Seelig, 'The little risks you can take to increase your luck', TED Talk, June 2018, at https://www.youtube.com/watch?v=PX61e3sAj5k; Stephen Senn, *Dicing with Death: Chance, risk and health* (Cambridge: Cambridge University Press, 2003); Ed Smith, *Luck: What it means and why it matters* (London: Bloomsbury, 2013); Nassim Nicholas Taleb, *Fooled by Randomness: The hidden role of chance in life and in the markets* (New York: Random House, 2005); Nassim Nicholas Taleb, *Black Swan: The impact of the highly improbable* (New York: Random House, 2007); Richard Wiseman, *The Luck Factor: The scientific study of the lucky mind* (London: Arrow, 2003).

2 Donald E. Brown, *Human Universals* (New York: McGraw-Hill, 1991), *passim*, and see especially pp. 130–41 for his synthetic description of an imagined 'Universal People' or 'UP', who manifest all the traits of his human universals (cf. p. 139 on fortune and misfortune). The risk of all universalisms, of course, is that they reinforce and naturalize – universalize, precisely – what are in fact historically specific, locally defined and deeply ideological norms (such as gender or racial hierarchies), in other words, that they are inherently conservative. Brown had been preceded by other anthropologists searching for traits common to all human cultures, starting with George Murdock in 1945, who included 'luck superstitions' in a provisional list of human cultural universals (George P. Murdock, 'The common denominator of cultures', in Ralph Linton, ed., *The Science of Man in the World Crisis* (New York: Columbia University Press, 1945), pp. 123–42 (p. 124)). The specialist debate in anthropology acquired a markedly higher profile, and generated some heat as a result, through the vigorous defence of them – and the inclusion of a list based on Brown's work in an appendix – found in Steven Pinker's widely read *The Blank Slate: The modern denial of human nature* (New York: Penguin, 2002); appendix at pp. 435–9. On the general problematic, see Theodore R. Schatzki, 'Human universals and understanding a different socioculture', *Human Studies*, 26.1 (2003): 1–20.

3 Words matter here: 'hap', from which we derive the verb 'to happen', is at root a Middle English word for luck, whence the term for a surprising circumstance, 'happenstance'. 'Hap' is also the title of an eloquent, bitter, early sonnet by Thomas Hardy, written in 1866, one of the key early entries in a canon of modern literature about luck, in which Hardy eloquently despairs of the Godless, causeless misery of pure misfortune in the world. If all there is in the world is pure 'hap', he reasons, then his life might just as well have led to good fortune ('bliss') as to bad: 'Crass Casualty obstructs the sun and rain, / And dicing Time for gladness casts a moan. [...] / These purblind Doomsters had as readily strown / Blisses about my pilgrimage as pain' (Thomas Hardy, 'Hap', ll. 11–14, in *Selected Poetry*, ed. Samuel Hynes (Oxford: Oxford University Press, 1994), p. 1).

4 See Chapter 3.

5 On the goddess Fortuna, see for example the remarkable work by the Spanish scholar José M. González García, *La Diosa Fortuna: Metamorfosis de una metafora politica* (Madrid: Antonio Machado, 2006).

6 There is an extensive body of iconography and scholarship on the *Atlas* project. See for example (including panel 48) 'Aby Warburg Mnemosyne Atlas', at http://www.engramma.it/eOS/core/frontend/eos_atlas_index.php?lang=eng.

7 See, for example, González García, *La Diosa Fortuna*, pp. 33–41, 93–102, or the group reading of the panel, Giulia Bordignon et al., '*Fortuna* during the Renaissance: A reading of Panel 48 of Aby Warburg's *Bilderatlas Mnemosyne*', *Engramma*, 137 (August 2016), at http://www.engramma.it/eOS/index.php?id_articolo=2975). On this Renaissance conjunction as marking the 'death' of Fortuna in the face of a new modernity, see Arndt Brendecke and Peter Vogt, eds, *The End of Fortuna and the Rise of Modernity* (Berlin: De Gruyter, 2017).

8 William Shakespeare, *Julius Caesar*, IV, 3, 269–76.

9 The best-known anthropologist of southern Italian magical belief systems was Ernesto De Martino: see in English Ernesto De Martino, *Magic: A theory from the south*, trans. Dorothy Louise Zinn (Chicago, IL: HAU Books, 2003); cf. also the short film *Superstizione* (dir. Michelangelo Antonioni, 1949). On Japanese beliefs and talismans of luck, see Inge Maria Daniels, 'Scooping, raking, beckoning luck: Luck, agency and the interdependence of people and things in Japan',

Journal of the Royal Anthropological Institute, 9.4 (2003): 619–38; on Yiddish traditions, see Ruth Wisse, *The Schlemiel as Modern Hero* (Chicago, IL: University of Chicago Press, 1971).

10 The serial origins of the eighteenth- and nineteenth-century novel have long fascinated literary historians and political thinkers, including the Marxist Antonio Gramsci, who saw the form as crucial for the dissemination of what he called a 'national popular' culture (see for example David Forgacs, ed., *The Gramsci Reader: Selected writings 1916–1935* (New York: New York University Press, 2000), pp. 364–5). For a recent reassessment, see Clare Pettitt, *Serial Forms: The unfinished project of modernity, 1815–1848* (Oxford: Oxford University Press, 2020). 'Myth' and 'narrative' also figure in the compendium of features of Brown's Universal People (Brown, *Human Universals*, pp. 132, 139).

11 For Gramsci on language, common sense, and his anti-picturesque notion of folklore as philosophical praxis, see for example 'Observations on folklore', in Forgacs, *Gramsci Reader*, pp. 360–2.

12 The debate on so-called 'punctuated equilibrium' in evolutionary science, as a critique of Darwin's 'gradualism', is associated with the 1970s work of Niles Eldredge and Stephen Jay Gould. It reached a wide public through Gould's remarkable work as a popular-science writer, and through fierce debate with figures such as Richard Dawkins and Daniel Dennett, in forums such as the *New York Review of Books*: see for example Stephen Jay Gould, 'Darwinian fundamentalism', *New York Review of Books*, 44.10 (12 June 1997): 34–7. Gould further explores chance and contingency in evolution in *Wonderful Life: The Burgess Shale and the nature of history* (New York: Norton, 1989); and cf. the influential earlier contribution to the understanding of the fundamental role of contingency in biology and life, Jacques Monod, *Chance and Necessity: An essay on the natural philosophy of modern biology*, trans. Austryn Wainhouse (New York: Alfred A. Knopf, 1971).

13 On this concept, see for example Georges Didi-Huberman, 'The surviving image: Aby Warburg and Tylorian anthropology', *Oxford Art Journal*, 25.1 (2002): 59–69.

14 See Ian Hacking, *The Taming of Chance* (Cambridge: Cambridge University Press, 1990). Weber introduced the notion of the 'disenchantment' (*Entzauberung*) of the world in his 1904 work *The Protestant Ethic and the Spirit of Capitalism*, developed further in a 1917 lecture. It has been qualified and criticized in recent studies of the persistence of forms of irrational belief within modernity, or so-called 're-enchantment', including luck beliefs and superstition: see for example Joshua Landy and Michael Saler, eds, *The Re-enchantment of the World: Secular magic in a rational age* (Stanford, CA: Stanford University Press, 2009); Stuart Vyse, *Superstition: A very short introduction* (Oxford: Oxford University Press, 2020), pp. 54–5.

15 The phrasing alludes to David Edgerton's critique of 'modernolatry' through a study of the surprising persistence of old, tried and tested ways in the history of technology: David Edgerton, *The Shock Of The Old: Technology and global history since 1900* (Oxford: Oxford University Press, 2007). The title was an allusion and a riposte to the influential documentary account of the 1980s of the 'make it new' modernism of twentieth-century avant-garde art, Robert Hughes, *The Shock of the New* (London: BBC, 1980).

16 See Daniel Kahneman, *Thinking, Fast and Slow* (New York: Farrar, Straus and Giroux, 2011), which describes a divide in human mental processes between 'System 1' and 'System 2', the former fast and intuitive, the latter slow and deliberative.

17 The best-known declaration of Machiavelli's pairing of virtue and fortune comes in chapter 25 of *The Prince* (1532). His reflections on the theme unleashed centuries of subsequent commentary and political theory: see for example glosses and commentary in Niccolò Machiavelli, *The Prince*, trans. and ed. Russell Price and Quentin Skinner (Cambridge: Cambridge University Press, 2019).

18 The lyrics are from the song 'Alexander Hamilton' and the reference earlier to the song 'My shot' (both in Lin-Manuel Miranda, *Hamilton*, 2015). The topos of the immigrant's arrival in America and thus the connection between race, exile and luck is sustained through much of the mythology of the 'poor and huddled masses' arriving at Ellis Island in New York in the nineteenth and twentieth centuries: for example, Georges Perec's remarkable documentary and book on Ellis Island talk of Jews and other migrants reaching there 'alive to exile and to luck' (Georges Perec and Robert Bober, *Récits d'Ellis Island: Histoires d'errance et d'espoir* (Paris: P.O.L, 1994), p. 60; and see also the 1980 documentary *Récits d'Ellis Island* (dir. Robert Bober) at https://www.youtube.com/watch?v=s6l2xFQztsM (accessed 26 July 2022).

19 The most commonly given source for the formulation of the phrase 'the American dream' is the epilogue to a 1930s work of popular history, *The Epic of America*, by James Truslow Adams, in

which the phrase is explicitly introduced as a product of the tension between the luck of birth and status, and the possibility (*occasio*) of acquiring new stature and self-fulfilling achievement: 'The *American dream*, that dream of a land in which life should be better and richer and fuller for every man [sic], with opportunity for each according to his ability or achievement. [...] It is not a dream of motor cars and high wages merely, but a dream of a social order in which each man and each woman shall be able to attain to the fullest stature of which they are innately capable, and be recognized by others for what they are, regardless of the fortuitous circumstances of birth or position' (James Truslow Adams, *The Epic of America* (Garden City, NY: Blue Ribbon Books, 1931), p. 404; emphasis in the original). The association between chance, America and democracy goes back to Tocqueville: 'Those living in the instability of a democracy have the constant image of chance before them' (Alexis de Tocqueville, *Democracy in America* (first published in French in two volumes, 1835 and 1840), trans. G. Bevan (London: Penguin, 2003), p. 643.)

20 E. B. White, *Here is New York* (New York: Little Bookroom, 1999), p. 19.

21 Helen Macdonald, *H is for Hawk* (London: Jonathan Cape, 2014), p. 177. The example of Macdonald is usefully resistant to a marked gender bias in luck stories that we have already rubbed up against in this chapter and that will recur through this book: that is, narrative topoi such as setting out to seek a fortune, challenging the elements and the vagaries of chance, playing games, taking risks, searching for adventure and so on are all relentlessly gendered male in Western and many other cultures; and most often they are voiced by male storytellers. Luck, however, remains a cultural universal, and there is space too for counter-traditions of female and indeed non-binary voices and experiences in luck stories, from Moll Flanders to Alice to contemporary luck stories, as we will see. And there is still space also, with all due caution against risks of essentialism, for alternative modes of luck itself that counter those masculinist topoi, less founded on risk and action, more attentive to incident, experience and interrelation. *H is for Hawk* might be a good case in point, structured as it is in intimate counterpoint to the work of a highly ambivalent male precursor, T. H. White, and his work *The Goshawk* (1951).

2
Word trees and etymologies

Luck is not only all around us, out there in the phenomena of the world, or at least in our perceptions of them. It is also a pervasive presence in our language. As we began to see in the previous chapter, it is almost impossible not to stumble across a near-synonym, a hidden etymology, a lexical association, a figural motif for luck, or something very close to it, in our everyday vocabulary. Even that verb, 'to stumble', and the phrasal verb 'to stumble across', are figures of chance encounter, of unexpected surprise and accident, and also of falling, all of which are closely tied to the language of luck. (They point to one of the reasons why a certain kind of bad luck story is strongly associated with comedy, why one of its elemental figures is the slip, the trip, the fall.) And from our language, as George Lakoff and Mark Johnson influentially argued, come the 'metaphors we live by'.[1] This chapter sets out to explore the lexicon of luck, its origins, its scope and variety, its figures and metaphors, primarily as it works in English, but with a dose of help from a handful of other languages (and so other cultures), where we find the boundaries between and roots of terms for luck and semantically similar terms are often set usefully askew from their Anglophone equivalents.[2] This is not intended as a dry philological exercise in etymology, however, but as a method for mapping this compellingly fuzzy conceptual field as it is enacted in the everyday, through our words (and the shadow of their origins). Language gives us a vivid insight into the stretched and malleable senses of luck, how it occupies our minds, our actions and so our understanding of the world. It also allows us to begin to map out the luck motifs that will underpin the chapters that follow in Part II and the stories, figures and spaces that each will explore.

Building the lexicon of luck is an exercise in drawing word trees or Venn diagrams with a variety of intersecting or concentric circles. We must start, of course, with the term luck itself, but very soon, as we shall see – indeed, we have already seen – 'luck' spills over in its very definitions and origins into closely related terms, each with its own origins and etymons. But for the task we have set ourselves here, this slipperiness is all to the point, as is the circulation of obscure or false etymologies, often born in folk associations and legend, because all of these feed into the living culture of luck and its stories. Furthermore, any journey towards a point of origin in language necessarily carries us across borders towards other languages, both older and contemporary, so that current usage and translation (or as close as we can get to it) look like alternative branches in an evolutionary tree, with shared stems or roots, hidden beneath variant prefixes and suffixes, tied up with both phonetics and morphology. Broadening out further still, we can link all these to semantic associations in the field of luck and witness the still more numerous overlaps and resonances these bring. And since luck is a commonplace and a universal, we find its lexicon as alive in the register of the concrete everyday, in the creative phraseology of colloquial argot and slang as we do in the rarefied register of the abstract. As is often the case in such word games – and all the more so in the lexicon of the everyday – the noun is inevitably the dominant part of speech here, an object or concept to grab on to and fix (at least apparently), but luck is also present as a qualifier, in its adjectival form, as we suggested in Chapter 1 (being lucky), a dynamic operator and, as we are intent on showing, a story-maker. So we need also, finally, to tap into the verbs of luck, its capacity to vivify and humanize a static, abstract (and indeed fantastical) notion, to insert it into time and space, into history and story.

All definitions are, of course, a game of smoke and mirrors, of words defining other words. But the semantics of 'luck' seem particularly, frustratingly, circular. Luck is never quite held distinct from its sister terms, and it would be a fool's errand to lay claim to any watertight *distinguo* in language and use. The key, primary cluster of closely interdependent terms in English is threefold: luck, fortune, chance.[3] We can as a start look at each of these in turn, and the web of connections that binds them together, starting with luck itself.

The OED gives a number of branched definitions for 'luck', as we would expect, but the core definition, the most common and current, is definition 2.a:

Luck, n.

[...]

2.a. The *chance* occurrence of situations or events either favourable or unfavourable to a person's interests; the sum of *chance* events affecting (favourably or unfavourably) a person's interests or circumstances; a person's apparent tendency to have good or ill *fortune*. (Emphasis added)[4]

It is immediately apparent here, if we look at the italicized terms, that chance, fortune and luck are inextricably tangled up with each other, as well as branching out from each other. Each is worth tracing to its origins. 'Luck' itself, the OED tells us, has its roots in Germanic languages, borrowed from Dutch (*luc*), or Middle Low German (*lücke*). Deeper etymology and earlier variant meanings are murky, we are told, but one variant form in German is of exceptional interest for the stretched field of association and meaning it points to, one that will resonate throughout our explorations of luck stories: from the Middle Low German *lücke* modern German derives its word for (good) luck, *Glück*, which also means happiness.

The possible congruence of luck with happiness is, to the Anglophone ear at least, as astonishing as it is sobering, since it brings luck close to a concept of quite fundamental importance in human life and in the history of philosophy, perhaps to the very purpose of our existence: a striving for the good life, our 'unalienable right to life, liberty and the pursuit of happiness', to use the words of the American Declaration of Independence. But perhaps we should not be so surprised after all, since the English words happy and happiness derive from the now archaic 'hap', which, as we have already seen, means, precisely, chance, fortune, luck. (The etymology of 'hap' takes us on a journey to another linguistic region beyond West Germanic, to early Scandinavian, where a closely similar term is found in each of Old Icelandic, Norwegian and Swedish, all *happ*.) In fact, there is an elaborate lexical tree made up of derivatives of and branches from hap, which is such that luck can be linked not only to happiness, but also to murkier zones of doubt, uncertainty and contingency: these include derivatives such as 'perhaps' or the related if antiquated 'perchance' (and analogously in Spanish *acaso*, Italian *forse* and so on). Luck, good luck at least, brings happiness, then, and this much seems uncontroversial. But conversely, there is already a more sombre and, it seems, implicitly secular philosophy embedded in this lexical chain, one that seems strikingly attuned to the modern, but which clearly has ancient roots in our language(s): happiness is a matter of pure luck, and the path from one to the other is steeped in doubt.

Turning from 'luck' to 'fortune' points us away from Northern European origins and towards the Latin and Romance roots of parts of the English language; to the French *fortune* and the Latin *fortuna*, or indeed as we have seen the goddess Fortuna, all related to a root term for chance, *fors*. Fortune does not, it seems, derive from the closely similar Latin *fortis*, for strong or bold, but the rigours of etymology have no power to resist false association and false etymology, or contiguity and the simple pleasures of puns. And so fortune and strength have long been powerfully linked in our language and culture, both current and inherited, as in the proverbial phrase 'fortune favours the bold', where the alliteration in English alludes to an older alliteration and pun in its Latin sources, famously for example in Pliny the Elder's *fortis Fortuna adiuvat*. (Machiavelli's pairing and contrast of *fortuna* and *virtù* also contains echoes of the classical bond between fortune and strength.)

'Chance' meanwhile also comes down to us from Romance, the OED giving a chain via Middle English, back to Old French (*cheance*) to late Latin *cadentia*, falling.[5] We can add a striking parallel instance from Italian, where the word for chance – or indeed sometimes luck, random conjuncture, circumstance and more – is *caso*, which shares the same root association with falling, but also has a vast set of generic functional meanings, much like the English 'case', for example in phrases such as 'to be the case', simply that which is, as well as a detective or medical, grammatical or theological 'case'; and other senses that go beyond English, such as a surprising outcome, and more. (In an interesting false-friend mismatch between Italian *caso* and English 'case', the derived Italian adjective *casuale* is strictly linked to its original meaning of chance or circumstance, rather than to the now dominant meaning of 'casual' in English as informal; but they share the same root and indeed the informal English meaning perhaps retains something of the irregular and unregulated force of chance.)[6]

As we have already noted more than once, a significant sub-sector in the language of luck, via its proximity to chance, shares an origin or an association, even if at times hidden in the mists of etymology, with falling, and we need to pay some further attention to this area. First of all, there is a neat and powerfully telling link back to the discussion of luck and its Northern European linguistic links to happiness, to remind us, if we needed it, of the entangled lines cutting across the vastly distant etymological geo-linguistic map that we are charting. Happiness derives from 'hap', but so too, as we have seen, does the base verb 'to happen'. And we have other terms in English, again now verging on the archaic, to link happening to falling; most directly the verb 'to befall'. But, remarkably, the same precise bond obtains in the case of chance, since its root in the Latin *cadere*, to fall, is also the root for a string of commonplace verbs and nouns, starting with *accidere* (*ad* + *cadere*), to happen. Indeed, early

Modern High German actually borrowed this formation in Latin to form another German term for luck or chance besides *Glück*, one that is linked to falling rather than happiness: *Zufall*. As *il caso* also suggested, then, luck or chance is at one level simply that which is, that which befalls, that which happens.

The Romance *cadere* or falling root is a hardworking etymon, and there is a spiralling set of English words that derive from it, beyond its catch-all association with happening. These include 'incident' terms, such as coincidence, accident, occasion, and, as is apparent from this list, they evince frequent and profound links to the terminology of luck and chance. Several are also dynamic drivers of luck *stories*, of circumstances and sequences of events in which a turn of chance, a surprising 'happening', lies at the root or the heart of a story. (They are also, we might add in anticipation of analysis in Part II, closely bound up with some of the characteristically random, unpredictable, luck-driven dynamics of the *modern* narrative, the modern novel, where encounters and coincidences seem to abound, in contrast with the driven destinies of, say, classical tragedy or conventional happy-ending comedies.)[7] Indeed, each one of them could be said to amount to a structural principle or a motif of storytelling. To come up against a minor event that triggers consequences (incident), to fall victim to a sudden injury or disaster (accident), to cross paths randomly for no reason (coincidence), to grab at a chance that comes along (occasion): all these have the potential to generate and drive luck stories, of vividly dramatic, even melodramatic, comic or tragic kind.[8] Simply insert infinite possible variants and variations, and enjoy.

One final branch or set of branches emanating from the etymological and narrative links from luck to chance to happening is worth noting. Some alternative words for happening point up potentially useful, new or expanded associations, not now or not only with falling but also with other kinds of movement, through space and through stories: so much so that these associations begin to suggest a core spatial or sequential dynamic to luck and luck stories that will prove crucial for our mapping of the field. One example of these would be the terms 'occurrence' and 'to occur', which come to us from another Latin root, *currere*, to run, with the prefix *ob*, 'against', to build a sense of running into, or running up against. (Another interesting false-friend association from Italian is illuminating here: *occorre* in modern Italian is an impersonal verb meaning 'is necessary', almost, then, the opposite of the random contingency of happening; but more than one philosopher and storyteller has noted the strange affinity of chance and necessity, or fortune and fate.) An analogous case might be the term 'succession', 'to succeed', which has an intriguing dual meaning: first and in a somewhat higher register, simply to come next, to be next in line (say as regards the Queen, or indeed the Logan family in the HBO drama *Succession*); and then, more commonly, to reach a positive outcome or a desired goal. A succession of events, then, morphs into or overlaps with a successful outcome; if the presence of luck in this pairing seems a little shady, it is certainly there in the OED definition of 'success', specifically definition 12.a: 'succeed, n. [...] To have the desired or a *fortunate* issue or conclusion' (emphasis added). Lastly, we might add to our list another base word, a prop for all talk of happening, the word 'event', noted above as rooted in *venire*, to come, and predicated on an idea of a sequence leading to an action, or an outcome (*e-venire*, out-come).

These etymologies – of occurrence, succession, event – all point to a *geometry* of luck, to luck as a *vector*. Luck falls, runs, moves in sequence in a line, in a notional space and for a notional time. Or perhaps it would be better to imagine that luck marks an 'incident' along that line of space-time sequence, an incursion, an interruption, possibly a deviation or a split, or an intersection of lines, a point of unpredictability along an apparently determined path.[9] Another, closely related term that also invokes a kind of intersection is contingency, a term which plunges us back into the realm of uncertainty, even fragility, that always hovers close by the lexicon if luck. Interestingly, the etymology of contingency adds a further sensory dimension to this geometrical and so also visual figure of coming together, since its root lies in a verb of touching (Latin *tingere*).

That line-geometry and vectors are fundamental to our understanding of luck and chance, and of how they are visualized and rendered into concept, figure and story, is confirmed by one of the oldest philosophical-scientific conceptions of the role of random chance in the universe, Lucretius' notion of the swerve, the *clinamen*. Lucretius suggests that the very world of nature and being itself is produced by random swerves in the falling linear motion of atoms.[10] Its close bond to modern science is confirmed in Darwin's famous tree figures representing the evolution of species created by random or chance genetic error and mutation.[11] And its force in modern storytelling is encapsulated in the remarkable power and resonance of the so-called 'forking-path' motif in modern fiction, derived from Jorge Luis Borges's 1941 story, 'The garden of the forking paths'.[12] All these analogous examples are so many line drawings of luck, and we will find their geometries repeated – and indeed confused and disrupted – across the wide and varied field of modern luck stories explored in Part II. Of course, these figures of simple linearity – of branches, swerves and forks – need to be taken with due caution as powerful figural simplifications, as archetypes. Luck is in reality rarely binary, more likely to be dizzyingly plural, and, again, this is a facet that modernity and its epistemologies have embraced and conceptualized with growing boldness, captured in the science of randomness and random (Brownian) motion, with its crazed unpredictable movement of atoms (random, etymology Old French *randir*, to run fast), or even more so in the quantum mathematics of simultaneity and uncertainty, in other words in new geometries of chance.

We are perhaps on a slippery slope here, for all the exhilarating energy and sense of playful connection generated by these chains of words and etymologies: happenings, events and all their myriad associations are so vast and loose as to risk losing all purchase on our specific quest to map the meanings and language of luck. But the associations are powerful nonetheless, perhaps precisely because of that capaciousness. And in fact our game of OED-led exploration around the terrain of the three sister terms of luck, chance and fortune has already taken us a long way, well beyond these three terms. Already, along the way, we have sketched out a lexical field of words that are, if not exact synonyms, then analogues for luck, strangely bound up with it, sharing some association or quality or some point of origin, and therefore, we can suggest, adding fuel to the fire of the storytelling and figural potential of luck. Thus far, these secondary associative terms have included happiness, uncertainty, strength or courage, events or happenings, accidents and coincidences, lines, sequences and successions, branches, swerves and forks, running and falling, irregularities and deviations.

And the game is not quite done. There is still ground to cover before the etymologies and word trees, their figures and associations, have been exhausted and have range enough to be crystallized into the map we are hoping to draw of the key motifs and patterns in the field of modern luck storytelling, the focus of Part II of this book. If the discussion thus far has been born of circles of association around our three core sister terms – chance, fortune and luck – we should not forget that there are several other near-congruent terms for luck, in English, in the handful of other languages we have touched on and in a few others besides, which add new and distinct layers of etymology, meaning and association to the field.

One set of such terms links luck to a sense of futurity, to the uncertainty of what might happen in the future and the fear and vitality this sense brings. Words we have noted before, such as 'venture' and 'adventure', already point in this direction, with a direct syntactical pointer in their Latin root in *venturus*, a future participle of the verb to come, that which will come about. In Spanish and Italian, among other languages, *ventura* carries with it meanings of luck and fortune as well as future (and in Spanish also, once again, happiness). And in popular and marginal culture, in the circus and the fairground, the figure of the fortune-teller or clairvoyant is a two-bit descendant of the prophet and seer of times to come, who occupies a powerful imaginary role as a conduit to our futures. Other, more technical, terms linked to luck and chance look to the future in their etymology and origin: stochastic is one example, an adjective to describe random events governed by probability, with its roots in Greek terminology for 'aim'. 'Probability' itself is another, with a root in verbs of showing and proof, which comes to mean the mathematics of calculating that which is likely to come to pass. And finally, the terminology of sortition, or drawing lots, has its roots in figures of binding (Latin *serere*, to tie), of bringing the unruly future into line, tying it down (with echoes of Machiavelli's infamous comments in chapter 25 of *The Prince* on the need to dominate and tame a female Fortuna). Modern Spanish uses *la suerte* as a standard term for luck, with this same etymology and sense of futurity built in.

This latter example of binding points to a profound paradox in the entire lexical field of luck, one which is as inevitable as it is confounding, but one that is also particularly useful for our exploration of a modern paradigm shift in the meanings and stories of luck: that is, the recurrent overspill of luck into its apparent precise opposite. In lexical terms, synonym and antonym seem all too often to coincide here; uncertainty, unknowability and the openness of chance and luck merge disconcertingly in both language and idea with the dead hand, the bound inevitability of certain fate, destiny and determinism. This was already clearly the case in classical traditions, when the whole function and purpose of the goddess Fortuna was to remind mere humans that their unknowable future was wholly controlled by the gods, or in the Christian tradition by God and grace. If Western modernity loosely aligns with a decline in faith (and it is a big if), there is certainly a decline to be seen in this complementarity between human uncertainty and divine predestination; but other 'higher' certainties have nevertheless taken the place of the latter, often associated with dark, controlling or conspiratorial hands of hidden power, or, more plausibly, with the unstoppable force of actuarial or probabilistic calculus. Number replaces gods or God in this luck dynamic, creating highly distinctive ruptures in the forms and figures of luck, but also typically hybrid, even uncanny, continuities.

Number, indeed, is another area of fundamental importance in the semantic field of luck, and in its stories. Sortition has its Germanic equivalent in English in 'lot', whence 'lottery'. And the history of lotteries, in the modern sense of the drawing of numbers as a form of gambling, as opposed to Athenian and later traditions of government by sortition, has been widely studied as both a turning point in the cultural history of chance and in the mathematical history of concepts of probability.[13] The etymology of 'lot' points to neutrally numerical terms found in several old languages for portion or part, indicating a process of division or sharing out. Here we are dealing with a sort of mathematics of small numbers, rather than the potential infinites of statistics and calculus, and this difference in scale and range – reminiscent of Kahneman's fast and slow aspects of our mental processes alluded to in Chapter 1 – is a key element of distinction between strict usages of luck and chance (see Chapter 3). Luck and luck stories, rooted in the human and the everyday, tend to deal in small numbers, even if only as metaphors for the calculus of vast, or rather infinitesimal, probabilities, and this is only confirmed by turning to another ludic and remarkably ancient and pervasive sector of the lexicon of luck: the language of dice.

Dice are ancient presences in human culture, objects of divination and of play, a form of basic technology designed to make random choices between a small number of possible outcomes, through numbers.[14] The English word (originally the plural of n. die) derives from another of those capacious Romance terms, this time from the Latin *dare, datus*, to give, that which is given. (We can compare this in the generality of its register and scope to 'fate', from Latin *fatum*, that which has been spoken, and indeed to our various discussions of happening, above.) Further Latin associations are to be found in the lexical fields of philosophy and aesthetics, where we find 'aleatory', from the Latin for dice, *alea*. We inherit from Latin the often misconstrued proverbial phrase, 'the die is cast', *alea iacta est*, supposedly Caesar's phrase for his point of no return as he crossed the River Rubicon and headed for Rome and his destiny. Caesar's dictum, the figure of the cast die, offers a resonant conjunction for a number of reasons. First, it gives us a sequential frame for understanding how those apparent antonyms, luck and destiny, can come to overlap and coincide: for Caesar, and for all our dice-rolling decision-making, *first* there is uncertainty, possibility, dreams of good and bad luck, *but then*, as a decision is made, an action taken, the future is bound, fate is sealed. It is, then, a useful sequence here in particular because it is both apparently causal – by rolling the dice, I seal my fate – and a compelling narrative form. Further, it captures in an image of the throwing, the casting of the die, another kind of falling and swerving, and thus another emblematic instance of the vector geometry of luck.

The language of dice finds other origins well beyond Latin and Romance, however. As is the case for much of our vocabulary of number, there are also strong Arabic roots and associations with dice words, roots that link strongly to our present-day language of luck. The key term here is the Spanish *el azar*, from which derive the French *le hasard* and English 'hazard'. The term came into Spanish originally as, precisely, a word for a dice game, a derivative of the Arabic for a die, *zahr* or *al-zahr*.[15]

As this sequence of connection from number to dice to hazard tells us, there is a further semantic field to open up here, another Venn diagram of overlapping lexical spheres that suggest how luck, especially here bad luck, is tied to the language of hazard, that is of danger and risk. That luck is shaded in darkness, permanently tinged with fear of injury, illness, death, is something we have noted earlier as a cause of its pervasiveness and (dark) fascination and which is vividly apparent in the vocabulary of danger (the latter's etymology lies in terms for 'domination'), much as it was in the association of luck with accident. Here too, ancient formulations and religions are linked to later vocabularies of belief in destiny and fate, through the language of astrology. Disaster and catastrophe, figures of when luck turns bad, derive from the language of the stars (*astro-*), as is also apparent in the terms 'ill-starred' or the Shakespearean 'star-crossed', from another, higher power traditionally assumed to determine or dominate our fate.[16] In the case of 'risk', the etymology is deeply uncertain and disputed, with roots possibly found again in Arabic, *risq*, a catch-all term for luck, lot, provision, or in Latin *resecum*, a crag or reef. In the latter, the association is clear: we have come full circle back to Warburg and the figure of Fortuna as a storm or as a tiller in a storm, to the danger of shipwreck. And indeed, early uses of risk also link to Warburg's mercantile gloss on seafaring and fortune, since they are typically, according to the OED once again, related to commercial danger, danger of loss of merchandise (and from these to the modern industry of insurance).

The shared semantic field of risk and danger thus points us towards one final, crucially important dimension of luck in language, which we have touched on in passing, but perhaps not with sufficient emphasis, that is to say, the economics of luck. The wheel of Fortuna casting us high and low is a metaphor for many realms of human experience, for power and greatness, for happiness and misery, for love and solitude, even for salvation and damnation, but it is also, possibly most often and most immediately in the venal human mind, a figure for wealth and poverty, or more materially for plenty and scarcity, food and hunger. The goddess's cornucopia is a figure of plenty in both these senses. Indeed, we should hardly need to be reminded that 'fortune' in modern English (and in most of the other languages we have tapped into thus far) is at least as common in its 'base' and concrete meaning, as wealth, riches, treasure, financial success, as it is in the more notional, magical meaning as a force of good and bad luck. Dice, lotteries, gambling, but also the risk of insurance, investment and return: all these are deeply embedded in economics and, it can plausibly be argued, in the economy and therefore also the ethos of capitalism, where production is driven by and aimed at profit and gain. If the Roman principle of fortune favouring the bold was at heart a military principle, in capitalism it is a formula for risk and commercial adventure, for what late twentieth-century capitalism would tellingly label venture capital.[17] 'Nothing ventured, nothing gained' might come to mind as an alternative proverb, and we have seen already how 'venture' intersects and overlaps in its etymology and meaning with notions of future, storytelling and luck. As with all the lexical strands we have been teasing out in this chapter, we will see in Part II how the economics of luck is pervasively present across the field of modern luck myths and stories.

*

Etymology is something of a rabbit hole, in which it is all too easy to get lost and disoriented, and where meaning can sometimes get lost in a web of lost or nonsensical connections. It is also somewhat hit-and-miss as a tool for scoping out a semantic field, since it is often confounded by outliers that do not tie neatly into its forest of word trees: a case in point in English would be the term 'serendipity', a neologism coined by Horace Walpole in 1754 to mean accidental happy outcomes, taken from a fairy-tale use of a Persian name for Sri Lanka.[18] (We will return to the link between luck and fairy tales in Chapter 8.) But etymologies are nevertheless fascinating in the proliferation of links and networks they throw up, some tenuous and loose, some dense and overdetermined, and their value is confirmed by how many of the hints and suggestions we have touched on here will resonate in Part II. But etymology is decidedly not meaning, nor does it give us a picture of actual usage in the living world of language. And so we need to take a further few steps along other paths of language before we leave such questions behind and turn to the stories. To get closer to real-world language use, we can tentatively pick out a few commonplace phrases and slang terms for luck, again mostly drawing on English. The colloquial is of course a vast and constantly changing sphere of language and language use, guaranteed to be out of date the moment any attempt is made to pin it down in writing, let alone in academic analysis. But, as with our forays into etymology, its usefulness here lies less in watertight scientific precision or in exhaustiveness than in its generative potential to anchor our thoughts on luck in real, material worlds.

First of all, it is worth noting the sheer malleability and accessibility of the word 'luck', and for once this is an area in which we can stick tightly to the word itself, rather than its sisters and close analogues. Luck is one of those simple, non-Latinate English words, end-stopped and monosyllabic, that easily and strikingly combine into idiomatic phrases, whether 'luck' itself or its derived adjective 'lucky'. So we have, to give just a flavour (the cumulative, disordered effect of the list is part of the point here): good luck, bad luck, in luck, out of luck, down on one's luck, to luck out, hard luck, tough luck, one for luck, best of luck, better luck next time, to strike it lucky, stroke of luck, lucky streak, lucky break, get lucky, beginner's luck, lucky star, lucky charm, luck of the draw, your lucky day, dumb luck, lucky devil, lucky beggar, happy-go-lucky. (There are many more.) And we can throw into the mix a rich series of terms and idioms that avoid the explicit use of luck or lucky, but that we intuitively understand are figures for the rough, tough or sometime joyous consequences of luck: to fall on your feet, to catch a break, break a leg!, to draw the short straw, to be in the wrong/right place at the wrong/right time, to beat the odds, touch wood. And this before trying to tap into slang or colloquial terms for luck, typically the hardest of all to trace and track, such as fluke, jinx, jammy, fingers crossed and hope for the best.

Trying to see the wood for the (word) trees in this flow of language, we can usefully identify a few clusters and patterns of association. Certain elements simply replicate idiomatically aspects of luck we have touched on before: sortition, falling, coincidence, risk. In others we see a distinctively strong material dimension in the elaborated everyday language of luck – luck is hard, tough, it breaks, it strikes, or indeed it is sticky and sweet (jam) – and this reinforces the sense we have come across before of luck as a zone of danger and struggle, and of low life (devil, beggar). But it also points to how, as we will see, the materialization of luck will be one of the main drivers of luck stories, with new imaginary forms in the modern set alongside millennial traditions of luck's objectification and fetishization, into wheels and blindfolds, horseshoes, clovers and unlucky numbers. Further, and echoing the latter, there is a clear line of connection to those forms of luck magic and superstition – charms, stars, touching wood, jinx (the word probably derives from a bird species, the jynx, used in magic spells) – that we touched on in Chapter 1. There are also nods to sex and sexuality: 'get lucky' can refer to money or just a generic lucky break, but it also has a (sexist) connotation of sexual conquest (indeed, the OED gives a now thankfully rare US slang idiom with a bluntly racist connotation: 'to change one's luck' defined as '(of a white man) to have sexual intercourse with a black woman, sometimes in the belief that this will bring good luck. Now *historical* and *rare*.' Many more still evoke the economics of luck, through fantastical dreams of somehow winning money by betting and gambling. And finally, it is interesting to note that the antonymic pattern we saw earlier at the level of high concept, whereby luck evokes and coincides with its opposite (for example fate), is also at work in this sphere of the everyday. In this case, however, it is a pointer to another mechanism of luck magic, the apotropaic, the act which averts or protects from bad luck. At times, this is carried out in popular language and culture through simple objects or gestures – fingers crossed – but it is also invoked in language itself through the play of antonyms, the superstitious augury: to wish someone good luck in the theatre, we tell them to 'break a leg'; in Italian, the most common good luck augury is *in bocca al lupo*, 'into the mouth of the wolf', to which the addressee replies ritually, *crepi il lupo*, 'hope the wolf dies'. All these lines of association seem to converge on a particular mix of the demotic and the magical, which provides a tonal key, as well as a source of narrative content, for a rich array of the stories we will come to examine (see Chapter 7).

One final note of cultural localization is useful, before we take the mass of lexical material that we have accumulated in this chapter and bend it towards the fields and figures of storytelling that will be our principal interest in Part II. A heavy dose of the language of luck in English, and particularly its more everyday, contemporary and vernacular iterations, seems to have something distinctly American about it, often distinctly American and male. The street language but also the ethos of modern luck intersects frequently with the topoi and the ethos of American life, particularly as it stands for or stands in for something essential in the modernity of the long twentieth century: Henry Luce's 'American century', or, as we saw in Chapter 1, the 'American dream' of James Truslow Adams or E. B. White. The lucky break, the man on the make, the gambler and the chancer, the lone cowboy trying his luck against the elements (or, more likely, against the native Americans), the democratic, free American dream of coming good, the guy hoping to get the gal: all of these, low and high, are topoi, clichés perhaps, of American culture (and its occlusions, we might add), a culture that came to colonize the rest of the world also as a global imaginary and the very definition of twentieth-century modernity, as much as it did America itself,[19] and all of them have elements of the luck motifs and luck stories we have been charting thus far. Capitalism itself too, as we have seen, lies at the base of many modern conceptions of luck, and of course America embodies twentieth-century capitalism in the collective imagination more than any other place and culture. Although this book did not set out to be about America and Americana, it is striking how often in Part II we will be pulled towards American stories and emanations of an American encounter with an idea of luck.

This aspect of American history and culture has been charted magisterially by T. J. Jackson Lears in his 2003 study *Something for Nothing: Luck in America*,[20] which gathers a vast array of cultural, anthropological and sociological sources, stretching from the Pilgrim Fathers in New England to African-American slave rituals and religious practices in the Deep South, to twentieth- and twenty-first-century art and Wall Street capital, all viewed in the light of what Lears sees as a millennial struggle within the very idea of America between an impulse towards management and control on the one hand, and an instinct for luck on the other, seen variously as synonymous with risk, magic or grace. Lears's focal point throughout is the archetypal figure of 'the Gambler', embodied in everything from the card sharp to the hedge-fund speculator, always looking to evade rules and restraints, and to win big:

> Debate about gambling reveals fundamental fault lines in American character, sharp tensions between an impulse toward risk and a zeal for control. Those tensions may be universal, but seldom have they been so sharply opposed as in the United States, where longings for a lucky strike have been counterbalanced by a secular Protestant Ethic that has questioned the very existence of luck.[21]

But as Lears himself hints, we can and should extract this history from the confines of America into an idea of Americanness that reflects something universal and also characteristically modern, something that certainly permeates the general field of modern luck as an archetype. The Americanness of American luck, that is, navigates well beyond American history. This is apparent not least in the telling way that the English (in fact, American) word *Lucky* circulated, often as a proper name, in cultures well beyond America and well beyond the English language in the twentieth century.

A few varied examples help make the point. During the Second World War and after, the fascination and cultural force, the glamour, for liberated Europe, of American soldiers and the new life they promised, was frequently encapsulated in cultural myths and objects, one of which was the Lucky Strike cigarette, born in the California gold rush, an essential symbol of the American dream, and of the crazed delusion, of 'striking it lucky'.[22] In liberated Europe, Lucky Strikes became an icon of freedom and also of modern erotic desire.[23] At around the same time, during the 1940s, another 'American' icon began circulating in European popular culture, this time, however, one that was entirely European-born: 'Lucky Luke' was a Franco-Belgian *bande dessinée* series and the name of its lead character. It was created in 1946 by the Belgian comics cartoonist Morris, who later collaborated on the strip from the 1950s until the 1970s with René Goscinny (subsequently co-creator of the *Astérix* series). The strip survives in other hands to this day. Lucky Luke is the archetypal lonesome, fast-shooting, horse-riding American cowboy hero, fighting villains and bonding with his horse. He is not especially lucky as such; his name is instead an indicator of his gritty, down-to-earth resilience and his decency, his easy-going Americanness, and perhaps also of the fact that he always comes through. The fighter and survivor association with Lucky is also there, more cynically perhaps, in the real-life and notorious Italian-American mafioso, 'Lucky' Luciano, whose nickname travelled with him into international folklore as a figure for the slippery, murderous gangster. And any and all of these, accompanied by all the dense punning and wordplay that Samuel Beckett was capable of packing into a couple of syllables, might lie behind the naming of his character Lucky who appears in one key scene only of his *Waiting for Godot* (*En attendant Godot*, first performed in 1953), tied by a rope to his fellow and master, Pozzo. Lucky's situation is something like that of a human slave or an abject beast of burden, weighed down also by all the useless logorrhoea and nonsense of Western thought and philosophy that his incoherent speech pours out over us. Beckett's Lucky is both an echo of the Aristotelian tradition (that link to happiness again) and a stock animal name (like Felix, from another Latin word for happy, lucky); and it is just one of many echoes and ironies in this cursed and suffering figure that his name both points to these high–low origins and is an inversion of the down-home, free American hero, or at least its reflection in the non-American imagination.

*

The lexicon of luck and the culture and myths that surround it are, as this chapter and the previous one have shown, vast, indeed uncontainable. But by dint of the sheer accumulation and of a play of intersections and reiterations traced in Part I, we can distil six pathways to explore, six intersecting motifs or patterns to track through the panoply of modern stories of luck over the course of the six chapters in Part II (Chapters 3 to 8). Each one will tap into ancient–modern motifs, human universal, high conceptual and intuitive notions of luck in the world, and into the new ways our modern world has configured it to tackle the universal challenges that chance and contingency, danger and possibility pose to each and every one of us.

Chapter 3, 'Lucky numbers', picks up on the centrality of number as a foundational aspect of human interactions with and intuitions about luck, from 'primitive' binary gambles between two options (fight or flight?), to the everyday 'science' of games, lotteries and risk, to the hyper-complexities of probability, statistics and even quantum physics. The chapter examines how modern stories of luck work to navigate the contingency and uncertainty of the modern through number games. The key focus of the chapter is on how simple 'lucky numbers' rub up against the unfathomable difficulties of modern experience, often governed by scales and systems beyond the scope of individual calculation, seen through stories of tossed coins, dice throws and deadly games of Russian roulette.

Chapter 4, 'Lucky lines, lucky places', looks at how modern luck and its stories are shaped by specific spaces and places, sites where luck tends to be activated and enacted, where forces of luck are intensified and where our openness to luck is somehow enhanced, and, similarly, at recurrent linear patterns or narrative geometries where space and luck narratives intersect. The chapter argues that these 'lucky places' and 'lucky lines' can be connected to modernity and to its own many new and often disconcerting spatial configurations. Examples of the latter explored in the chapter include the train station, the bar, the border town, and the generically urban.

In Chapter 5, 'The luckiest man', the mythical force of modern luck stories is the key central focus of interest, and in particular the modern archetypes or modern 'heroes', who capture something of the essence of our struggles with contingency and luck. A key instance of this modern mythology is shown to be the figure of 'the luckiest man' or 'the luckiest man in the world', which is shown to be at work in a series of texts from superhero comics to film melodramas to socially engaged plays. Conversely, the chapter also examines the opposite figure, also a quintessential embodiment of the modern, the anti-heroic figure of the preternaturally unlucky man, the loser.

Luck stories frequently intersect as we know with stories of sex, danger and violence, with war and death, and thus with some of the darkest shadows within modernity. Chapter 6, 'Moral luck and the survivor', explores this nexus by picking up on a singular and uncannily compelling narrative figure, in some ways linked to the archetypes of Chapter 5, who seems to embody the scale of modern war, modern technology and their related catastrophes: the figure of the survivor. The survivor exists in storytelling on a rising scale of improbability – and thus of luck – from the survivor of an accident, of car, train or plane crashes, all the way to the most extreme case of the survivors of genocide. These figures of 'lucky survivors' pose intractable moral questions about agency and responsibility encapsulated in the problem of 'survivor guilt'.

Chapter 7, 'Luck and the low life', charts how modern luck stories have often found their natural level in low-life settings and shady corners. From the gambling den to the racetrack, from underworlds to peripheries, luck seems to belong in the modern imagination to the margins. And there is both an aesthetics and a politics to this, since the recourse to luck and gambling is often a last resort for the marginalized, for those outside the legal economy and systems of control. The chapter looks at 'demotic' storytelling from the gamblers of 1920s New York to the racetracks of twenty-first-century California and other places in between.

Finally, in Chapter 8, 'Early style and child's play', the focus turns to combine the modern field of cultural production with the internal formal features of luck narratives analysed thus far. It acknowledges that luck as a motif and facet of narrative is itself somewhat marginalized, condescended to and devalued, and sees this manifested in its typically 'minor' place in literary and film careers, in its confinement to genre spaces, and in its particular prevalence in the field of children's literature. The chapter examines the dynamics behind these positionings and interrogates what they might tell us about the location of luck stories in the modern cultural field writ large.

The book concludes with a brief 'Afterword' reflecting on the intense cultural work being done by and to stories of luck, chance and contingency today at the tail end of the long twentieth century, from constraints placed on luck in the digital universe of Google and Facebook algorithms, to the games of number and risk thrown at us all since early 2020 by the Covid-19 pandemic. Shared, shifting stories of luck, in other words, continue to be a profoundly necessary aspect of our navigation of the everyday uncertainties of the contemporary.

Notes

1. George Lakoff and Mark Johnson, *Metaphors We Live By* (Chicago, IL: University of Chicago Press, 1980).
2. Most of the reference points here are to languages, and thus concepts, of European origin, which reflects my own limitations. There is an extended field of work on language and beliefs

about luck in non-European cultures: see for example two remarkably rich special issues of the journal *Social Analysis*, co-edited by anthropologists Giovanni da Col and Caroline Humphrey: *Cosmologies of Fortune: Luck, vitality, and uncontrolled relatedness*, 56.1 (2012); and *Future and Fortune: Contingency, morality, and the anticipation of everyday life*, 56.2 (2012); see also Lisa Ann Raphals, 'Fate, fortune, chance, and luck in Chinese and Greek: A comparative semantic history', *Philosophy East and West*, 53.4 (October 2003): 537–74.

3   Here as an example is one lucid attempt to make the distinction between fortune and chance in early modern literature, in relation to human individuality or selfhood: 'In medieval, Renaissance, and Restoration texts, fortune had generally been viewed in relation to individual desires and ambitions, and it invariably implies a larger, governing (though often obscure) supernatural design. Chance, on the contrary, is impersonal, arbitrary, and subject to statistical quantification, while its effects on human aspirations are random and incidental' (Brian Richardson, *Unlikely Stories: Causality and the nature of modern narrative* (Newark: University of Delaware Press, 1997), pp. 23–4).

4   See OED, s.v. 'Luck', at http://www.oed.com/view/Entry/110864 (accessed 26 July 2022)(emphasis added). This chapter makes extensive use of the remarkable resources and sources of meaning, etymology and historical usage found in the online OED, as well as etymological dictionaries of English, Latin and other languages I am able to read. Also useful are the thesaurus and word-tree entries such as those to be found in the *Cambridge Dictionary*'s SMART vocabulary clouds (see for instance 'Good luck and bad luck', at https://dictionary. cambridge.org/topics/chance-and-possibility/good-luck-and-bad-luck), or the word-maps of the *Visual Thesaurus* (at https://www.visualthesaurus.com/).

5   Jacques Derrida, in one of his sparkling and more accessible essays, reflected on the etymologies and associations of luck with chance, falling, transgression. See Jacques Derrida, 'My Chances / *Mes chances*: A rendezvous with some Epicurean stereophonies', trans. Irene Harvey and Avital Ronell, in *Psyche: Inventions of the other, vol. I* (Stanford, CA: Stanford University Press, 2007), pp. 344–76.

6   Modern English does preserve an echo of the earlier usage in 'casualty', the victim of an accident or misfortune. Thomas Hardy's 1866 poem 'Hap', quoted in Chapter 1, retains the etymological meaning, when it uses 'Casualty' ('Crass Casualty') as a synonym for 'Hap' (or luck). In contemporary political theory, Adriana Cavarero offers powerful reflections on the ethics of contemporary violence by linking the term's etymology to the incidental and innocent victims of war or terrorism. to the randomness of their suffering (Adriana Cavarero, *Horrorism: Naming contemporary violence*, trans. William McCuaig (New York: Columbia University Press, 2011), pp. 74–5). On chance, *caso* and *casualità* as principles of epistemology and (micro-)historical research methods, see the fascinating reflections by Carlo Ginzburg in 'A proposito di Nondimanco / Il caso, i casi', *Doppiozero*, 12 April 2019, at https://www.doppiozero.com/materiali/il-caso-i-casi, where Ginzburg notes that in the 1950s his earliest associations of the term 'case' were with Freud and Sherlock Holmes; and 'Conversations with Orion', trans. Giovanni Zanalda, *Perspectives* 45 (May 2005), at https:// www.historians.org/publications-and-directories/perspectives-on-history/may-2005/ conversations-with-orion.

7   On this link between chance, encounter and the modern novel, see for example Jean-Dominique Biard, 'Chance encounters as a novelistic device', *Journal of European Studies*, 18.1 (March 1988): 21–35; Romano Luperini, *L'incontro e il caso: Narrazioni moderne e destino dell'uomo occidentale* (Bari: Laterza, 2007). More broadly, chance as a key factor in the modern novel, following on from Darwin's principle of random variation as a driving force in evolutionary change, was widely explored in George Levine's influential study *Darwin and the Novelists: Patterns of science in Victorian fiction* (Chicago, IL: University of Chicago Press, 1988).

8   The concept of the accident has a long history in philosophy and literature, starting with Aristotle, examined in Ross Hamilton, *Accident: A philosophical and literary history* (Chicago, IL: University of Chicago Press, 2007). There is another false or proximate etymology that is suggestive here: 'incident' and related words seem to veer close in etymology and meaning to 'incision', from the Latin *caedĕre*, to cut. Even though this is in fact quite distinct from the root in *cadere*, we will see that there is indeed a geometry of luck vocabulary that is strongly associated with intersections, with lines in movement cutting across one another and thus with encounters between people, places and events.

9   The bond of time to chance is already evoked in a much-quoted verse from Ecclesiastes (9: 11), 'the race is not to the swift, nor the battle to the strong, neither yet bread to the wise, nor yet

riches to men of understanding, nor yet favour to men of skill; but time and chance happeneth to them all' (Authorized Version).

10 On Lucretius and the *clinamen* and its role as one of the hidden roots of modern epistemology and science in early modern Europe, see Stephen Greenblatt, *The Swerve: How the world became modern* (New York: W. W. Norton, 2011). And on the influence of Lucretius on modern literature, especially on the experimental literature of chance, see Warren F. Motte, 'Clinamen redux', *Comparative Literature Studies*, 23.4 (Winter, 1986): 263–81.

11 On the role of chance in Darwinian and later twentieth-century re-elaborations of evolutionary theory (the so-called 'modern synthesis'), see Francesca Merlin, 'Evolutionary chance mutation: A defense of the modern synthesis' consensus view', *Philosophy, Theory, and Practice in Biology*, 2.3 (September 2010), at http://dx.doi.org/10.3998/ptb.6959004.0002.003.

12 Jorge Luis Borges, 'El jardin de senderos que se bifurcan' (1941), in English as 'The garden of forking paths', in *Collected Fictions*, trans. Andrew Hurley (London: Allen Lane, 1998), pp. 119–28. For more on 'forking-path' narratives, see Chapter 4.

13 On the history of lotteries, see for example Gherardo Ortalli (ed.), *Lotteries, Lotto, Slot Machines: The luck of the draw: A history of games of chance* (Rome: Viella / Fondazione Benetton, 2019).

14 On the archaeology and history of dice, which stretches back at least as far as 2000 BCE, see for example Marco Dotti, *Il calcolo dei dadi: Azzardo e vita quotidiana* (Milan: O barra O, 2013), pp. 33–45.

15 The same connection of dice to *hasard* governs the great poem of formal play and avant-garde experimentalism in late nineteenth-century, early high-modernist European literature (and the source of one of the epigraphs to this book), Stéphane Mallarmé, *Un coup de dés jamais n'abolira le hasard* ('A throw of the dice can never cancel chance') (1897).

16 Bad luck and unlucky or ill-fated people seem to attract an especially vivid array of locally specific, colloquial terms that are often comic or bordering on the obscene, in stark contrast to 'noble' unfortunates such as Romeo and Juliet. In Chapter 5, where this figure is explored further, we will come across terms such as the loser, *schlimazel*, *klutz*, *sfigato* and *chèvre*, and this is just a small illustrative sample of a vast field.

17 In the late twentieth century, the concept of risk was the subject of particular attention in the social sciences, stimulated especially by the work of Ulrich Beck, who conceived of risk as central to contemporary thinking on the economy and the political sociology of late capitalism. For Beck the 'risk society' is a late modern society whose subjects and institutions are compelled to organize and govern themselves according to prevalent and increasingly overwhelming and unpredictable external risks, dangers and insecurities (see Ulrich Beck, *Risk Society: Towards a new modernity*, trans. Mark Ritter (London: Sage, 1992)). We might usefully further link this conceptualization to our idea of luck and luck stories as constitutive of the experience of modernity. On the mathematics of risk in contemporary life, see for example Michael Blastland and David Spiegelhalter, *The Norm Chronicles: Stories and numbers about danger* (London: Profile Books, 2014). On risk from a more historical perspective, see Peter L. Bernstein, *Against the Gods: The remarkable story of risk* (New York: John Wiley & Sons, 1998).

18 Umberto Eco collected his essays on the uses of error and accident in the history of human knowledge under the title *Serendipities: Language and lunacy*, trans. William Weaver (New York: Columbia University Press, 1998). See also Mark de Rond and Iain Morley, eds, *Serendipity: Fortune and the prepared mind* (Cambridge: Cambridge University Press, 2010); Telmo Pievani, *Serendipità: L'inatteso nella scienza* (Milan: Raffaello Cortina, 2021); and compare a recent entry in the proliferating subgenre of self-help luck books, Christian Busch, *The Serendipity Mindset: The art and science of creating good luck* (London: Penguin, 2020).

19 Henry Luce, publisher of *Life* magazine, famously claimed the twentieth century as 'the American century' (Henry Luce, 'The American century', *Life*, 17 February 1941). On American cultural imperialism, with a particular focus on Europe, see Victoria de Grazia, *Irresistible Empire: America's advance through twentieth-century Europe* (Cambridge, MA: Belknap Press of Harvard University Press, 2005); David Ellwood, *The Shock of America: Europe and the challenge of the century* (Oxford: Oxford University Press, 2016).

20 T. J. Jackson Lears, *Something for Nothing: Luck in America* (London: Penguin, 2003).

21 Lears, *Something*, p. 2. There is a longstanding tradition of critical association between capitalism, chance and gambling, for example by Walter Benjamin, whose unfinished 1930s *Arcades* project describes capitalism (quoting Paul Lafargue) as a 'giant international gambling

house' (Walter Benjamin, *The Arcades Project*, trans. Howard Eiland and Kevin McLaughlin (Cambridge, MA: Belknap Press of Harvard University Press, 1999), p. 497). In the same period, the board game *Monopoly,* launched commercially in 1935 by Parker Brothers, used 'Chance' cards as one of its central features, driving the speculative acquisition or loss of property and capital.

22 The iconography of 'striking it lucky' or 'striking it rich' transferred from the gold rush to another quintessentially American, and also wider global, modern fantasy of striking oil, modern liquid gold. This luck fantasy is vividly captured in Ryszard Kapuściński's portrait of the last Shah of Iran, *Shah of Shahs*: 'Oil kindles extraordinary emotions and hopes, since oil is above all a great temptation. It is the temptation of ease, wealth, strength, fortune, power. […] The concept of oil expresses perfectly the eternal human dream of wealth achieved through lucky accident, through a kiss of fortune and not by sweat, anguish, hard work. In this sense oil is a fairy tale and, like every fairy tale, a bit of a lie' (Ryszard Kapuściński, *Shah of Shahs*, trans. William R. Brand and Katarzyna Mroczkowska-Brand (New York: Vintage, 1992), pp. 34–5).

23 A particular famous, indeed scandalous press photo of 1947 showed film star Lucia Bosé in bed with a Lucky Strike (see Carl Ipsen, *Fumo: Italy's love affair with the cigarette* (Stanford, CA: Stanford University Press, 2016), pp. 107–8). Cf. more widely, Richard Klein, *Cigarettes Are Sublime* (Durham, NC: Duke University Press, 1994).

Part II

3
Lucky numbers

Our modernity is decidedly an age of numbers, especially of unimaginably large numbers and of number determinism. The nineteenth and twentieth centuries ushered in an age of statistics, probability and actuarial calculation, the twenty-first century one of big data and digital surveillance capitalism.[1] But luck and luck stories do not see it that way, or rather do not *tell* it that way. Luck stories are steeped in numbers, in number lore and number games, in bets, odds, risks and guesses, but they are, typically, either wilfully blind to the determinism of large numbers, or vague and loose when the counting goes high. In luck stories, old notions, back-of-the-envelope calculations and small numbers, just like the human individuals that use them, come up against and clash with the higher systems that control them, and this clash is what makes them characteristically modern.

There are good anthropological or evolutionary reasons for this, as Kahneman and Stanislas Dehaene among others have investigated, since it seems that our brains and our senses, our 'mathematical minds', have evolved to deal with small, visible and reckonable numeric orders in the phenomenal world – from nothing (although zero as a number is a relatively recent invention, perhaps from third-century India), to one, two, possibly as high as six – above which we tend to resort intuitively to loose categories such as the many or the uncountable.[2] We certainly struggle to grasp, from the moment we encounter them as schoolchildren, the complexity of large numbers and calculation, let alone the newly discovered scales of astronomy and cosmology or indeed the infinitesimally small measures (and quantum states of being) of atomic and subatomic physics. And these large numbers already point towards questions of probability, chance and luck, if we think for example of the challenge of understanding the infinitesimal improbability of the very existence of a cosmos that contains a single planet with all the conditions necessary for the evolution of life, let alone of human life.[3]

And it is not only our maths that fails us in such contexts; it is also and perhaps above all our languages, shaped in their counting by the same small-number brains that determine our numerical perceptions. This is the system clash – another iteration of Kahneman's System 1 and System 2 – from which many modern luck stories flow, generating uncertainty, plurality of perspective, success and failure, comedy and tragedy. Numbers feel lucky, feel like they work as keys to deciphering our world or unlocking our future success, but they most often fail us. This chapter looks at the fragile workings of these modern lucky numbers.

Rick Blaine is sitting at his bar in Casablanca in late 1941, alone, after hours, drunk and disconsolate. His old friend Sam comes to offer support, but cannot shake him. Rick is 'waiting for a lady', his former lover Ilse Lund, who abandoned him in Paris the year before and has now turned up in Casablanca with her new partner, Resistance war hero Victor Laszlo, looking for papers, transit letters, to escape the Nazis. This is, of course, *Casablanca* (dir. Michael Curtiz, 1942), Rick is Humphrey Bogart and Ilse is Ingrid Bergman. And Rick's drunken monologue in this scene, including one of the most quoted lines in film history, is among other things a stripped-down tale of unlucky numbers:

RICK: They grab Ugarte [a black-market dealer], then she [Ilse] walks in. Well, that's the way it goes. One in, one out. ... Sam.
SAM: Yes, boss?
RICK: If it's December 1941 in Casablanca, what time is it in New York?
SAM: What? My watch stopped.
RICK: I bet they're asleep in New York. I bet they're asleep all over America. ... Of all the gin joints in all the towns in all the world, she walks into mine.

'One in, one out', the time in New York, the bet on night and day: these are all nonsense numbers, with no purchase in reality, no real cause or effect, spoken out of the bottle. They lead up to Rick's melancholic, rough-and-ready calculus, 'Of all the gin joints in all the towns ...'. This is a probability equation – What are the chances? How unlucky can you get? – but the numbers are a feint, a mask for Rick's bitter love story and a foreshadowing of his unlikely redemption, which will form the dramatic climax of the film, for the causes of love, sacrifice and patriotic heroism.

This much-quoted moment from *Casablanca* gives us a telling insight into the shadow-workings of simple numbers in modern luck stories, since in fact numbers themselves are hardly mentioned at all ('one', 'all', dates, time), but the stories are nevertheless pulled by their undertow and by their intuited link to luck. They capture something essential in an emotion and a narrative situation and space (and indeed we will come back to the film as a whole as a tale of convergence of fortune and misfortune in a single space in Chapter 4). It is no coincidence that Rick's calculation takes place in wartime, in 1941: the world war, the global journey the scene takes us on from Paris to Casablanca to New York, the imaginary glance over 'all the towns in all the world', the shift in scale from the vast world out there to the bar table and bottle in here – all this sense of scale makes possible the melodrama and the romance (consider another famous number line of Rick's: 'I'm no good at being noble. But it doesn't take much to see that the problems of three little people don't amount to a hill of beans in this crazy world'). And this is what makes the rough play of numbers something modern, or rather ancient–modern, as we put it in Part I, a perception of two vastly incommensurate scales clashing and the narrative human drama at the heart of it.

Rick's Bar is a good place to start an exploration of lucky numbers, because it underscores how the numbers in modern luck stories tend to be phantasmatic. Even when they are decidedly present *as numbers*, we need to be wary of treating them as anything more than a feint towards the higher mathematics, anything more than an intuitive arithmetic that lets luck do its work as a human and storytelling device in the face of multiple modern confusions of cause and effect, agency and responsibility. A powerful case in point where numbers as numbers are to the fore is Tom Stoppard's 1966 play, *Rosencrantz and Guildenstern Are Dead*, riffing with postmodern verve on two minor characters in *Hamlet*. Rosencrantz and Guildenstern were already born in Shakespeare's play under the sign of 'fortune', as their opening ribald banter on their first encounter with their supposed friend Hamlet in Shakespeare's play shows:

> HAMLET: My excellent good friends! How dost thou, Guildenstern? Ah, Rosencrantz! Good lads, how do ye both?
> ROSENCRANTZ: As the indifferent children of the earth.
> GUILDENSTERN: Happy, in that we are not over-happy;
> On fortune's cap we are not the very button.
> HAMLET: Nor the soles of her shoe?

ROSENCRANTZ:	Neither, my lord.
HAMLET:	Then you live about her waist, or in the middle of her favours?
GUILDENSTERN:	Faith, her privates we.
HAMLET:	In the secret parts of fortune? O, most true; she is a strumpet. What news?[4]

Stoppard's play, in playful echo of that banter, sets its protagonists from the outset in a realm of 'suspended' fortune. It opens with a famously baffling, comic scene of the two eponymous heroes betting on the toss of a coin. Guildenstern tosses, Rosencrantz calls and it comes up heads, every single time, 92 times in a row. The sheer absurdity of the scene, and Guildenstern's perplexed mock-philosophical reflections on it (Stoppard's stage directions indicate Guildenstern is 'well alive to the oddity of it. He is not worried about the money, but he is worried by the implications; aware but not going to panic about it'),[5] gradually nudge the audience towards a marking out of the pair's strange entrapment. They find themselves in a predetermined world, a universe pre-written (by Shakespeare), one in which the apparent workings of fortune and misfortune, agency and drama are suspended, figured by the stalling in the simplest of binary number distributions, the purest of all luck games: heads–tails, win–lose, 1–0:

GUILDENSTERN:	It must be indicative of something, besides the redistribution of wealth. (*He muses*.) List of possible explanations. One: I'm willing it. Inside where nothing shows, I'm the essence of a man spinning double-headed coins, and betting against himself in private atonement for an unremembered past. (*He spins a coin at ROSENCRANTZ*.)
ROSENCRANTZ:	Heads.
GUILDENSTERN:	Two: time has stopped dead, and a single experience of one coin being spun once has been repeated ninety times … (*He flips a coin, looks at it, tosses it to ROSENCRANTZ*.) On the whole, doubtful. Three: divine intervention, that is to say, a good turn from above concerning him, cf. children of Israel, or retribution from above concerning me, cf. Lot's wife. Four: a spectacular vindication of the principle

that each individual coin spun individually (he spins one) is as likely to come down heads as tails and therefore should cause no surprise that each individual time it does. (*It does ...*)[6]

Guildenstern deploys a smattering of notions – from economics, theology, the science of space-time, probability (he follows up this monologue with a long syllogistic reflection on probability, the probability of probability and 'un-, sub- or supernatural forces')[7] – but the surprise, and the comedy, remain. Rosencrantz's hyperbolic, metastasized luck is a figure of a bind; the pair are stuck, their games and their speech repetitious or specious, their existences, we begin to realize, tenuous, unchanging, like simulacra of a vital, changing reality (and in this, as in many other respects, they are akin to the pseudo-couples of *Waiting for Godot*, Vladimir and Estragon and Pozzo and Lucky, to whom, as Vivian Mercier famously put it, 'nothing happens, twice').[8] They are, in other words, as the title tells us, already dead. And the 'lucky' coins are a glitch in the system, a clue that tells us that this is not quite life as we know it. (We will return below to the figure of the glitch.)

The link from simple numbers to matters of life and death, posited in mock-metaphysical style by Stoppard, is staged even more explicitly in one of the most stark and powerful number motifs in the modern cultural armoury, another apparently simple game of numbers that has generated luck narratives, and luck clichés, of remarkable intensity: the game of Russian roulette.

The origins of Russian roulette are obscure. Some sources point to the literature of the duel and especially Mikhail Lermontov's *A Hero of Our Time* (1841), others to an obscure 1930s short story in the American illlustrated magazine *Collier's*.[9] But in its most familiar form, at least, we can certainly say it is dependent on a modern invention, a piece of modern technology, the six-barrel revolver, itself a powerful emblem of the American West and its mythologization in the genre of cowboy books and films.[10] (Russian roulette is not to be found in conventional cowboy stories, however: it is too stark and too nihilistic a staging of luck, perhaps.) Place a single bullet into a six-barrel revolver, spin the barrel and shoot the gun against your temple. The odds, the lucky numbers, could hardly be more stark or more simple: 5-to-6 you live, 1-to-6 you die. And whatever its origins, the figure of Russian roulette has taken on powerful symbolic, even mythical, resonance in some corners of contemporary culture, none more so than in two American films that bookend the fretful, heated politics of the 1970s, each containing standout sequences that play a version of this game of bullets and numbers, and each one as a result rising to iconic cultural status – and intense controversy – so that in some sense they can be said to have distilled in figural form a contemporary topos of luck. Through this distillation, they came to channel contemporary anxieties around violence and war, both in reality and in representation, linking the urban and intra-national violence of the American city of the 1970s of one case, to the global, colonial and geopolitical violence of the recently ended Vietnam war of the other. The films in question were *Dirty Harry* (dir. Don Siegel, 1971) and *The Deer Hunter* (dir. Michael Cimino, 1978).

The two films are of profoundly contrasting kind in several respects: in genre (cop movie, war movie), in artistic pitch and style (popular entertainment, new Hollywood director's cinema) and in the biographies, generations, acting styles and iconic associations of their leading men (Clint Eastwood, Robert De Niro). But they share a series of key features, starting with the common iconic status of those stars as leading figures of the masculinity of the post-studio era in Hollywood.[11] In their Russian roulette sequences specifically, the films share further crucial features and are thus in implicit dialogue with each other, through hidden generic markers – deriving from the western, above all – that point to their capacity to engage with profound problems of an (American, modern, masculine) identity in crisis. This holds not only for Eastwood and De Niro, who already at the time of the making of these films shared in their back catalogue defining iconic roles as vigilante heroes: Eastwood's spaghetti western hero known as 'the man with no name' in Sergio Leone's so-called 'Dollars trilogy', 1964–6, and De Niro's Travis Bickle in *Taxi Driver* (dir. Martin Scorsese, 1976). These figures are both avenging cowboy-angels, come to cleanse degenerate towns in latter-day American Gomorrah. And the presence of common markers between *Dirty Harry* and *The Deer Hunter* is borne out also in that shared fetish-object, the six-shooter, onto which the dramatization of luck is relentlessly projected in the defining sequences of both films.

The earlier of the two, *Dirty Harry*, starts and ends with Eastwood's detective Harry Callahan and his virtuoso, single-handed take-down of two criminals: at the start of the film a street thief (played by Albert Popwell), in a sequence that sets out to establish Harry's credentials as a maverick, ice-cool, vigilante cop who does not play by the rules (but does relish play), and subsequently, at the climax of the film, the serial killer 'Scorpio' (Andy Robinson), the film's principal villain, very loosely based on a true-crime case, who dies in a set-piece reprise-cum-inversion of the earlier sequence. In both sequences, following a shoot-out, Harry/Eastwood ends up filmed from an angled camera from below, looming tall over the fallen criminal, Smith and Wesson .44 Magnum in hand, offering the perp (the illusion of) a chance to gamble between life and death, a mock duel between the criminal and the law, apparently governed not by right and wrong, or strength and weakness, but by luck. In both cases, Callahan delivers his signature monologue, part of which was quoted in Chapter 1, including the catchphrase that would propel the character to the status of popular icon. The two serial variants start as follows, delivered by Eastwood with a series of contemptuous, knowing smirks, in his trademark husky drawl:

> I know what you're thinking: 'Did he fire six shots or only five?' Well, to tell you the truth, in all this excitement, I've kinda lost track myself. But being this is a .44 Magnum, the most powerful handgun in the world, and would blow your head clean off, you've got to ask yourself one question: 'Do I feel lucky?' Well, do you, punk?

This is a tricky variant on Russian roulette: the thief has to calculate whether or not he is staring at certain death – one bullet left – or whether all six bullets are spent and his chance of dying is now zero. In the first sequence, the trembling, crushed villain caves, letting his tensed hand, hovering near his own handgun, drop away, giving up on the mock offer of the duel. Callahan picks up the weapon and turns to walk away. But his victim (and his audience) need to know whether he has won or lost – whether he played the game and read the odds right, or lost on a nothing, on a bluff: 'Hey, I gots to know,' he says. Callahan turns back, walks back up to point-blank range and shoots ... a blank. He laughs, either because he knew he was bluffing, or, more likely given his devil-may-care persona, because he genuinely neither knew nor cared: because he is a creature of luck.

Eighty-two minutes of screen-time further on, Callahan has cornered Scorpio. The time, his smile has given way to a spitting snarl and a heavily punctuated delivery of a near-identical script:

> I know what you're thinking, punk, you're thinking: 'Did he fire six shots or only five?' Now, to tell you the truth, I forgot myself in all this excitement. But being this is a .44 Magnum, the most powerful handgun in the world, and would blow your head clean off, you've got to ask yourself a question: 'Do I feel lucky?' ... Well, do you, punk?

In a neat and pleasurably inevitable symmetrical inversion, which only underlines Callahan's – or his Magnum's – preternatural embodiment of luck, Scorpio gambles the other way and grabs his gun. This time, Callahan shoots for real and kills him, the bullet's impact arcing the serial killer's body through the air and into the murky water behind. The inversion makes Callahan, or the Magnum or the movie, an embodiment of a kind of transcendent, violent natural justice: the weak survive; the truly evil must die; the roll of the dice, the numbers will know which is which and Callahan is a spirit or god of this force of luck.[12]

Seven years and several *Dirty Harry* sequels later, Michael Cimino released his epic Ukrainian-American, working-class, Vietnam war movie, *The Deer Hunter*, which in one of its defining motifs takes the staging of Russian roulette to a paroxysmal pitch of literal and metaphorical intensity. Cimino somehow transformed this foolish game into one of the defining modern icons of risk, violence, fragility and the absurdity of war, in particular through one infamous sequence played out in the infested waters of a South-East Asian river. Cimino's luck sequence does not spell out in words the rules of the game, nor what is at stake, as *Dirty Harry*'s set-piece monologue had, but the gun and the game of luck, the sheer terror and confused violence of the scene, do frantic visual and aural work in order to show, to feel (and make the audience feel) what is at stake.

The key sequence takes place over 16 excruciating minutes, as De Niro's character Mike and his two fellow conscript soldiers from Pennsylvania – Steven (John Savage) and Nick (Christopher Walken) – find themselves held in a squalid Vietcong prison shack, made of bamboo rafts and cages, by, above and below a swelling river. One by one, the prisoners are forced to play Russian roulette to the death in front of their baying captors. The camera angles from above, below and within the watery, darkened, backlit, slatted spaces were deployed with remarkable force by director of photography Vilmos Zsigmond to build the sequence's confusion and impossible tension. First, the three Americans are forced to look on, as the Vietcong play their game with fellow Vietnamese prisoners, imagining along with the spectators that it will soon be their turn. When Mike, Steven and Nick are hauled up in pairs, there is a frenzy of barked orders, slaps and screams, pointed pistols and spun barrels, hysterical grimaces, smiles and tears, introjected and projected violence and moments of hyperventilating and mutual goading. The prisoners are forced to play Russian roulette against each other, while the guards bet piles of cash on the outcome. The dead are dumped into the river and then the next victim is dragged up from the swamp, until finally, as Mike and Nick face each other, the whole scene and its tensions explode into a gun battle that leaves the Vietcong dead and the American trio just about alive and escaped, floating downriver on a tree branch.

The scene comes around halfway through the three-hour film and displays in grim essence many of its central concerns, with war, violence, masculinity and mortality. And all of these are staged – and to a degree de-historicized and universalized – through the distilled power of the force and terror of pure luck. The scene became notorious for a number of intersecting reasons: for its sheer horror, for the virtuoso acting of De Niro and Walken, for its fantastical reimagining of historical violence (Russian roulette was never a tool of torture in Vietnam), for its broad-brush, quite probably racist, portrayal of the Vietcong (all baying, undifferentiated and pure evil).[13] As in *Dirty Harry*, it is undoubtedly the matrix of the pure, fatal luck of numbers underpinning the scene that gives it its driving force, its axis of connection to the spectator: there is no simpler nor more terrifying nor more universal question than the binary calculation offered up by Russian roulette: is there a bullet or not? Death or life? In so far as the question and scene amount to a duel with death itself, they are pitched somewhere between *Dirty Harry* and *The Seventh Seal* (dir. Ingmar Bergman, 1957), in which the Knight (Max von Sydow) sits down with Death itself to play a game of chess for his very life.

The Russian roulette sequence is *The Deer Hunter*'s centrepiece and its objects and motifs of luck ripple outwards throughout the film, both proleptically and analeptically, making it just as much of a structuring presence and synecdoche for the whole as the equivalent sequences in *Dirty Harry*. Looking forward in the narrative, Russian roulette itself recurs later on, marking in particular the arc of Walken's character Nick, persisting as a pathological weight on his mental equilibrium, an immoveable, obsessively revisited trauma that follows him to inevitable death. It is as if Nick's survival in the river camp cage was a mirage, a mere dilation of time, an illusory delay in the flashpoint moment of his death (in this not unlike Rosencrantz and Guildenstern, who are already dead). After reaching a hospital in Saigon, Nick is taken up by mysterious gambling guru Julien Grinda (Pierre Segui), who grows rich on Nick's drug-addled compulsive need to keep playing Russian roulette, now in the city's drug and gambling dens, and on his apparently magical ability to keep winning. Somehow he stays alive – although mentally he is lost in a state close to catatonia – until Mike returns from America to search him out, only to witness face to face his first and last failure with the bullet, his death a close reprise of the prison-camp scene, with the same baying noise, money, guns and tension (and, indeed, ethnic stereotyping) as the first time. (The replaying of the sequence closely recalls the structure of the binary reprise in *Dirty Harry*, in both cases the first ending in life, the second in death.) Nick, his head in a red bandana, rather than the white bandage he wore in the prison-camp scene, only recognizes Mike moments before the fatal shot, and he does so through another talismanic motif of luck in the film, which had been established proleptically in its opening part set back in Pennsylvania: the eponymous motif of the deer hunter and (again) his gun.

Just before dying, Nick looks at Mike one last time. As a flicker of a memory of their hunting trips back home plays across his eyes, he smiles and says, 'One shot.' (Note once again the simple number.) The reference is to the long arc of the film's first part, to the steelworks town the men come from, the wedding sequence of Steven and Angela (Rutanya Alda), scenes of men working, drinking, celebrating and fighting, culminating in a lyrical mountain-top expedition to hunt for deer. In a moment of marked symbolic weight, the beautiful animal is taken down with 'one shot' from Mike's rifle, according to his purist principle of the 'right' way to hunt and kill, a principle that will be shattered and grotesquely parodied in the incessantly repeated shots of the Russian roulette sequences, and by extension in the grotesque history of the Vietnam war as a whole. The opening part is pregnant with fear and excitement for the future, both for the marrying couple (and other couplings and relationships, especially Mike's with Linda, played by Meryl Streep) and for the imminent draft to Vietnam, and with the freedom, danger and elemental proximity to death that the deer hunt encapsulates. In a vein of heavy allegory that characterizes much of Cimino's work, all this sense of (shattered) future and fragile present is shot through with intense communal and homosocial bonding at the heart of a dark, but also somehow celebrated, masculinity. And the motifs of masculinity, the gun and Mike's 'one shot' are all tied to the motif of luck, and thus also to the Russian roulette and to the unravelling of Nick's life, as the film arcs through its first elegiac and ultimately tragic progress.[14] In fact, the talisman of luck had already been woven in closely and explicitly during the wedding sequence of the opening part, in one of its most resonant ritual, communal moments. At the wedding party, the happy couple, Angela and Steven, drink together according to Ukrainian tradition from the entwined double wine cup. The MC grandly and joyfully declares, 'Angela and Steven, if you don't spill a drop, it's good luck for the rest of your life.' The couple drink long and slow, to a crescendo of cheering and applause. Only the camera seems to notice, in a cutaway to close-up, two bloody drops of red wine splashing on Angela's pure white dress. Luck seems to give way to fate here, in a portentous pairing we have come across before, seeping like a poisoned red stain across the canvas of the film. The symbolic connection to blood and death, and to Nick's red bandana (widely used in the posters and marketing of the film), is all too clear.

*

The deadly 1-in-6 calculation of Russian roulette does a great deal of symbolic and narrative work in just a handful of scenes and sequences in these films, staging and distilling, within the confines of each one's register and genre, some rather profound questions, to do with agency and control but also masculinity, violence and war, in a cultural moment in 1970s America of profound fracture and destabilization. One-in-6 odds match in lucky numbers another, even more familiar, indeed ancient, talisman of luck that we have come across before, in Chapter 2, the six-sided die. We can therefore follow the same set of numbers and some of the same questions – of luck and loss of self, of freedom, survival and moral danger – through a parallel case study of luck storytelling with numbers, this time replayed through the figure of dice. The work in question was another 1970s American cultural product: a strange and in some quarters cultishly successful, psychosexual, metafictional, satirical novel of 1971 by Luke Rhinehart entitled *The Dice Man*.[15]

The Dice Man is set in a Manhattan world of work, sex and Freudian psychoanalysis. Over the course of the novel, its protagonist, also named Luke Rhinehart, becomes a subversive visionary and mock-revolutionary prophet of luck, profoundly subverting along the way all the individuals and institutions, the mores and morals of his comfortable, modern middle-class world. Luke is a successful but dissatisfied psychoanalyst, stuck in a rut in career and marriage, a cliché of mid-life crisis and a 'sophomoric'[16] yearning for a life that is more real, more alive. One day – 'D-day', as he comes to call it (for 'dice day') – he stumbles upon the solution and the radical revolution that propels the whole novel: after a desultory game of poker, he finds a die under a sofa and decides on a drunken whim that if he throws a one, he will go to the apartment on the floor below and rape his friend, fellow psychiatrist Jake's wife, Arlene. He throws a one, thus unleashing the entire philosophy, life system, anti-psychiatry and cult of the 'Diceman'.

Luke will live from now according to the throw, the rule, of the dice. In gradually increasing degrees of audacity and submission, for his every single action, Luke will draw up for himself a list of options and let the die decide. *Alea iacta est*, indeed. The upshot is a freewheeling anarchic chaos and apparently absolute freedom, the destruction of all sense of self, of need, of human relations, mores and institutions all around him: in his professional practice, in the hospital and prison where he works, in the TV forum on religion in which he earnestly appears, in his marriage and family, and so on. Luke experiments with himself, with his children – who tellingly take to the game with the joyous innocence of as yet unformed selves, for whom play trumps all regulated morality – with his lovers and his wife, with his patients. Gradually, he acquires a following, the 'dicepeople', sundry devotees, from teenagers, managers, writers, all of whom feel released from their neuroses by the self-abnegating power of the dice. They drop out of their lives to experiment in his so-called CETREs, 'Centers for Experiments in Totally Random Environments'.[17] The dice become a fully fledged cult phenomenon and Luke its guru. And this book is framed internally, in the novel's elaborate metafiction and self-commentary, as itself a 'cult' novel, part manual for living, part autobiography, part sacred text for the 'Way of the Dice'.

The Dice Man is frequently disturbingly violent, pornographic and abusive – and profoundly misogynistic, as is apparent from its founding act of 'dice' rape. The apparently 'random' luck choices Luke selects for the dice are persistently sexualized, and often degrading and humiliating. Indeed, his submission to the will of the Dice culminates in an extended sequence describing a brutal, sexualized murder of a woman. The squalid nature of these choices reflects, of course, Luke's drives and so they are far from random, pointing to one line of origin of all modern luck stories in Freudian ideas of free association, slips and errors and the hypothesis of their reflection of subconscious drives and impulses.[18] But Rhinehart's – and 'Rhinehart''s – project is also proffered as politically subversive, in a mode typical of certain 1970s subcultures (and as prone to degradation into the corrupt power of sects and secret societies). The cult and the novel share an ambition to diagnose something fundamental, and fundamentally corrupt, in the American or modern condition – 'Being an American, I had to kill,' Luke calmly explains[19] – as well as a form of spiritual cure for this condition (and a parody of both). *The Dice Man* frequently refers to and quotes from an imaginary new work of Holy Writ, *'The Book of the Die'*, in effect a patchwork of the Psalms and the Gospels, Lao-Tzu, Zen, Blake, Nietzsche's Zarathustra and more, all adapted to substitute the figure of the godhead with the Die, with Chance:

> In the beginning was Chance and Chance was with God and Chance was God. [...] There was a man sent by Chance, whose name was

> Luke. The same came for a witness, to bear witness of Whim, that all men through him might believe. He was not Chance, but was sent to bear witness of Chance. That was the true Accident [...]. And Chance was made flesh [...], and he dwelt among us, full of chaos, and falsehood and whim.[20]

At various moments, Luke asserts that he is God, Jesus, the Tao, that he has created a radically new form of human (non-)consciousness, the 'Totally Random Man'.[21]

Luke's monomaniacal diceworld creates a vision of a world governed by pure luck, a vision that both contaminates and subtly reflects the modern world that surrounds him. But the (mock-)philosophical grounding of the diceworld remains rooted in the problem of the self, of agency and its profound uselessness. Luke's most profound dissatisfaction, he realizes ultimately, is with the dogma of the singularity and consistency of the self itself and in this he taps into anxieties that go back at least as far as the crises of identity and selfhood of high modernism. His most radical and transformative intuition is into a form of freedom from this dead weight of the self through flux, change and inconsistency, through a Whitmanesque multitude of selves. Through the whim of the dice, of a game of luck, layer upon layer of foundational meaning and existential substance are stripped away from the self: responsibility and control, but also guilt, pride, fear, a sense of past and future, social networks and relations, morality, subjectivity itself. All disappear, sacrificed to the new godhead:

> It was the Goddam sense of having a self: that sense of self which psychologists have been proclaiming we all must have. What if [...] the development of a sense of self is normal and natural, but is neither inevitable nor *desirable*? [...] Men have admired Prometheus and Mars too long; our God must become Proteus.[22]

Patterns and consistency must be replaced by a childlike openness: 'I am he who can play many games,' he reflects, 'fearless, frameless, egoless'. Even temporality, past and future, birth and death, cease to make sense: 'I am born anew at each green fall of the die, and by die-ing I eliminate my since. [...] Living flows.' The pressures of social convention dissolve, the self in the family and in the public sphere is rendered meaningless: 'My goal was to destroy all sense of an audience; to become without values, evaluators, without desires.' In an asymptotic trajectory, Luke imagines moving towards the 'infinitely multiple personality', a state of pure randomness, of ungraspable saturation in change and luck.[23]

Ultimately, the Dice Man's utopia imagines living all the throws of the dice at once; what he calls the 'six-sided man' becomes a preliminary step towards the infinite-sided man.[24] As one of Luke's patients, O. B., complains, every choice or action he is forced to make through the dice in fact shuts off myriad, indeed infinite, other selves and futures, for no good reason:

> I feel I ought to write a great novel, write numerous letters, be friendly with more of the interesting people in my community, give more parties, dedicate more time to my intellectual pursuits, play with my children, make love to my wife, go hiking more often, go to the Congo, be a radical trying to revolutionize society, write fairy tales, buy a bigger boat, do more sailing, sunning and swimming, write a book on the American picaresque novel[. ...]
>
> And do all these things seriously, playfully, dramatically, stoically, joyfully, serenely, morally, indifferently – do them like D. H. Lawrence, Paul Newman, Socrates, Charlie Brown, Superman and Pogo.
>
> But it's ridiculous. When I do any *one* of these things, play any one of these roles, the *other selves are not satisfied*.[25]

Luke's crusade is against the *one* and for the *many*. In this, he resembles some of the plurally fractured heroes of European high modernism, such as Luigi Pirandello's Vitangelo Moscarda, protagonist of his 1926 'numerical' novel, *Uno, nessuno e centomila*, 'One, no-one and one hundred thousand', a perfectly encapsulated description *avant la lettre* of Luke in his diceworld. Moscarda too ends the novel in some sense dissolved euphorically, and possibly insanely, into the infinitely multiple possibilities of selfhood.[26]

The liberation of the dice is also, finally, distinctly political, because the dice are inherently pluralistic and anti-totalitarian:

> Our Western psychologies try to solve O. B.'s problems by urging him to form some single integrated personality, to suppress his natural multiplicity and build a single dominant self to control the others. [...] [I]n dice theory we attempt to overthrow the totalitarian personality.[27]

The revolutionary import of the Dice Man's absurd experiments is multilayered: his assaults on conventions of psychology, religion, law, medicine and morality, on the family, gender and sexuality, normality and deviance are freewheeling and unstoppable. The diceworld brings with it, however, its own unfreedom, its own despotism. Its reasons are inscrutable, its attitude to the effect on human lives indifferent, its power overwhelming: the arbitrariness of its power chimes with a Kafkaesque inscrutable law, governed by an absurd unreason. Indeed, Luke compares the power of the dice, and its impenetrable justice, to the terrible God of the Book of Job, beneath whom Job, for all the relentless suffering that has befallen him, is forced to admit his infinitesimal ignorance of cause, meaning, worth, higher justice. The lucky throw of the die is as much a vessel of tyranny as of freedom.[28]

*

The play of lucky numbers, of ones, twos and sixes, set against the backdrop of the terrors and confusions of modern history and the modern scales of calculation of vast numbers that defeat us. Such is the governing dynamic of the luck stories and their motifs that this chapter has explored: tossed coins, spun barrels, rolled dice, each one representing fragile, degraded or hyperbolic gestures of control against those larger and deeper overwhelming forces, systems of numbers or systems of ideology. Sometimes – although it is mostly a deluded hope – the single lucky number can come good, can upturn the governing order, can be a glitch that defeats the system. In this sense, there is a shadow of this number play to be found in perhaps the most iconic science-fiction work of the turn of the millennium, *The Matrix* (dir. the Wachowskis; the first film was released in 1999, with two sequels in 2003 and a further one in 2021), in which the system of virtual-reality-driven subjugation of humanity by the titular Matrix is broken by Neo (Keanu Reeves), 'the One', revealed to be a random rogue element of code in the system, capable of saving it or destroying it, its makers and all of humanity. Neo is a glitch, an element that is somehow both random, a figure of luck, and systemic, that both subverts but also integrates and corrects the system[29] – and indeed, much of the paradoxical play of *The Matrix* series spins around the ambiguity of whether Neo is there to destroy or save humanity and the Matrix. This play of the 'one' against the 'system' is, we might say, the structuring dynamic of lucky number narratives, and the often disorienting shift or flip of perspective between them is a key dynamic potential energy within them.[30]

One vivid final illustration of the figures and threads of the argument of the chapter is to be found in the shape of a documentary television programme, first broadcast in February 2008 on the British network

Channel 4, conceived and presented by the illusionist Derren Brown. The programme was entitled, appropriately enough, *The System*. I was first alerted to it by an uncanny link to the discussion at the start of this chapter of the opening scene of *Rosencrantz and Guildenstern Are Dead*, since the programme contains a sequence in which Brown is filmed tossing a coin 10 times in a row and the coin comes up heads all 10 times. The sequence is there to illustrate the main challenge and theme of the programme, whether or not Brown can create a 'system' capable of predicting the outcome of horse races, just as he can apparently 'control' the outcome of a coin toss. In a compelling and deftly constructed story, Brown tempts one ordinary woman called Khadisha to bet her life savings (and more) on a sequence of races, by predicting the winner of a first race 24 hours in advance. Brown gets that winner right, winning Khadisha's confidence, and, astonishingly, he goes on to pick all five subsequent winners also. Along the way, Khadisha is persuaded to bet larger and larger sums of money, money she does not really have but has managed to scrape together from family and friends. There is a twist on the final race when the wrong horse seems to win and this is played for maximum melodrama and tears – this is after all a programme with a compelling storytelling arc, as well as a magician's sense of trickery and wonder – but in the end Brown, and so Khadisha, triumph.

How is it done? Brown takes care to explain (most of) his illusion and the explanation is precisely a play of numbers, of arithmetic, of luck and probability tamed, and of the optical and narrative discrepancies of perspective created in the contrast between individuals and systems. In fact, the personal tale of Khadisha is a trick of partial vision and perspective: all of the six horse races were chosen in advance as races with six runners (those 1-in-6 chances again). Brown and his team had in fact persuaded not only Khadisha, but 7,776 ($6 \times 6 \times 6 \times 6 \times 6$) people to take part, and each of them was assigned one of the six horses in the first race, in equal groups. A sixth of the group inevitably and randomly received a correct prediction: their horse won so the rest fell away, so 7,776 became 1,296. And so on for each subsequent race, as 1,296 became 216, became 36, became 6, became one, Khadisha. In this closed and extremely laborious system, one person must necessarily come through and win. There was in other words no chance involved in 'The System', just a large number of disappointed people and a probabilistic certainty of a single winner. (Brown also explains that his run of 10 coin tosses coming up heads was similarly a segment of thousands and thousands of filmed coin tosses, run on for hours and hours until the law of statistics and probability came good and a single run of 10 heads turned up. Again, it was an optical illusion born of a partial perspective and a great deal of labour.) But the illusion of a magical good luck created by our partial vision remains extraordinary. It is an example of what Kahneman calls 'availability heuristic' (Kahneman, *Thinking*, pp. 129–36), the natural tendency we have to only see data that is easily or proximately available to us to see, and to interpret the world accordingly. And it is not all wrong, of course: for Khadisha, for one ordinary individual struggling to get by and to make ends meet in real life, tempted to gamble their precious resources while terrified of the risks, it remains the case that, despite everything, *for her* this was still a moving story (*a story*) of winning against remarkable odds (1 in 7,776), of pure good luck.

Notes

1. See Hacking, *Taming*; Shoshana Zuboff, *The Age of Surveillance Capitalism: The fight for the future at the new frontier of power* (London: Profile, 2019).
2. See Kahneman, *Thinking*; Stanislas Dehaene, *The Number Sense: How the mind creates mathematics* (Oxford: Oxford University Press, 1997).
3. On this particular form of cosmological-scale thinking, see for example Geraint Lewis and Luke Barnes, *A Fortunate Universe: Life in a finely tuned cosmos* (Cambridge: Cambridge University Press, 2016).
4. William Shakespeare, *Hamlet*, II, 2, 242–54.
5. Tom Stoppard, *Rosencrantz and Guildenstern Are Dead* (New York: Grove Press, 1967), p. 11.
6. Stoppard, *Rosencrantz*, p. 16.
7. Stoppard, *Rosencrantz*, p. 17.
8. Vivian Mercier, 'The uneventful event', *Irish Times*, 18 February 1956. Stoppard's game with the 'lives' of fictional characters and the uncanny balance his play strikes between predeterminism and freedom recalls the modernist theatre of Luigi Pirandello as much as that of Beckett, for example *Six Characters in Search of an Author* (1921), in which the six characters on stage are famously compared with the 'real' actors who are tasked with playing them and declare that in comparison they (the fictional characters) are 'less real, perhaps, but more true!' (Luigi Pirandello, *Six Characters in Search of an Author and Other Plays*, trans. Mark Musa (London: Penguin, 1995), p. 12). (Stoppard translated Pirandello's 1922 play *Henry IV* in 2004.) We will return below to Pirandellian modernism, and further examples of cod-numerology in it, for its deconstruction of selfhood through contingency.
9. On the duel, see John Leigh, *Touché: The duel in literature* (Cambridge, MA: Harvard University Press, 2015); Joseph Farrell, *Honour and the Sword: The culture of duelling* (Oxford: Signal Books, 2021). The short story was Georges Surdez, 'Russian roulette', *Collier's, the National Weekly*, 30 January 1937. Surdez was a Swiss-American pulp writer of adventure stories mainly centred on the French Foreign Legion and 'Russian roulette' was one of these. The story itself points to an origin of the game in the First World War Russian army on the Romanian front, but it is quite possible Surdez invented this and the name himself.
10. See the classic structuralist study, Will Wright, *Six Guns and Society: A structural study of the Western* (Berkeley: University of California Press, 1975).
11. See Stella Bruzzi, *Men's Cinema: Masculinity and mise en scène in Hollywood* (Edinburgh: Edinburgh University Press, 2013). Bruzzi discusses both *The Deer Hunter* and *Dirty Harry* (pp. 53–60, 86–94).
12. The *Dirty Harry* films have been studied previously, alongside another Eastwood vehicle directed by Don Siegel, *Coogan's Bluff* (1968), for their investigations into ethics and luck: see Joel Deshaye, '"Do I feel lucky?" Moral luck, bluffing and the ethics of Eastwood's outlaw-lawman in *Coogan's Bluff* and the Dirty Harry films', *Film-Philosophy* 21.1 (2017): 20–36.

13 On the controversy, see Peter Biskind, 'The Vietnam Oscars', *Vanity Fair*, March 2008, at https://www.vanityfair.com/news/2008/03/warmovies200803, and Steven Biel, 'The *Deer Hunter* debate: Artistic license and Vietnam War remembrance', *Bright Lights Film Journal*, 7 July 2016, at http://disq.us/p/2izosqx. The Vietnam war – and protest against it – became closely associated with luck also because of the system of lottery conscription, used especially in 1969–70, to select young men for military service: see for example a recent novel that uses the Vietnam lottery and its contrasting impact on a group of young friends and their futures as its founding conceit: Richard Russo, *Chances Are …* (New York: Alfred A. Knopf, 2019); and cf. Wesley Abney, *Random Destiny: How the Vietnam War draft lottery shaped a generation* (Wilmington, DE: Vernon Press, 2019).
14 Mike's 'one shot' bears interesting comparison, for their intersecting stories of immigrants and race, masculinity, life chances and American dreaming, with *Hamilton*'s 'My shot', referred to in Chapter 1.
15 Luke Rhinehart (pseudonym of George Cockcroft), *The Dice Man* (1971) (London: HarperCollins, 1999). Rhinehart / Cockcroft claimed he had experimented by living with the same rules as his fictionalized character, but it should be noted that he was an inveterate self-mythologizer. On the author and the book's cult status, see the piece by French novelist Emmanuel Carrère, 'Who is the real Dice Man? The elusive writer behind the disturbing cult novel', *The Guardian*, 7 November 2019. The novel was the subject of analysis and also critique of its illusory utopia of pure luck by Jean Baudrillard, *L'Échange impossible* (1999), in English as *Impossible Exchange*, trans. Chris Turner (London: Verso, 2011); 'The Dice Man', pp. 58–66.
16 Rhinehart, *The Dice Man*, p. 64.
17 Rhinehart, *The Dice Man*, p. 433.
18 In *The Psychopathology of Everyday Life* (1901), Freud pays sustained attention to mishaps, to slips or omissions in both action and language, and to what he calls 'chance actions' (*Zufallshandlungen*) or faulty actions, carefully distinguishing between external and internal kinds: 'I believe in external (real) chance, it is true, but not in inner (psychical) accidental events.' The former are construed as meaningful only by the superstitious; the latter are necessarily meaningful for psychoanalysis as, like all parapraxes, they are symptomatic of unconscious processes. Paradoxically, Freud points out, the superstitious person and the psychoanalyst share a common resistance to the meaninglessness of chance: 'the compulsion not to let chance count as chance but to interpret is common to both of us' (Sigmund Freud, *The Psychopathology of Everyday Life* (1901), trans. James Strachey, Vol. 6 of *The Standard Edition of the Complete Psychological Works of Sigmund Freud* (London: Vintage, 2001), pp. 257–8). Against this kind of symptomatic, 'metaphorical' reading, and therefore in favour of simply seeing chance as chance, Susan Sontag argued in *Illness as Metaphor* for treating illness as without meaning, as simply the manifestation of its physical symptoms and the misfortune of their occurrence ('nothing is more punitive than to give illness a meaning', Susan Sontag, *Illness as Metaphor* (New York: Farrar, Straus and Giroux, 1978), p. 58).
19 Rhinehart, *The Dice Man*, p. 453.
20 Rhinehart, *The Dice Man*, pp. 6, 525.
21 Rhinehart, *The Dice Man*, pp. 136, 237, 267. On Tao, *I Ching* divination and the uses of chance in an array of twentieth-century avant-garde experimentation with random or aleatory creativity in art and music, see Margaret Iversen, ed., *Chance* (London: Whitechapel Gallery, 2010); Denis Lejeune, *The Radical Use of Chance in 20th Century Art* (Amsterdam: Rodopi, 2012).
22 Rhinehart, *The Dice Man*, pp. 146–7; emphasis in the original.
23 Rhinehart, *The Dice Man*, pp. 153, 152, 158, 198, 267.
24 Rhinehart, *The Dice Man*, p. 268.
25 Rhinehart, *The Dice Man*, p. 316; emphasis in the original.
26 Luigi Pirandello, *Uno, nessuno e centomila* (1926), in English as *One, None and a Hundred-Thousand*, trans. Samuel Putnam (New York: Dutton, 1933).
27 Rhinehart, *The Dice Man*, p. 316.
28 Rhinehart, *The Dice Man*, pp. 236–7. We will come back to Job as a figure for bad luck in Chapter 5.
29 The pairing of glitch and feature in information and systems theory maps neatly onto the pattern of the chance, random or lucky exception as both a disturbance and an integral element of a higher order of number as explored here. On the figure of the glitch, see the Dutch artist and theorist Rosa Menkman's *The Glitch Moment(um)* (Amsterdam: Institute of Network

Cultures, 2011), which includes her *Glitch Studies Manifesto* (p. 11). The related category of 'noise' in systems has been examined in a recent work by Daniel Kahneman, Olivier Sibony and Cass Sunstein, *Noise: A flaw in human judgment* (London: William Collins, 2021). In the vein of a conception of luck as linked to random flaws in complex systems, we might also consider here the function of luck in the human body and the 'causes' of human illness and death: Atul Gawande, for example, talks of bodies failing, of things falling apart 'in the way all complex systems fail: randomly and gradually' (*Being Mortal: Illness, medicine and what matters in the end* (London: Profile Books, 2014), p. 33).

30 *The Matrix* has been the subject of much philosophical enquiry. See, for example, William Irwin, ed., *'The Matrix' and Philosophy: Welcome to the desert of the real* (Chicago, IL: Open Court, 2002), and *More 'Matrix' and Philosophy* (Chicago, IL: Open Court, 2005).

4
Lucky places, lucky lines

Modern luck and its stories are compounds of a variety of different base elements, combining at different layers above, beneath or at the narrative surface. These can take the form of motifs and patterns, such as the lucky numbers of Chapter 3, or the stock characters and archetypes, or recurrent (moral) quandaries that will be the focus of later chapters. This chapter instead pitches its enquiry at the level of setting or ground, examining how luck stories are generated and shaped by, among other things, particular spaces and places, sites where luck seems to find itself at home, where the forces of luck seem to be triggered into action and where an openness to luck is somehow enhanced or accelerated (much as E. B. White posited that New York might be a space for people who are 'willing to be lucky'). These places need not be named nor even real – we are as likely to be looking at typologies and imagined spaces as real modern settings – but, as the link to New York suggests, such 'lucky places' are often connected in some way to modernity itself and to its many, disorientingly new spatial (and indeed spatio-temporal) configurations. The exploration can also extend to take in the spatial and geometric lines, the matrices of a spatial configuration, that were flagged up in discussion of the vocabularies of luck in Chapter 2. This chapter thus also encompasses a discussion of some typical linear patterns of luck stories, the narrative geometries where line and luck intersect.

A good place to start this mapping of the places and lines of luck narrative is where we began the previous chapter, in and with *Casablanca*. Previously, we listened to Rick's drunken lament asking how on earth Ilsa had happened to stumble upon his bar of all bars, hearing it as a pregnant evocation of all our intuitive luck calculations, the maths-without-numbers and the cod probabilities that we often compute to ask questions of our everyday misfortunes. Rick's reflections on his 'outrageous fortune' resonate with a far more sustained and centrally prominent thread running through the film, which centres, precisely, on its setting or its concentric circle of settings – Rick's Bar, Casablanca, all the ports, airports and borders and possible escape routes out of (or indeed, as the film's ending suggests, back into) Nazi Europe – and on all the forces of luck that converge on these. This focus on setting and place begins with the very first frames of the film.

Casablanca's portentous, slowly delivered opening monologue is spoken first over a turning globe, then over a map tracking a journey from Europe to North Africa, underscored by newsreel footage, and closed out over a bustling local street market in Casablanca. It sets the scene, literally, for the movie's plotline, but also and at the same time, paradigmatically for the spatial configuration of Casablanca as a place of luck and destiny (which are perhaps the same thing, as we have seen), of dreams of mobility and escape, and the stark reality of stasis and suspension, of waiting outside time and history:

> [*Voiceover*] With the coming of the Second World War, many eyes in imprisoned Europe turned hopefully, or desperately, toward the freedom of the Americas. Lisbon became the great embarkation point. But not everybody could get to Lisbon directly, and so a tortuous, roundabout refugee trail sprang up. Paris to Marseilles, across the Mediterranean to Oran, then by train, or auto, or foot, across the rim of Africa to Casablanca in French Morocco. Here, the fortunate ones, through money or influence or luck, might obtain exit visas and scurry to Lisbon; and from Lisbon to the New World. But the others wait in Casablanca … and wait … and wait … and wait.

Casablanca, then, is a place of entrapment and imprisonment, and only luck or power ('money or influence or luck') can get you out. The film is peppered with background subplots of the agents and victims of these forces: criminal black marketeers, elderly German exile couples, innocent young Bulgarians, Free French resistance fighters and anti-Nazis, as well of course as Vichy officials and Nazis, all obsessed with finding, negotiating or blocking off routes to that 'lucky' escape. And so the site of the film, distilled and concentrated into Rick's Bar at its centre, with Rick in turn at the Bar's centre as its presiding, indifferent household deity, becomes a site for the negotiation of luck. This situation and its consequences are played out in both the literal criminal black-market economy and in a more generalized game of fortune and misfortune, going on in hiding from the institutions and high politics of Casablanca's official status, in the corners, bars and hidden spaces of Rick's and Casablanca. Life stories and life-lines converge on Rick's and either get stuck there or find an escape route out, and this either/or too is governed by a kind of geometry of luck – who meets whom, who coincides with whom, who pays off or indeed who sleeps with whom – so that Rick's own lament ('of all the gin joints …') is in fact not so out of place nor so exceptional after all. All the lines converging on his bar are lines of improbable chance.

The film flags this combination of suspension between movement and stasis in several different ways: cinematographically, through the turning searchlights that pass back and forth over the street-scene exterior stage set and the bar façade, underlining the impossibility of hiding and the total surveillance of the site, and narratively, through the classic plot device of what Hitchcock called the 'MacGuffin',[1] a magical, mysterious object that all the key characters are obsessively chasing, in this case some letters of transit signed by none other than General de Gaulle himself, which in theory guarantee any holders safe passage to the Americas. And it is striking that the letters, talismans of that luck of the 'fortunate ones' evoked in the opening voiceover, are letters *of transit*, since journeying, transition, the dynamic of movement (and its interruption) are the dominant vectors of the film that establish its status as, among many other things, a luck story.

Luck, then, its forces, objects and dynamics, are the frame, the origin and the condition for *Casablanca*'s unique atmosphere of suspense and tension, and for its rousing and patriotic final resolution, for its strange alliance of repetition, cynicism and indifference on the one hand, and dramatic change, high principle and heroism on the other, and thus the ground also for Rick's final transformation into a hero. As if to underline the point, the film is peppered with playful allusions to luck and its tropes, including the handful we have already seen in the opening monologue and in Rick's soliloquy. First and most persistent of all, there is a buzz in the background of this film throughout – literally hidden away, behind secret doors, and repeatedly played out in the dialogue of the screenplay – of gambling, of roulette, bets and dubious dealings. Behind those doors, Rick hosts an elegant, illicit casino, raking in cash against the hopeless dreams of the exiles and demi-monde of Casablanca. It is a hidden operation, but also an open secret, always kept under the watchful eye and feigned ignorance of the venal French police chief Captain Renault (Claude Rains). (Rick lets Renault win at roulette every now and then, to persuade him to turn a blind eye.) The state and space of useless gambling captures nicely something of the suspended quality, the waiting stasis of the inhabitants of Casablanca, stuck playing the same old game, the wheel turning and turning, plotting useless deals and conspiracies, while never getting anywhere. Until and unless, that is, on rare occasions and apparently quite out of his world-weary, cynical character, Rick reveals himself to be controller and demigod of the players' luck and destiny, as well as a 'rank sentimentalist', as his maître d' Carl (S. Z. Sakall) will call him: Rick takes pity on a penniless young Bulgarian couple at the roulette table and whispers, with a nod to the croupier, to bet on number 22. Twenty-two comes up and Rick tells the husband to bet again on 22. Of course, it comes up again. The editing work is eloquent and complex here, as the camera cuts back and forth between the central two-shot of Rick and the young man, and a series of astonished onlookers – the croupier, the young wife, Carl, Captain Renault – as though a law of nature were being shattered: a breach in Rick's rock-hard carapace of cynicism, that is, rather than the remote probability of 22 turning up twice in a row. (There is a distant echo, or rather an anticipation, of the recurrent coin tosses in *Rosencrantz and Guildenstern Are Dead*.) The shutters come down again after the second bet: Rick tells the man to take his winnings and clear out, and when the wife tries to hug him in thanks, the old Rick is back and the response is lapidary and sarcastic: 'He's just a lucky guy.'

In fact, Renault as much as Rick seems to be the household deity of this place of luck and gambling, and of all the dirty dealings in Casablanca. These are ostensibly centred on merely corrupt exchanges of money and of sex (Renault is an inveterate womanizer and prone to offering papers and other favours in exchange for sex, a trait presented by the film as somewhat rascally, but nothing worse), but actually stand as code for higher struggles of resistance, freedom and desperate survival. Renault's flexible dealings contrast with his other analogue (beside Rick), his counterpart-cum-enemy, the Nazi major, Strasser (Conrad Veidt), overlord of quite another order of law and violence that will not turn a blind eye, nor do deals, nor watch the vagaries of chance play out and will look for whatever advantage can be found. (Renault notes of himself, 'I have no conviction, if that's what you mean. I blow with the wind and the prevailing wind happens to be from Vichy.') Unlike Renault, Strasser in his Nazi rigidity sees no play, no margin for manoeuvre in leaving things to chance and adapting accordingly. After all, as he tells Laszlo to his face, he (Laszlo) has 'so far […] been fortunate in eluding us' and it is now 'my duty to see that you stay in Casablanca' and no longer be so fortunate. In this way, we might say, different orders of law and duty, of police and totalitarian order, each underpinned by a different model of the state, ethos and social bonds, stand off against each other in *Casablanca*, each with a different battle to be fought in alliance with or against luck.

Luck also plays a pivotal and recurrent role in the love story, and the love triangle, at the heart of the film. Rick's lament for his rotten luck that Ilsa 'had to walk into' his 'gin joint' turns out to be an echo and an inversion of one of the romantic flashback sequences in the film set in Paris more than a year earlier, with a dapper Rick head over heels in love with Ilsa. We hear him asking her incredulously: 'I was wondering [...] why I'm so lucky? Why I should find you waiting for me to come along?' The answer, at the time, is that there had been another man in her life, but that he is now dead. Unbeknownst to Ilsa at the time, however, and unbeknownst to Rick for long months until Ilsa reappears in his bar in Casablanca, the unlikeliest and unluckiest of turns had defeated Rick's luck: Ilsa's other man – Laszlo – was not dead after all, but was sick and needed Ilsa, and with him lay the hopes of the anti-fascist cause, and so Ilsa abandoned her true love Rick waiting for her at the train station ('A guy standing on a station platform in the rain with a comical look on his face because his insides have been kicked out'). Ironically, given what we noted above about duty and luck in relation to Strasser, Renault and Rick, another kind of duty here seems to supersede the luck of two lovers' paths crossing in Paris and of the two of them being, at that moment, alone. And it takes their paths crossing again by chance for this imbalance to be resolved.

Luck, finally, turns up in another incidental but powerfully resonant site in the film, at Sam's piano. Sam (Arthur 'Dooley' Wilson) is another sometime partner, soulmate and alter ego for Rick, to set alongside Renault and Ilsa and maybe even fellow bar owner and inveterate dubious dealer Ferrari (Sidney Greenstreet), each one a figure of some aspect of Rick's past or future, his dark or light side, his overdetermined hard-soft heroic character. Sam is the oldest and most loyal of them all, holder of the secrets of Rick's past love for Ilsa in Paris, captured in the signature love song 'As time goes by', and probably of Rick's even murkier American past hinted at occasionally in the film. But Sam's real set-piece number in the film – a playful band showstopper belted out for all the folks at Rick's Bar and all the film's audience, at a crucial plot-point moment, since the noise and clatter accompanying the song are perfect cover for Rick to hide the infamous letters of transit in Sam's piano – is not 'As time goes by', but another song, 'Knock on wood'. The title and refrain refer, of course, to an ancient and widespread folk figure of luck, touching wood to ward off bad luck, and the song is nothing but a euphoric, percussive chant and response on and around all things lucky. Its lyrics progressively evoke being in trouble ('"Who's got trouble?" "We got trouble." "How much trouble?" "Too much trouble."'), being unhappy ('Who's unhappy?', etc.), being unlucky, having nothing, being happy, being lucky. And the answer to each chant and refrain is a simple 'knock on wood'. It is as if all the anxious, dark dealings, all the ambiguities and dangers presiding over the luck-space of Rick's Bar and of Casablanca, are channelled just for one moment into this euphoric, magical, musical transformation of misery into luck.

*

As the trail across the map beneath the opening monologue in *Casablanca* and the film's talismanic letters of transit suggest, spaces and sites in luck stories are often tightly bound up with spaces of journey and travel, spaces of transit where different arcs and trajectories meet, and thus encounter and transformation are possible. And as *Casablanca* again suggests, these journey-and-encounter narratives carry with them an intense power of affect; they are often transformative because love and desire are operative in these suspended, but mobile, places in ways that are somehow heightened, intensified, open to surprising twists of fate. It is worth adding that such places of suspension are also often spaces of storytelling, or, better, spaces *for* storytelling: spaces where people meet, where especially travellers meet, and often, even more narrowly, where strangers on a journey meet and stories are told, whether stories of how they got here and where they are going, or stories of fortune and misfortune, or perhaps simply stories to while away the time. This latter purpose is an ancient motif, of course – Boccaccio's fourteenth-century brigade of storytellers in the *Decameron* have travelled to rural safety to escape the Black Death in Florence, to swap stories of love and Fortuna; Chaucer's *Canterbury Tales* too are tales told to pass the time, on a journey of pilgrimage. And the motif finds a characteristically modern iteration in locations such as Rick's, in taverns, saloons and bars. A studied example of this convergence of journeys on a shared site of storytelling is to be found in one of Italo Calvino's playful experiments in form, *The Castle of Crossed Destinies* (1973): in this two-part work, Calvino imagines a group of travellers mysteriously thrown together in the middle of a dark forest, in the first part in a castle and the second in a tavern. In an even greater, unexplained mystery, they lose their power of speech and so swap stories with the use of nothing but a deck of Tarot cards, which are reproduced on the pages of the novel. Calvino was intent on exploring the structural patterns of storytelling embedded in the archetypal figures of the Tarot cards and the combinatorial, generative power of the cards to recreate and retell myths and legends through sequence and association. But the premise, as in *Casablanca*, is doubly saturated in luck patterns: the chance convergence of journey-lines in this suspended, magical site creates the condition for both encounter and narrative (and indeed for narratives of luck).[2]

The bar of *Casablanca* and the tavern and castle of *The Castle of Crossed Destinies* are points of suspension in multiple journeys. A further, complementary thread of modern luck narratives are staged instead within more dynamically mobile spaces of journeying. These spaces include the airport, the train station, the road-stop or junction, or indeed the vehicles and vessels of their associated journeys, the plane, the train and the automobile. These all offer modern iterations of a traditional motif of luck and travel, which Aby Warburg's iconology saw as embodied in the figure of the ship, but it is striking to note that they all supplement the traditional motif with markers of urban modernity: on the one hand the fluid spaces, temporalities and technologies of the urban modern, and on the other the social disaffection, the anonymity and the replicability that led Marc Augé to include them in his influential category of the '*non-lieu*', the 'non-place'.[3] The category is typically one of critique of the emptied-out texture of late capitalist society, but in the frame of luck narratives it is interesting to note that it is precisely the modern fluidity and non-specific anonymity that allow for unpredictable intersection and change.[4] They render them sites that make place for luck.

It is not hard to find examples of luck stories in transit.[5] We can limit ourselves for now to focussing on trains and train stations, as they are architectural spaces and technological drivers of nineteenth-century capitalist modernity that have been set in parallel by cultural historians to both the novel and film as paradigms for modern perception and storytelling.[6] Railways are also, of course, technologies of modern empire, of conquest and control, whether in British India or America, and as such occupy a powerful place in the narrative imaginary of such histories: a striking recent instance was Colson Whitehead's novel *The Underground Railroad*, which fantastically literalized the mythical railroad of the title, in history a loose, secret network of routes to escape from slavery in the early nineteenth-century South, in Whitehead's imaginary version an actual subterranean train line with mysterious hidden stations on the way northwards. The terrifying experiences of the novel's hero, Cora, as she escapes along the railroad and stops at towns along the way, until fear of recapture, murder, sterilization or rape force her to move on, are regularly tied to dynamics of luck, not least because her companions consistently think of her as a talisman of good luck, because years before her mother Mabel had been the only one of them to escape and stay alive. But Cora resists doggedly standing for luck: '"You think I'm a lucky charm because Mabel got away. But I ain't"'; 'Jesus had not blessed [Jasper …] with looks

[…] or with luck. Luck least of all. He and Cora had that in common'; 'She wasn't a rabbit's foot to carry with you on the voyage but the locomotive itself.'[7] Cora does not want to be luck for others, she needs to have luck herself, to ride the railroad to freedom.

More concretely rooted in historical space, the structures and movements of modern train stations and trains propel the crowds and individuals in them to move in a bewildering combination of Brownian chaos and regulated flow, governed by barriers, guards, permits and controls. These are also spaces, again as with the 'moving picture', where motion comes bound together with emotion or affect,[8] we might say with happiness, recalling the shared etymologies of happiness and luck. Within this contingent space, random encounter seems not only possible but inevitable.

A powerful case study, for its pared-down narrative and its intense emotional impact, is the British film *Brief Encounter* (1945), directed by David Lean and written by Noël Coward.[9] The secret romance narrated by the film between a reserved British couple, Alec and Laura (played by Trevor Howard and Celia Johnson), is made possible by trains and train stations and the chance encounters and the chance for planned secret encounters they create. Alec and Laura first meet by chance in a train station refreshment room, when Alec helps remove a piece of grit from Laura's eye, then again outside a chemist's in town. She misses her train home one evening and dreams of bumping into Alec again, before they meet for a third time in a restaurant, and from there a more intimate connection develops when they go to the cinema together. As the romance develops, there are further near misses, again at the station café and on the platform, as trains arrive and leave, and farewells are enacted at train windows. Their final meeting and poignant interrupted parting take place back in the station café, their emotion excruciatingly suppressed by the awkward and unlucky arrival of a chattering friend of Laura's. In fact, both the train station settings and the luck of the meetings are a thin thread running throughout the film. The more detailed substance and sustained attention in terms of screen time are taken up elsewhere, as their romance blossoms through wanderings around other places and other planned and, precisely, no longer chance, encounters. The station, at least after the first meeting, is turned into a far more melancholy place, inevitably a prelude to parting, to yet another transition for Laura back towards her dull domestic life, her unfortunate 'real' existence. But that initial space of luck, and the opening up of a temporary possibility of fantasy and desire, of happiness, is the framing condition and catalyst for all the rest, and at each one of its momentary reappearances in the film this is further underscored. Despite its limited screen time, then, the resonance and affective weight of the space of transit permeates the mood of the film.[10]

A similar pattern of framing and mood – of mobility, openness, possibility and melancholy – can be observed in other railway stories, including other lucky love stories. Perhaps the most emblematic example in recent cinema is to be found in *Before Sunrise* (1995), the first of the so-called *Before* trilogy, directed by Richard Linklater (*Before Sunset*, 2004; *Before Midnight*, 2013). In *Before Sunrise*, two characters, Céline and Jesse (Julie Delpy and Ethan Hawke), meet on a train between Budapest and Vienna. Their chance encounter leads to an impulsive decision to get off the train together in Vienna and spend the night wandering around the city. The next day, back at the station, as Céline leaves, they agree not to contact each other but to meet again in the same place in six months' time. Again, the train and the openness to the potentiality of luck is the condition for the film's sustained romance, for its conversations and evolving human connection, and indeed for the subsequent narrative arc of the trilogy, each one of which is structured around shared wandering. The space of luck and transit sets the paradigm.

In *Brief Encounter*, the camera returns again and again to shots of railway station clocks, suggesting that these specific spaces of luck are also spaces of regulated and constrained temporality, a constraint that seems bound up with and perhaps itself unleashes the possibilities and dangers of the romance. After all, Laura and Alec's love is made possible in no small part by the relentless, cyclical regularity of weekly trips to town, every Thursday, and by train timetables and guard's whistles. As Mary Ann Doane has argued, this regulation of space-time is a defining characteristic of capitalist modernity, a mechanism for taming contingency, except in those instances (or fantasies) when contingency escapes its bounds, instances that for Doane are captured in some essential way in the temporality of cinema.[11] In *Before Sunrise* and its sequels, too, temporal constraint is structurally and affectively central: departures loom as soon as encounters occur, with Jesse and Céline only ever together on screen for strictly delimited periods, one night or one afternoon, a contemporary reprise of the Aristotelian unity of time. (Longer, regulated cycles of time, instead, connote dull domesticity, whole lives lived together, no space and no time for luck.) Lucky space is, in fact, lucky space-time, just as we saw, in Chapter 2, that there was a space-time geometry, a vectoring in the lexicon of luck. And thus it is no surprise that narratives rooted in these spaces of transit are also, in key instances, narratives that play games with time, with the relentless closure of regimented time and the fantasies of plural, alternative timelines.

Both space and time are at stake in a potent and highly influential subgenre of modern narrative experimentation linked to luck, the forking-path narrative, derived from (or at least taking its most common label from) a 1941 story by Jorge Luis Borges, 'The garden of the forking paths', noted in Chapter 2.[12] The story has a complex *mise-en-abyme* spy-story plot, centred on a lost labyrinthine book by a Chinese scholar that contains potentially infinite worlds, as every action or event is imagined as a bifurcating path, 'an infinite series of times, a growing, dizzying web of divergent, convergent and parallel times'.[13] Borges's intuition here seems to coincide with or uncannily anticipate everything from multiverse theories of space-time in quantum physics, to the matrix of hypertexts and video-gaming, to the literature of the counterfactual or 'what if' narratives that Catherine Gallagher and others have studied (from their eighteenth- and nineteenth-century origins in philosophy and studies of warfare, to waves of historical genre fiction imagining the South winning the American Civil War or the Nazis winning the Second World War), to Robert Frost's much-quoted image of the forking path in 'The road not taken' ('Two roads diverged in a wood, and I – / I took the one less traveled by').[14]

The paradigm in Frost and some other cases suggests a form of agency and thus apparently the opposite of unwilled, indeterminate luck – each forking-path moment seems to present in essence a binary choice, left or right, to act or not to act, to kill or not to kill[15] – but taken together their infinite number and their interweaving of infinite potential timelines seem to drain away that agency (just as the narrator of Borges's story chooses a dramatic final act – to kill – but only at the price of regret and imminent execution). If all paths are possible and indeed extant in parallel, to choose any one in particular, to be on one path rather than another, amounts to something random, arbitrary, ineffectual, hardly even action at all, pure luck. (The same paradox points towards the problematics of responsibility and so-called 'moral luck', which will be discussed in Chapter 6.)

We might point here for comparison to two powerful contemporary film narratives founded on a single binary choice that seems to open out onto entire devastating futures, but in practice dissolves as the narratives develop into something far more fuzzy and blurred, both in narrative structure and in concept. The first is the choice at the patriarch's sixtieth-birthday party between the yellow and green envelopes in Thomas Vinterberg's *Festen* (1998) and the second Neo's choice between the red pill and the blue pill in *The Matrix*. These are apparently 'choices' between knowledge, truth and agency on the one hand, and ignorance, delusion and blind oblivion on the other, but both films seem to suggest that ultimately these are hardly choices at all, given their uncontrollable and in any case inevitable consequences.

Luck stories, then, intersect with the forking-path paradigm in a variety of modes and settings, not least in their spaces and lines of transit. It is no coincidence that the central image of Borges's story is the path, alongside the garden and the labyrinth, an image of line and deviation, and of travel, nor that the story contains a train sequence, in which the narrator luckily eludes a chasing British spy by just catching a departing train.[16] And the specific motif of catching or missing a train recurs in later iterations of forking-path narratives that similarly, uncannily, stick close to the journeying motif. In popular cinema, this is most often associated with the 1998 romantic comedy *Sliding Doors* (dir. Peter Howitt), which tracks two parallel possible stories of the couple at its centre depending on whether or not the woman (Gwyneth Paltrow), at one ostensibly random moment, does or does not make it through the doors of a London Underground train as they slide shut. The title has become proverbial in English for the life-changing consequences of the infinitesimal chance variation of a moment, here in the form not of a chosen act but rather of a random, chance event. And of course, the image is another one of train travel: we are back in the 'lucky' space of the train. The same spatial motif and play on chance, and the same motif of trains and stations, recurs in an earlier film that is widely taken to be the model for *Sliding Doors* and the modern paradigm for forking-path film narratives, Krzysztof Kieślowski's 1987 film *Blind Chance*.[17]

Przypadek, the Polish title of *Blind Chance*, is a term for chance that shares the latter's etymology associated with falling or befalling, as well as the parallel meaning, with the same root origin as chance, of 'case': that is, both that which is the case and case in grammar (see Chapter 2). And there is a clear residue of that double origin in the plot and structure of the film, which involves forking-path narratives and motifs of both falling and accidents. The film follows three parallel hypothetical life stories of its protagonist Witek (Bogusław Linda), each pivoting on whether or not he catches a train from Lodz to Warsaw, which is determined by whether or not he crashes into a man drinking beer at the station, stumbling or swerving or knocking the man over, as he runs for the train. The three scenarios envisage profound variations in Witek's destiny from this moment onwards, which weave together individual, emotional and moral life choices with the charged political realities of late-period Communist rule in Poland, just as the first rumblings of the

Solidarity trade union and opposition movement were emerging. (The film was made in the early 1980s, but its release was delayed by censors for several years for political reasons.) Witek variously becomes a Communist party official, an anti-Communist and Christian activist (but possibly also an informant), and a medic who refuses to get involved in politics on either side.[18] Other biographical patterns and variations emerge also: he forms a relationship with one of three different women; he has a child or he does not; he takes a plane to Paris or he does not. The film ends on that aeroplane with a crash that has been foreshadowed through earlier narrative hints, not least in the confusing prologue that runs before the train-station sequence is first introduced. Several of the characters from different segments seem to converge on the plane's departure, suggesting, much as in Borges, and indeed *Sliding Doors*, that the multiple bifurcations of forking paths and alternative timelines are in fact a surface illusion, noise occluding a higher-order continuity and determined inevitability.

Blind Chance, like *Brief Encounter*, stages its train-station sequences as a matrix for the film's deeper engagement with the problematics of luck, freedom and constraint. The chance binary – catching or not catching the train – is a framing condition, again, that allows the film to function, generates the narrative form and the conceit of the parallel narratives, and levers open the otherwise thickly realist alternative film biographies of Witek. But luck, contingency and agency also feed into those biographies, in a way that Kieślowski will develop with ever-greater philosophical depth in his later, French films, in particular *The Double Life of Véronique* (1991), whose dual narrative structure picks up in significant ways on the potential energies of *Blind Chance* and dwells at length on matters of contingency and coincidence, this time through a somewhat mystical dimension of a narrative steeped in death, magical connection and doubling.

As David Bordwell and others have explored, *Blind Chance* and *Sliding Doors* sit alongside a series of late twentieth-century films that offer variations on the forking-path topos, playing games with time, space and multiple simultaneous futures, all underpinned by the workings of luck and chance.[19] Another key case in this field is Tom Tykwer's *Run Lola Run* (*Lola rennt*, 1998), a film in which the relentless, breathless, urban running of the protagonist Lola (Franka Potente), echoing Witek's sprint for the train, could be said to stand in for the travel motif, as she attempts to save her boyfriend against all the odds, in three different parallel or divergent scenarios. Besides the running, the film offers further motifs, such as clocks, traffic accidents and roulette wheels, which we have seen circulating in the other case studies, motifs that mark out spaces and temporalities of luck. And, in Henriette Heidbrink's analysis, Lola's repeated, time-limited sprints are packed full of an excess of what she calls 'dissipative' coincidences, so that 'the programmatic application of unmotivated coincidences makes the matter of chance turn thematic'.[20] Heidbrink places particular emphasis on Lola's scream, which in the third version of her story seems through its sheer visceral force and frenzied energy to stretch the bounds of reality and allow her to control the ball on the roulette wheel, to bend pure luck to her will – an energy generated by the video-game time constraint of the film – and so to win twice. The number is 20 here, not 22, and Lola's scream is a long way from Rick's surreptitious wink to his croupier in *Casablanca*, but the dynamic interplay and the pattern of luck in the two scenes are identical: Lola/Rick saves a young man by bending the spinning wheel to their 'magical' will, by tricking luck, deviating chance through willed intervention.

Bordwell notes in these films an acute sensitivity to the infinite possibilities of the Borgesian labyrinth, in time, space and storytelling, but also a kind of reining in of their dizzying shapelessness. Instead of infinite possibility, *Blind Chance* and *Run Lola Run* offer a mere three alternative timelines, although these are admittedly multiplied or at least complicated by the secondary repetitions, intersections and variations that cut across them. *Sliding Doors* offers fewer still, only two, but here supplementary complications come from the complex parallel intercutting of the two strands along the way and the archly constructed points of convergence in the plots, culminating in the point of repetition and closure when the two storylines reconverge against the backdrop of two new 'sliding doors' of a hospital lift at the end.[21] Bordwell links this process of limitation, this shirking of the radical potentiality of the multiverse, to the very nature of narrative:

> Narratives are built not upon philosophy or physics but folk psychology, the ordinary processes we use to make sense of the world. [...] [T]he shortcuts, stereotypes, faulty inferences, and erroneous conclusions to which we are prone play a central role in narrative comprehension. In following a plot we reason from a single case, judge on first impressions, and expect, against all probability, that the rescuer will arrive on time because we want it that way. [...]
>
> Since we bring folk psychology to bear on narratives all the time, why should parallel-worlds tales be any different? Consider the counterfactuals we might spin in ordinary life. If I had left the

parking lot a minute or two later, I wouldn't have had the fender-bender that became such a nuisance to me for the next month. This sort of homely reflection on short-term outcomes, in which only small things change, seems the basis of *Sliding Doors*, [...] and *Run Lola Run*.[22]

Bordwell's turn of phrase here, his talk of 'folk psychology', 'ordinary process', 'shortcuts' and 'homely reflections', is more than somewhat condescending, but in fact he captures rather precisely the affinity of the epistemological and narratological field of luck with an everyday mode of philosophical thinking that we noted in Chapter 1, via Gramsci, as constitutive of how luck stories do their thinking. The same applies to the very notion of a disappointed falling away from the infinite, paradoxical numbers of quantum uncertainty towards the everyday numbers of two or three or six possibilities in these forking-path stories, a number pattern already flagged up in Chapter 2 and replicated in the patterns we have seen in this chapter of places and lines of luck storytelling. These narrative paradigms are perhaps to be read less as inadequate simulacra of higher complexities than as their everyday manifestation and as evidence of the deep interplay between these two layers. They point forcefully to the ways in which luck stories, the games they play, and the pleasures they give, stage the clash between our from-below perception and the destabilizing impact of the modern.

Forking-path films offer a formalist paradigm for luck narratives, plottable as linear constructs. They can be grouped together with a cluster of late twentieth-century films that use metacinematic frames and philosophizing structures to play games with time, place and space in a series of distinct but overlapping ways.[23] All of them share something of the triggering potential of moments of luck and their deterministic inverse, through lines parallel and perpendicular, levered into varied conventional genres including comedy, romance, adventure and crime, each with its theme of self-discovery or self-making, or indeed self-unmaking or ruin. We might include here *The Truman Show* (dir. Peter Weir, 1998), a film in which all apparent contingency and agency in the life of its protagonist Truman Burbank (Jim Carrey) is shown to be a hidden, fake, TV construct, or several films from this same period built around multiple narrative strands converging on and spreading outwards from the site and story of a car crash, including Alejandro González Iñárritu's *Amores Perros* (2000) and Paul Haggis's *Crash* (2004). An inverse example, where luck rather seems to be suspended and stripped away, is *Groundhog Day* (dir. Harold Ramis, 1993).

Like *Sliding Doors*, *Groundhog Day* is a film whose title has become proverbial and another that replays parallel stories of a single life, although in this case the plot tracks endless iterations and variations of a single day in the same life, of curmudgeonly reporter Phil Connors (Bill Murray). Murray's character, among many comic tropes played out and 'folk psychological' lessons learned over the course of his endlessly repeated day, which lead him eventually towards happiness and love – and a life once again free from repetition – learns to tame luck, as he realizes he can avoid stepping into puddles, save people from accidents, incidents and misfortunes, and use every trick and snippet of foreknowledge in the cause of conquering Rita (Andie MacDowell), leaving nothing to chance (except love itself, of course). *Groundhog Day* creates an inverse or anti-luck space, circumscribed within the magical space-time of Punxsutawney, the town in which the film is set and where Phil becomes inexplicably trapped in his time-loop. It is a world in which luck is eliminated, allowing a new myth to take shape: repetition, the dilation of time and the transcendence of luck remake Phil, through a control experiment of trial and error, into a kind of downbeat, mock-philosophical god, into a good, happy and thus lucky man.[24]

One final example is worth looking at, as something of a counterexample to the reductive numerics of Bordwell's 'folk' storytelling of luck through merely a handful of forking or intersecting timelines. An early film by Austrian director Michael Haneke self-consciously presents itself, in its title and in its highly fragmentary structure, as a work which seems to be governed by no overarching pattern of connection at all, no parallelism or simultaneity, nor any imagination of the 'what if' (although like *Blind Chance* it starts with what turns out to be a proleptic premonition of its violent end). The film is called *71 Fragments of a Chronology of Chance* (*71 Fragmente einer Chronologie des Zufalls*, 1994) and the number 71, indicating the number of disconnected sequences in the film, is in a sense a parody of a Borgesian infinity, a random number chosen as a nod towards something 'countless'. The film proceeds as a confusing jumble of elements, of chance snatches of characters and lives. Here too, as in *Blind Chance*, the film converges on a final act of violence – in this case a deadly, random city shooting, carried out by one young man we have encountered along the way – that seems to gather the fragments into a single moment. Although this echoes Kieslowksi's plane explosion and other patterns of chance convergence following in the wake of lines of divergence, Haneke's culmination is not one 'caused' or rendered meaningful by preceding sequences. The final act, just like the preceding 71 fragments, simply 'is'. The disconnectedness of the fragments is underlined by the use of brief black-screen interstices between them and their status as randomly snatched elements of the contemporary by Haneke's use of real news footage of reports about global conflicts.

Thomas Elsaesser has commented that the title of Haneke's film is 'not so much a title as a program, a motto, albeit one to which Haneke is dedicating his creative life', because of its careful performance of a contradictory balancing act between control and contingency.[25] Elsaesser points to a sequence in which the young man, and later shooter, plays a game of pick-up-sticks with his friend, as a possible forking-path moment, when he might have lost the gun that he later happens to have with him when he snaps at the bank. The same man is also seen playing a relentless game of table tennis against a machine that shoots ball after ball at him, non-stop, against a building sense of anxiety and exhaustion. The coercion to play the game, to return the ball, drains it of all sense of play, sport and contingency, and this seems to be a figure also for very contemporary anxieties that lead to violence. The game is mechanized, repetitive, rhythmically psychotic. (Indeed, the game that turns violent looks ahead directly to Haneke's later work of 2007, *Funny Games*.) Elsaesser posits that the inversion of the forking-path paradigm in Haneke points ultimately, in the context of late twentieth-century Germany, to a profoundly difficult historical question, one posed by another filmmaker, Alexander Kluge, that is not so much the 'what if?' question of the counterfactual, but rather the 'how' question of historical memory:

> A more directly historical reference comes into view, however, if one compares Haneke's chronology of contingency with a famous saying by another German director, Alexander Kluge: 'Tausend Zufälle, die im Nachhinein Schicksal heissen' ('a thousand coincidences that afterwards, in retrospect, are called "fate"'), a phrase which in Kluge functions as an answer to the always present, if implicitly stated, question, 'How could it have come to this?', where 'this' invariably stands for the German disaster of the Nazi regime, World War II, and the Holocaust.[26]

In Chapter 6, we will return to the dark history of the Holocaust and the way it seems to hold a strangely powerful position in the imagination of modern luck and its stories.[27] Here it has emerged as a shadow behind certain more abstracted spatial patterns and archetypes that are to be found permeating the field of modern luck stories. Certain spaces draw out luck and the perception of the possibility of change, and therefore a vibrant interplay of fortune and misfortune. We have dwelled on bars and taverns, on trains and train stations, but many other such sites could have been selected, sites of movement, travel and transit. And for all the formalist, even abstract, focus of the discussion – lines, geometries, convergences and divergences, infinites – there are profoundly, often dark and intensely human ('folk', ordinary) life experiences shadowing these narrative forms. After all, our lucky lines and lucky places must also include borders and seas, which in the geopolitical moment of the early twenty-first century cannot but invoke the Mediterranean as it has become a vast site of risk, mortal danger, flows of people and intense geopolitical crisis, throwing up too many harrowing tales of death and survival, also in their way stark contemporary instances of luck stories.[28]

Notes

1. See Ken Mogg, *The Alfred Hitchcock Story* (London: Titan, 1999), p. 101; 'What's a MacGuffin', at https://hitchinfo.net/faqs.html.
2. Italo Calvino, *Il castello dei destini incrociati* (1973), in English as *The Castle of Crossed Destinies*, trans. William Weaver (New York: Harcourt Brace Jovanovich, 1979). On the literature of the chance encounter, see Luperini, *L'incontro*.
3. Marc Augé, *Non-Places: Introduction to an anthropology of supermodernity*, trans. John Howe (London: Verso, 1995). As it happens, Augé is also the author of a fascinating memoir-essay on *Casablanca*, discussed earlier: Marco Augé, *Casablanca: Movies and memory*, trans. Tom Conley (Minneapolis: University of Minnesota Press, 2009).
4. This fluidity suggests potential connections with Manuel Castells's notion of the 'space of flows' in later network societies (e.g. Manuel Castells, *The Information Age: Economy, society and culture. Volume 1: The Rise of the Network Society* (Oxford: Blackwell, 1996)).
5. The focus here will be on trains, but it is fascinating to note, in the context of car travel, the early history of the automobile and stories of chance encounters on the road, that one of the earliest words invented to describe what is now known as 'hitchhiking' was 'lift-luck', from the title of a 1910 travelogue, Tickner Edwardes, *Lift-Luck on Southern Roads* (London: Methuen and Co., 1910).
6. On these links between trains and the forms and history of the novel and early cinema in the late nineteenth century, see for example Remo Ceserani, *Treni di carta. L'immaginario in ferrovia: L'irruzione del treno nella letteratura moderna* (Genoa: Marietti, 1993); Giuliana Bruno, *Atlas of Emotion: Journeys in art, architecture, and film* (London: Verso, 2002), pp. 73–127; and more broadly, on the railway and modern perception, Wolfgang Schivelbusch, *The Railway Journey: The industrialization and perception of time and space in the 19th century* (Berkeley: University of California Press, 1986).
7. Colson Whitehead, *The Underground Railroad* (New York: Doubleday, 2016), pp. 46, 203, 238.
8. See Bruno, *Atlas*, pp. 15–72.
9. See Richard Dyer, *Brief Encounter* (London: British Film Institute, 1993).
10. That this deployment of incidental train (and other transitory) encounters is intensely generative of narrative energy across a wide transgeneric spectrum and well beyond romance, is confirmed by a comparison with the near-contemporary psychological crime novel *Strangers on a Train* (Patricia Highsmith, 1950) and subsequent film (dir. Alfred Hitchcock, 1951), in which the apparently 'perfect' murder is forged by two strangers meeting on a train, who agree to carry out each other's murder, thereby confounding all possibility of detection. Once again, we might point to a narrative resonance with Carlo Ginzburg's intersecting, dual meaning of *caso*, as criminal case and luck or chance (Ginzburg, 'A proposito di Nondimanco / Il caso, i casi').
11. Mary Ann Doane, *The Emergence of Cinematic Time: Modernity, contingency, the archive* (Cambridge, MA: Harvard University Press, 2002).

12. Borges, *Collected Fictions*, pp. 119–28.
13. Borges, *Collected Fictions*, p. 127.
14. Robert Frost, *The Road Not Taken and Other Poems*, ed. David Orr (London: Penguin Books, 2015), pp. 87–8. On Borges, narrative and the multiverse, see for example David M. Baulch, 'Time, narrative, and the multiverse: Post-Newtonian narrative in Borges's "The garden of the forking paths" and Blake's "Vala or The four Zoas"', *The Comparatist*, 27 (May 2003): 56–78. On counterfactual narratives see Catherine Gallagher, *Telling It Like It Wasn't: The counterfactual imagination in history and fiction* (Chicago, IL: University of Chicago Press, 2018); Christopher Prendergast, *Counterfactuals: Paths of the might have been* (London: Bloomsbury Academic, 2019). For a beguiling study that takes Frost's poem as a starting point for a wider enquiry into the imaginary sphere of 'unled lives', paths not taken through choice or chance, see Andrew Miller, *On Not Being Someone Else: Tales of our unled lives* (Cambridge, MA: Harvard University Press, 2020).
15. In this iteration, the forking path had already been dramatically staged in medieval Christian literature in Dante's early fourteenth-century *Comedy*, in which a devil laments that a soul, Bonconte da Montefeltro, has been saved from the torments of hell by the smallest of tears at the moment of death, enough of a willed expression of repentance for God to save him ('You'd prise him from me for one little tear / and carry off his everlasting part?', trans. Robin Kirkpatrick, *Purgatorio* V, ll. 106–7). His father Guido was not so 'lucky'; a demon carried him off to hell (*Inferno* XXVII).
16. Borges's 'A survey of the works of Herbert Quain', another story that appeared in the same collection as 'The garden of forking paths', imagines a reverse-time novel starting in a train station (Borges, *Collected Fictions*, pp. 107–11).
17. On the parallels between *Blind Chance* and *Sliding Doors*, see Karen Mann, 'Kieślowski's narrative conscience: Physical time and mental space', *Quarterly Review of Film and Video*, 19.4 (2002): 343–53, which, however, does not point to direct influence. Others have talked more openly, if loosely, of the latter as a 'rip-off' of or 'stolen' from the former (see for example Agnieszka Holland, interview, on DVD / Blu-ray edition of *Blind Chance*, Criterion, 2015).
18. The context of the Cold War and its ideologies are pertinent here. As Steven Belletto has shown, certain paradigmatic conceptions of the contrasting ideologies, of West and East, and their narratives of themselves and the other, were operatively associated with chance; the West saw freedom in figures of chance or luck in contrast to the rigid totalitarian control and design planning of the Communist bloc. See Steven Belletto, *No Accident, Comrade: Chance and design in Cold War American narratives* (Oxford: Oxford University Press, 2011). This binary recalls rather closely the contrast drawn in Chapter 3 between Captain Renault and Strasser, Vichy and Nazi Germany, in *Casablanca*.
19. David Bordwell, 'Film futures', *SubStance* 31.1 (2002): 88–104. (Bordwell's essay is followed by responses from Edward Branigan, 'Nearly true: Forking plots, forking interpretations', *Substance*, 31.1 (2002): 105–14, and Kay Young, '"That fabric of times"', *Substance*, 31.1 (2002): 115–18.) Cf. also Slavoj Žižek, 'Run, Isolde, run', in Slavoj Žižek and Mladen Dolar, *Opera's Second Death* (London: Routledge, 2002), pp. 197–225, and 'Chance and repetition in Kieślowski's films', *Paragraph* 24.2 (July 2001)): 23–39.
20. Henriette Heidbrink, '1, 2, 3, 4 futures: Ludic forms in narrative films', *SubStance* 42.2 (2013): 146–64 (pp. 135, 156).
21. Something of the same limitation is part of Jean Baudrillard's critique of *The Dice Man* referred to in Chapter 3, whose six pre-constituted choices for every action are hardly a prefiguration of an infinite freedom (Baudrillard, *Impossible*, pp. 78–9). To explain the point here, Baudrillard plays on Mallarmé – 'a throw of the dice – countless throws of the dice – will never abolish this initial determination' – and calls this kind of limited freedom of decision 'dé-cision', punning on the French word for 'die', *le dé*.
22. Bordwell, 'Film futures', pp. 90–1.
23. The focus is on films here, but there is a rich field of writing within contemporary literature that plays comparable games. See for example a number of British works of fiction: the experimental formal devices in a pair of novels by Kate Atkinson, *Life After Life* (2013) and *God in Ruins* (2015), which tell alternative life-and-death stories of its protagonist, Ursula Todd, starting from an 'original' version in which she dies at birth, strangled by her umbilical cord; works by Ali Smith using parallel timelines and formally intersecting narratives (e.g. *The Accidental*, 2005, *How to be Both*, 2014); and Laura Barnett's *The Versions of Us* (2015), which follows three

possible life stories pivoting on a moment of accidental encounter. (Compare also Paul Auster's novel, *4 3 2 1* (2017), which tells four alternative versions of its protagonist's life story.)

24 This contrary play of the singularity of luck against repetition recalls a structural distinction that holds in inverse form in both narrative – reliant on the single event, the encounter, the coincidence – and the epistemology of science in a Popperian sense, which requires reproducibility as a condition of knowledge and truth ('non-reproducible single occurrences are of no significance to science' (Karl Popper, *The Logic of Scientific Discovery* (1934) (Abingdon: Routledge, 2002), p. 66). Haruki Murakami plays with this principle in his 2013 novel *Colorless Tsukuru Tazaki and His Years of Pilgrimage*, trans. Philip Gabriel (London: Harvill Secker, 2014), commenting on the mysterious one-off harmony between his five protagonist friends: 'The whole convergence was like a lucky but entirely accidental chemical fusion, something that could only happen once. You might gather the materials and make identical preparations, but you would never be able to duplicate the results' (p. 5).

25 Thomas Elsaesser, 'Performative self-contradictions: Michael Haneke's mind games', in Roy Grundman, ed., *A Companion to Michael Haneke* (Oxford: Wiley-Blackwell, 2010), pp. 53–74 (p. 67).

26 Elsaesser, 'Performative', p. 69.

27 In the context of Kluge and Germany's post-war reckoning with its dark modern history, memory, and the ways in which this issue might intersect with luck, chance and fate, it is instructive to look at the beguiling work of W. G. Sebald, whose semi-fictional narratives are carefully built on the fragile residues of genocide, war and destruction and whose structures are steeped in patterns of coincidence. This is not least the case in his 2001 novel *Austerlitz* (trans. Anthea Bell (London: Hamish Hamilton, 2001)), which is steeped in the history, memory and architecture of trains and train stations. Contingency in Sebald is widely discussed and analysed in Carole Angier, *Speak, Silence: In search of W. G. Sebald* (London: Bloomsbury Circus, 2021). And from Sebald, there is much potential to extend further the link between coincidence and a certain postmodern mode of literary narrative, perhaps best incarnated in the work of Paul Auster, for example in *The New York Trilogy* (1985–6) and *The Music of Chance* (1990); see Steven E. Alford, 'Chance in contemporary narrative: The example of Paul Auster', *Lit: Literature Interpretation Theory*, 11.1 (2000): 59–82.

28 Among the myriad stories of transit and migration to emerge from the Mediterranean refugee crisis, there are compelling examples gathered by the ERC project 'Bodies across borders: Oral and visual memory in Europe and beyond' (2013–18; https://cordis.europa.eu/project/id/295854), which asked its participants to draw maps and line drawings to narrate their journeys, thus encapsulating the stories' mobility, lines of chance, trauma and loss, and dreaming, much like the map and the journey-line that opened *Casablanca* and that opened this chapter too. See Luisa Passerini, ed., *Conversations on Visual Memory* (Florence: EUI, 2018), at https://cadmus.eui.eu/handle/1814/60164.

5
The luckiest man

Intacto is a Spanish film of 2001, directed by debut filmmaker Juan-Carlos Fresnadillo. The film is set in and around Madrid but moves for its climactic sequences to the lunar landscapes of Fresnadillo's native island of Tenerife. It imagines a conspiratorial secret society of men and women naturally endowed with good luck.[1] Once initiated into the sect, these people gamble against each other, with their very luck and often their lives at stake. They aim to earn or steal the luck of others by challenging them in a series of bizarre and dangerous games, in which the winners somehow absorb and take over the failed luck of the losers, in a fantastical zero-sum game. If you win, your luck was by definition greater and stronger than your rival's. For the successful player, a sequence of ever more demanding and terrifyingly dangerous challenges leads on to one final set-piece challenge, one-on-one against the mysterious guru and founder of the sect, Sam, played with his familiar gloomy charisma by Max von Sydow. Sam lives isolated in the secret, lightless basement of his casino in Tenerife, from where he presides, godlike and silent, over this remarkable secret world of luck, one which exists in parallel to and in between the lines of the urban, modern everyday world, of which it is both a magical exception and an invisible essence.

In a knowingly self-conscious construction, Fresnadillo and his co-writer Andrés Koppel fill their film with a compendium of ancient–modern tropes of risk and luck. Thus, the young protagonist of the film, Tomás (Leonardo Sbaraglia), is recruited into the secret society of lucky people after emerging as the sole survivor of a plane crash. Similarly, we learn that his lover did not board the same flight by pure chance of circumstance, and subsequently that his police pursuer, Sara (Mònica Lopez), is herself the miraculous survivor of a car crash in which all her family died. There are recurrent sequences and shots in the casino on Tenerife, Sam's lair, of a roulette wheel, the modern wheel of fortune, as well as glimpses of televisions showing a 'Wheel of Fortune'-type quiz show. The sect's games are, of course, games of pure chance, including the iconic example, which was heavily used in the marketing trailer and posters for the film because of its clearly recognizable figural topos of luck, of the players running blindfold (*'Fortuna caeca est'*). The image is taken from one 'enchanted forest' game that has the players running at high speed through an archetypically dense, dark and mysterious forest. The winner, the luckiest runner, is the one left standing after all the others have violently smashed headfirst into a tree.

Plane crashes and car crashes, random decisions, casinos and roulette wheels, TV quiz shows and blindfolds, and the final challenge of all, the ultimate test in this imaginary ladder of rising risk, danger and 'pure' luck is a single round of Russian roulette (see Chapter 3) against Sam. Sam, of course, always wins (until he encounters Tomás, that is). Each time, he appears in his basement to confront wordlessly his latest challenger, always emerging wearily and resignedly the winner, his opponent lying dead behind him. Sam, as Tomás and the audience are informed at one point by one of his henchmen, as if no more needs to be said in explanation, is *'el hombre más afortunado del mundo'*, the luckiest man in the world.

*

Stories of modern luck often coalesce around a specific archetype or category of character, much like the motif of the 'last man' in post-Romantic apocalypse literature – the topos of an imaginary human figure in literature who somehow captures the essence of a theme and its mythical narrative force for modernity.[2] One of the most compelling and powerful of these is the figure of the 'luckiest man', or in various commonplace variants the luckiest man alive, the luckiest man in the word, as embodied by Max von Sydow in *Intacto*. (The figure is almost invariably, as in most modern luck stories, gendered male.) All myths are hyperbolic, in their essence and nature, and thus it makes sense that luck myths and their story cycles should coalesce around fantasies of extreme, unlimited good (or bad) luck, but any given culture and moment is likely to reimagine this fantasy in new ways and with new inflections. How, then, this chapter asks, does modernity imagine the greatest luck of all? What does the experience of such ultimate good luck look like, on whom is this gift bestowed, and what do stories about such figures tell us about 'ordinary' human lives, as they struggle with the messier modern realities of meagre scraps of luck, of everyday contingency and uncertainty?

There is a dual polarity in how we might conceive of modern luck as embodied in its maximal form by a given archetype or character. We can return to some of the characters encountered in earlier chapters to illustrate the point and to map out the two poles. We might recall, for example, Helen Macdonald in *H is for Hawk* or, say, Luke Rhinehart's 'Dice Man' imagining a hyperbolic immersion in the vagaries of luck: they dream of giving themselves up entirely – ceding their very sense of self – to the instinct of the hawk or the throw of the dice. The figure of 'the luckiest' here stands for something like 'saturated in luck', 'lost to luck', 'nothing but a string of impulses'. Agency dissolves into purely random effect and affect, a kind of undetermined chaotic motion of action and consequence, of repeat arbitrary action. Although this dream of self-dissolution is a powerful thread in the modern cultural imaginary, and binds to luck in intense ways, it is the exception rather than the rule, by no means the dominant form of the 'luckiest man' topos. This is because a second topos of extreme good luck tends more frequently and easily, more legibly somehow, to accrue around something like its opposite, around modern versions of figures of heroically strong selfhood, figures of invulnerability. These are figures who are preternaturally or magically immune from the 'slings and arrows of outrageous fortune' and therefore represent a fantastical ability to resist, whether that means to resist simple misfortune or failure, or, more profoundly, to resist all harm, danger, illness and ultimately even death. This mythical figure, rather than being a modern variation on the goddess Fortuna, or a man lost to the throw of the dice or merely on an unstoppable lucky streak, is instead somewhat closer to the figure of a modern Achilles, divinely, magically immune to harm.[3] This chapter explores instances of such luck stories, built around these modern Achilles, and probes what their magical invulnerability (as well as their inevitable points of weakness, their Achilles' heels) has to tell us about modern luck and the dynamic of modern luck stories.

To begin to sketch out the magical modern figure of the luckiest man, the modern Achilles, we can start with another contrast, this time taken from a cultural zone of kitsch and commerce, a contrast between superheroes and losers. As many critics (and fans) have pointed out, the pantheon of DC, Marvel and other twentieth-century superheroes, invented in 1930s America and reborn to dominate the mass culture of the early twenty-first-century mediascape, represents in many different ways, from cultural function to cyclical, serial narrative form, a reprise of ancient myths, heroes and gods.[4] And one of the most intriguing of those echoes is one posited between Superman and Achilles: both are blessed with a 'magical' invulnerability that is narrated and explained in the myth-world through their birth story and specifically through their parents; both are cursed with a narratively determining, myth-generating single and secret weakness; both are caught between their innermost impulses as warrior-heroes and lovers.[5] But if Achilles can in a sense be construed, as we have suggested, as a displaced figure of hyperbolic good fortune, divinely protected from the all-too-human curses of vulnerability, injury and death, this does not seem to work anything like as well for Superman. Superman seems in the end more Hercules than Achilles, his warrior virtues rather more lying in his superhuman strength, speed, vision and the like, more immovable *virtù* than uncanny *fortuna*, to return to the Machiavellian dyad.

There is a slippery relation in evidence here between luck and (super)power: can luck be distilled and materialized, even in a magical universe, into a specific superpower? Or is it by definition too uncertain, too ubiquitous and shape-shifting for that, so that luck cannot constitute a superpower as such? The superhero universe has shown it is well aware of this constitutive problem, while also being fascinated by it, and its confusions are borne out by the fact that luck effects have typically been relegated there to occasional, odd corners and unachieved depictions. Indeed, this is a good example of a persistent tendency in luck stories not to interrogate too closely or too deeply its core defining notion, to leave luck half-baked in its imaginings, so that it is left to float, morph and modulate in our imaginations. (See Chapter 8 for more on this 'half-baked' aspect of luck.) A good example is an early, rare instance of a female superhero created in 1940 by no less a figure than Will Eisner, a caped crime-fighter called Lady Luck, dressed in green (a lucky colour in several cultures, associated with fertility and growth) and wearing various lucky charms.[6] But Lady Luck did not quite stand up as a creation: she was a masked figure with no superpowers as such (although this was by no means unheard of), and the name seems more derived from a familiar stock phrase than used as a meaningful descriptor for Brenda Banks. Indeed, the character did not last beyond 1946 (before later revivals).[7] Similarly, a string of minor Marvel characters tapped into the talismans and nomenclature of luck traditions: dig deep enough and you can find characters such as Black Cat, Roulette, Longshot, Shamrock, and the X-Force mutant Domino, who is able to manipulate probability to generate good luck for herself and bad luck for her enemies. Finally, in 2016, another titan of the comics world, Stan Lee, created a detective-cum-superhero franchise for British television called *Lucky Man*, one of his very last creations before his death in 2018.[8]

The titular detective in *Lucky Man*, Harry Clayton, is a gambling addict whose new power of luck is bestowed on him by way of an ancient irremovable magic bracelet, the hyperbolic luck effect of which seems to be primarily to drive the plot towards ever more danger, ever more sinister criminals, and ever more improbable plot twists and escapes for Harry. Again the fit is awkward, the 'power' of luck a vessel for everything and nothing that Harry gets away with or from. But, as in the other cases, this adds to the evidence that luck is a key force eating away at the edges of the imaginary universe of the superhero. Indeed, pre-transmission publicity material for *Lucky Man* suggested a kind of summary quality of luck in relation to the overarching idea of superpowers as a whole, at least for its creator Lee. Lee was asked by fans which superpower he would personally like to have, and he replied 'luck', as if it might be a power that transcends all others.[9] Who needs laser vision or the power of flight and the like, if you simply know that everything will go your way?

At the other end of a putative scale of luck as a source of strength and a force for good, we can contrast these few and thinly convincing 'lucky' comic-world superheroes with an example from Hollywood cinema of a 'lucky' loser, and what's more, a bully and a creep. The character in question is Biff Tannen (Thomas F. Wilson), the love-to-hate, dim-witted villain of the *Back to the Future* film series (dir. Robert Zemeckis, I–III, 1985–90), and the sometime nemesis of our hero Marty McFly (Michael J. Fox), and indeed Marty's father, George. Biff is transformed in one of the cycle's alternative timelines into a stunningly rich and successful tycoon. He manages this through a glitch in the time-travel narrative: unbeknownst to Marty and his mad-scientist companion Doc Brown (Christopher Lloyd), Biff in 2015 steals from a bin an almanac which contains the results of sports events going back years into the past, which he proceeds to give to his 1955 self, who starts laying bets, leading to the accumulation of an astonishing fortune. Marty learns this grim fact as he returns from 1955 to an alternative future version of 2015 and finds himself visiting the 'Biff Tannen Museum', where he watches a celebratory video that includes a flash of an old image of the *Hill Valley Telegraph* newspaper with the glaring headline, accompanied by Biff's smiling face: 'Biff Tannen. Luckiest Man on Earth'.

Biff's time-travel story, the loser transformed into 'the luckiest man on Earth', does some interesting work here. Rather like Derren Brown's illusory 'system' for predicting the future in *The System* (see Chapter 3), it takes us to the heart of the association between luck and futurity, and the play of temporality more generally, that we had already noted from the etymologies of luck in Chapter 2. Play games with time, all these examples suggest, and you play games with luck. Both Brown and Biff are cheating time, and cheating luck, by playing the numbers with an unfair advantage and by playing time backwards. Furthermore, both flag up another crucial recurrent feature in modern luck stories: a pattern in which 'genuine' luck, absolutely open randomness, is a kind of utopia, a dream of equality and possibly even democracy, but often also a kind of delusion, a symptom of a world of hidden control, tricks and deceptions, and rigged systems.[10] The 'luckiest' man, here, is the one who is immune to luck, whether through good or ill, and thus, strangely enough perhaps, closer to the Superman paradigm after all.

The other pattern we can discern in the falling off from superhero to loser, as contrasting figures of the luckiest man, is a characteristically modern arc of descent from gods and kings to the travails of the ordinary man, and the tragicomic or absurd bathos that accompanies it. This is perhaps rather too much to load onto the shoulders of Biff Tannen, but it can usefully point us in the direction of the next step in our discussion, a work from the mid-1940s and thus a moment pitched somewhere between the birth of the superheroes and the world of the 1950s that *Back to the Future* parodically reimagines, as the Ur-time of modern American 'happy days', where the roots of its shared modern prosperity and values lay.

One of the boldest and clearest statements of the hypothesis that tragedy has moved from the courts of kings to the humble homes of the modern man was Arthur Miller's 1949 piece 'Tragedy and the common man'.[11] By 1949, Miller was well on the way to gaining his reputation as one of the great dramatists of his day, following the success of *All My Sons* (1947), and *Death of a Salesman*, which opened in the same month in 1949 as the essay appeared. Indeed, 'Tragedy and the common man' was written in defence of the 'low' tragic hero of that play, Willy Loman. These dramas would be followed in short order by *The Crucible* (1953) and *A View from the Bridge* (1955), mature works that would together see Miller probing profound problems of morality, family, masculinity and economy, along with questions of freedom, identity and self-making, all with their origins (like Superman) in Depression- and war-era America. But a few short years earlier, in a now largely forgotten play, Miller had woven many of these same threads into a play explicitly centred on the problem of luck. The play was entitled *The Man Who Had All the Luck* (1944), and it merits close attention.[12]

The play is set in a 1930s Midwestern American town and centres on the Beeves family: David, his brother Amos and their father Pat. Pat has trained Amos since childhood as a baseball pitcher, drilling him to the point of obsession, and now a big-time scout is coming down from Detroit to watch Amos pitch in a live game. But the scout spots a fatal flaw in Amos's game, one created directly by Pat's relentless home-training (Amos tightens up when confronted with the noise of a real crowd). Amos's story, then, is a tragicomic one of the small cause of a life ruined and of the dreams of ordinary families – and of fathers, especially – and the damage they leave behind. Pat's obsession, his vicarious dream of success for Amos, destroys his golden son (a pattern that recurs in Miller's mature plays). And several core motifs of modern luck, good and bad, are deployed in this cautionary tale: the luck of sports and the game, the random spin of luck on which a whole life turns – one pitch, one game, one scout's visit – and the way in which, once again, that spin turns out not to be random luck at all, but a systemic flaw (in character, strategy, imagination, even in the breeding itself). The game was rigged against Amos from the start.

But Amos is not the hero of *The Man Who Had All the Luck*, nor its central focus as a modern luck story. The eponymous hero, the man with all the luck, is his brother David, whose problem is that he somehow always falls on his feet (to use one of our commonplace 'falling' luck phrases). Miller gives no explanation for this fact, magical or otherwise, and neither we nor David himself can fathom it. Indeed, he cannot come to terms with the guilt of repeatedly escaping from predicaments (in love, work, prosperity), with a sudden, unlikely bound towards success, happiness and a brighter future, and all of this in the face of his brother's untimely, leaden failure. David's is the strange curse of the lucky man.[13]

David Beeves, we learn, is struggling to make a go of his job as a car mechanic and simultaneously struggling to pluck up the courage to ask the terrifying father of his sweetheart Hester for her hand in marriage. Suddenly, randomly, the father is killed in an off-stage car accident; shortly after, a new mechanic, Gus Eberson, appears from nowhere to help with the cars, like a grubby *deus ex machina* in overalls. Thus all obstacles to David's business and marriage success fall away. At the end of the play, David's struggles turn again: Hester gives birth to the son he feared he would never have and his crazy high-risk venture in mink breeding is saved from disaster, when he accidentally, luckily, weeds out a hidden poison in their feed.

David's story, David's luck, like Amos's misfortune, is on a cusp between the absurd and the tragic: Miller commented later that he was undecided whether he should end the play on David's ultimate double good luck, or instead with his suicide, as if the two were equivalent resolutions for this study in luck as unearned success or failure.[14] Luck is a curse in either case, because it is a trial and a trap set against David's sense of agency and self-making. And David's lucky fate is constantly glossed and exacerbated by its brotherly contrast to Amos: a variant on Cain and Abel, the question of who we are and how much we make ourselves and what forking paths we take, is, as Miller puts it, 'pre-eminently a brother's question'.[15] Unlike Amos's and Pat's singular obsession with baseball, David turns this way and that – he is the fox to Amos's hedgehog – but he is baffled by his inability to call down upon himself a deserved disaster, to pay any debt whatsoever for his good fortune. David is a small-town Achilles who cannot fathom how he has come by the role of hero in Miller's two-bit, unheroic world.

Miller's underlying concerns, shared with his mature plays to come, are all here: agency and responsibility, money, work and family, self-making and an individual's fragile moral place in the modern world, in the face of poverty, labour and an uncertain future. The luck of the title provides the material and imaginary matrix of that uncertainty. And a series of sometimes odd metaphors and idioms for luck runs through the play to give us the shape of Miller's nascent worldview seen through this matrix.

The primary struggle in the play is to find a language and a set of actions to understand a man's responsibility in the world and this is couched by Miller as a question of whether to make or wait for one's own luck (a modern Hamlet's dilemma). A key – and rather odd – metaphor that he uses more than once is of the jellyfish, proffered by a minor character, Shory, a wheelchair-bound Great War veteran, crippled not heroically on the battlefield as it turns out, but in an absurd accident in a prostitute's hovel:

> DAVID: How do you know when to wait and when to take things in your hand and make them happen?
> SHORY: You can't make anything happen any more than a jellyfish makes the tides, David.[16]

And later:

> SHORY: A man is a jellyfish. The tide goes in and the tide goes out. About what happens to him, a man has very little to say.[17]

David is caught between waiting (like a frog, Hester accuses him, with her own zoological metaphor) and acting, and then feeling guilty for his good fortune, blurred between causality and chance. He eventually acts, asking for Hester's hand, but only after the accident removes her father from the scene. Similarly, once Hester is pregnant, he waits for and expects the child to be stillborn, and wills his minks to die because he feels the need to be punished for his good luck, to restore some moral balance in the world, but in the end a healthy boy is born and the minks flourish.

Pat is similarly torn between acting and waiting: he trains Amos for 12 hard years, but nervously holds off calling out the scout, dreaming that Amos will be discovered as if by some natural, organic force (luck?):

> PAT: I've picked up the phone a lot of times ... but I ... I wanted it to happen ... naturally. It ought to happen naturally, Dave.
> [...]
> DAVID: I mean ... can you *just wait for something to happen?*[18]

This comes at a crucial, tragic turning point in the interplay between Amos's and David's luck when we learn that David has secretly called out the scout himself ('Where's the jellyfish could've done that?' he boasts),[19] thus unknowingly bringing ruin down on his brother.

The traditional icon that we saw in Warburg's *Mnemosyne Atlas* of man or Fortuna as the sailor at the wheel, navigating the tides and storms of the seas (just like those jellyfish), reminds us that imagery of luck has long also been a code for the negotiation between the human and the 'natural', the rhythms and organic flux of the world. This binary is reinforced and reworked in Miller's play by the crucial interweaving of two supplementary semantic and metaphorical fields, running intricately parallel to each other through the play and intimately bound up with notions of fortune: economy (through motifs of money, work, property, luxury, investment and return) and reproduction (through motifs of childbirth, sickness, infertility, impotence and fidelity).

David's garage, the fortunate routing of a new highway right past its door, his work with Gus, his accidental acquisition of Hester's father's property, his remarkable success with the minks: all these are material markers of success, profit, magnetically drawn to David, in a post-Depression America overshadowed by poverty and scarcity of production. There is luck and risk in all of these, but also rules and calculations, so that they run in close, at times ironic, metaphorical parallel to the theme of games and sport in Miller's play, from Amos's baseball to others' games of pinochle, claviash and rummy.[20] Problems of fertility, in contrast, run as a seam of instability, of uncontrolled luck, and dangerous secrecy, working to undermine apparently clear lines: J.B., another town store owner, thinks his wife is too old to conceive, until, late in the play, he is crushed to learn this was no stroke of bad luck after all, but his wife's deliberate deceit, since she could not trust him to stay sober. For J.B., the failure to reproduce is the very death of the future: 'No kids. Isn't that something? You die, and they wipe your name off the mail box and … that's the ballgame.'[21] David and Hester, once married, have their own worries about infertility, until it turns out that they just needed to wait. Shory's wheelchair-bound impotence also turns out to have been a product of a site of infidelity and sexual risk, the brothel, a bathetic turn from the soldierly, martial tradition of metaphors of luck, force and danger.[22]

At telling cruces in the play, these parallel threads of fertility and economy, as markers of 'success' or 'luck', perhaps the ultimate good luck, intersect. This is most marked in Pat's moulding of Amos, from childbirth to the forging of a destiny, a future, against plural, random chance:

> PAT: An infant in his mother's arms. I felt his body and I saw it was strong. And I said to myself, this boy is not going to waste out his life being seventeen different kind of things and ending up nothing. He's going to play baseball.[23]

Pat is taking a life and 'moulding it to fit the thing you want':[24] he is breeding, in other words, to forge an identity and to make success and money, just as you would a racehorse, or indeed a mink. The pseudo-calculus of the one thing versus the 'seventeen different kinds of things' – the fox and the hedgehog again – echoes the play of the one and the many in the lucky number stories we encountered in Chapter 2. And it is reprised in other number games in Miller's exploration of economy, fertility and luck. The mink breeding, for example, is laid out as an all-or-nothing gamble because of the high risk to high return ratio in mink reproduction statistics (it is almost impossible to get them to breed, but if they do, they breed massively and at vast return). Gus comments acidly, 'A business! That's a slot machine'.[25]

At the core of David's near-fatal descent into a kind of insanity, before his one last stroke of luck, we witness his obsessive conviction that luck itself must have its own economy, a zero-sum calculus, that all his successes must be paid for, must balance out somehow, according to an imagined, but quite untenable, natural law that he needs to hold true, even if it means losing his unborn child. This starts out in David's mild optimism for Amos – 'Things even up, I guess in the long run'[26] – and spirals down into a visceral need for a price to be paid:

> DAVID: I just didn't like the idea of me getting everything so steady, and him [Amos] waiting around like … I mean you get to wondering if your own turn isn't coming.
> PAT: Like what do you mean?
> DAVID: A loss … a big unhappiness of some kind.[27]

And, finally, to a blind faith in a curse, a conviction that catastrophe will out:

> DAVID: You'll never meet a man who doesn't carry one curse … at least one. […] A man is born with one curse at least to be cracked over his head […] as if a law was written in the sky somewhere – nobody escapes!
> […]
> AMOS: Nobody escapes […] except you![28]

The natural law fails. This is how David has all the luck, which undermines the very inner being and moral core of his self. This is above all a crisis of 'moral luck', of moral responsibility for actions and consequences beyond your control.[29] Nothing is his own doing and nothing bespeaks his own sense of self and self-building, if everything comes by luck, especially if the luck is always good:

> HESTER: It's good to be lucky. Isn't it?
> DAVID: Isn't it better to feel that what you have came to you because of something special you can do? Something, something … inside you?[30]

It is ultimately Gus, the Austrian mechanic, who sees through David's madness. He is the one who guesses that David is betting everything on the minks. Perversely convinced his unborn child is dead, David's moral calculus 'knows' the mink will breed in recompense. He is using death and loss as his stake in a bet, calling down and welcoming a curse on his head. Gus is soberly critical: 'I do not bet on dead children.' He alone strikes a balance between morality, luck and agency, declaring that there is no law, no calculus and no moral sense to actions and consequences: 'Are you mad! There is no catastrophe upstairs [where Hester is in labour], there is no guarantee up there for your mink.' As J.B. puts it, 'It always happens senseless.'[31] When David and Hester's baby boy is healthily delivered, David cannot touch him for shame at already having betrayed him, for having offered him up for dead at the altar of his luck calculus. The child is the literal embodiment of his luck, his fertility, his success – and his curse.

Gus slowly emerges as Miller's voice of reasoned reflection in the play's strange and strained stress-testing of agency and responsibility. He sees that David's luck, even his extreme, relentless, unbreakable chain of 'all the luck', is no vessel of individual worth, nor of morality; even his luck is part of the tide in which we swim. Agency resides not in your luck, for Gus, in a kind of gritty downbeat existentialism, but in your response to contingency: as he says, 'Whether you lay there or get up again – that's the part that's entirely up to you, that's for sure.'[32]

Gus the European is also able to reflect as an outsider on David's luck and America: in welcoming catastrophe, he sees, David is reviving a morbid old European attraction to disaster, millennial catastrophism and guilt, and he is betraying an American freedom to take life and luck as he finds it, to ride on its tide, to grab its chances, guilt-free, no price attached, what Jackson Lears calls a form of 'grace':[33]

> GUS: David, you broke my heart. This is from Europe, this idea [that we pay for our luck]. This is from Asia, from the rotten places, not America.[34]

In his later work Miller would test to destruction the impossible strains that David's extreme good luck put the Beeves family under, starting with his next, breakthrough play, *All My Sons*. There, the theme of luck is no longer front and centre, no longer a mysterious unexplained but central driving force of characters' choices and destinies; but it is profoundly operative nevertheless, sublimated within Miller's frontal assault on the American dream of work and family, masculinity, self-making and success.[35]

The motif of the luckiest man, or the modern Achilles, is among other things a device for interrogating the problem of how magic has survived into the modern imaginary of luck and how we tell stories about it. *Intacto*'s Sam, Stan Lee's Harry Clayton, Arthur Miller's David Beeves, are all, as we have seen, endowed with some kind of magical good luck. How this has come about has considerably less narrative force in their respective stories than the profound consequences of their supernatural or preternatural gift (although we will come back to the 'how' in Sam's case in Chapter 6). They are thus exceptional or extreme cases, descendants of gods as we have suggested, but they are all in their different ways also studiedly ordinary; and this suggests that, at one level, the luckiest man motif is simply an extension or a distillation of all those minor, propitious or apotropaic acts, those rituals and superstitions that persist in our lives (touch wood, cross yourself, make the sign of the horn, throw salt over your left shoulder), the millennial magic of everyday life designed to protect us from bad luck and to attract good fortune. If the magic works, you are Achilles for a moment, safe for now, at least in your own perception. Imagine, these stories propose, that this same magic of the everyday were total and permanent. In other words, these stories are both impossible myths of the superhuman and fantasies within the grasp of our everyday, although, as Miller shows, if the fantasy were to work, profound disorientation would ensue, the modern everyday would clash starkly with the fantasy. This is a pattern we can find recurring in other modern luck stories, where some magical gift of luck, again taken as a given, an unexplained precondition at the origin of the story, plays out as a curse, or more lightly as a comic complication, or as a baffling block on identity and self-fulfilment, against the backdrop of a contemporary, 'disenchanted' everyday.

Two popular, somewhat formulaic Hollywood films from the 1990s provide good illustrations of this phenomenon, perhaps precisely because of their middlebrow slickness and watchability: *29th Street* (dir. George Gallo, 1991) and *Fearless* (dir. Peter Weir, 1993). *29th Street* is a warm-hearted, Italian-American working-class family comedy, starring Anthony LaPaglia as Frank Pesce Jr, a lucky guy (we never know quite why), and Danny Aiello as Frank Sr, his put-upon, unlucky but loveable father. The set-up has more than a few distant echoes of Miller's family in *The Man Who Had All the Luck*, replayed in a sentimental, comic key, dosed with some clichés about Italian-American life (mobsters, an overbearing mother and family, spaghetti with meatballs), and several other familiar clichés and motifs from luck stories.[36] It tells Frank Jr's life story – LaPaglia's voiceover narrating throughout – as a series of good luck twists, in flashback from the moment when his city lottery ticket is about to win and win big, an event that for some reason is disastrous for him. (It turns out this is because the ticket is tangled up with Frank Sr's gambling debts to the Mob.)

Fearless has a touch more pretension than Gallo's film to be taken seriously as an exploration of human psychology, but it too is premised on serial luck motifs and one ordinary man's 'magical' good luck. In this case, Max (Jeff Bridges) survives an air crash unscathed at the start of the film. As a result of this extraordinary good luck, he is catapulted into a near-fugue state of detachment and overweening confidence, as if he were invulnerable (like Achilles), and his personality and personal relations are turned upside down as a result. He asks himself, and the film asks us to imagine: was he somehow predestined to survive, is he immune from harm? Or rather, is his state of mind, is asking the question itself, indicative of a psychopathology caused by Max's random and miraculously extreme good luck, by an impossibly close brush with death? Max seems to suffer from something like the opposite of David Beeves's guilt of the lucky man.

When luck at its extreme descends upon ordinary lives, these examples again suggest, the upshot is destabilization, not necessarily triumph at all. (We could fill a further book, after all, with compelling tales, both true and fictional, of lottery winners or the suddenly rich whose lives are torn apart as a result of their amazing good fortune.)[37] And this is one of the reasons why, as was clear from the strange juxtaposition we noted above between Superman and Biff Tannen, the step from the hero to the loser is not so great a leap as we might initially imagine. As a final thread of discussion in this chapter, therefore, we need to turn from the figure of the luckiest man to his direct opposite, in many ways a more pervasively commonplace figure in stories of luck ancient and modern, the loser or the unluckiest man.

We saw in Chapter 2 how deep the etymological seam runs in English, linking the vocabulary of luck to the semantically similar 'hap' which has been subsumed into several commonplace modern words, from 'happiness' to 'happen' to 'perhaps'. In modern English usage, however, 'hap' has remained a particularly marked presence in the realm of the unlucky, in terms such as 'mishap' and 'hapless'. The hapless, the accident-prone, the perennially unlucky are a common source of comedy and of surprising fascination in our culture. If, however, the luckiest of all fascinate us because of their hopeless distance from our everyday lives (or at least so it seems) or for the frisson of possibility in imagining we could be one of them, the hapless are more likely to feel like our all too familiar twins or siblings, one step away from our own travailed existence with its inevitable accidents, uncontrolled slips, and unlucky turns. How this comes to be manifest in modern stories is suggested by the foundational early role of the accident-prone in the history of the central medium of twentieth-century figuration and narration, and of modernity itself, the cinema. The hapless clown and the accident, after all, played an elemental role in the birth of film, through its comic or fantasy shorts, its emergent comedy film stars, and through the mode of slapstick that was established from the very birth of the medium. Keaton, Chaplin, Laurel and Hardy and others rose to become genuinely mythical and defining examples of film stars and the dynamic potential of film itself, so much so that the influential characterization by film historian Tom Gunning of early cinema as a 'cinema of attractions', in contrast to and preceding the 'narrative cinema' of later eras, included the rhythmic succession of gags, pratfalls, missteps and crashes as an alternative and precursor to linear story as means of drawing audiences to this magical new medium.[38] Slapstick is a mode in which everything goes wrong, for no particular reason, in other words the very essence of extreme bad luck, of mischance as comedy (until, in full comic mode, everything finally comes right).[39] We see this, famously, in Laurel and Hardy's 1932 short *Music Box* (dir. James Parrott), in which an attempt to deliver a piano up a flight of stairs fails, crashes and falls in a series of random comic mishaps.[40] Two further striking examples are the 1921 American hit *Seven Years Bad Luck*, directed by and starring French star Max Linder, and Hal Roach's 1925 production *His Wooden Wedding*, starring Charley Chase. Both play around with slapstick, superstition (breaking a mirror in the former, getting married on Friday the 13th in the latter), hoaxes and trickery; both use journeys by boat and train (modern luck motifs, as we know from Chapter 4) to sustain and extend their comic stories into a second act; and both tell luck stories of love and marriage, first disastrously confounded and then happily reconciled.

Later film comedy has largely eschewed the form of slapstick and the figure of the slapstick loser, along with other stock comic figures of the silent era, but not entirely. The hapless hero, the loser, remains ripe for occasional revival or reinvention. It was at the root of the extraordinary international success of the bumbling Inspector Clouseau, played by Peter Sellers in a series of six film comedies, most directed by Blake Edwards from 1963 to 1978 (plus a seventh using out-takes after Sellers's death). The slapstick loser was literally revived in silent-movie form in the hugely successful comedy character and global franchise, Rowan Atkinson's *Mr Bean* series, in shorts, features and indeed cartoons (1990–2015); it was at least an influence in the establishment of Woody Allen's comic persona in his early films of the late 1960s and 1970s, where physical comedy (for example that of the incompetent bank robber in *Take the Money and Run*, 1969; or in the fight with a lobster in *Annie Hall*, 1977) was combined with neurosis to create a kind of contemporary psychoanalytical variant on the loser figure, in no small part derived also from Yiddish traditions (and vocabulary) of the schlimazel, the schlemiel, the nebbish, the klutz.[41] Both Allen's and Atkinson's protagonists, it should be noted, tend to be self-consciously situated in modern, urban settings, New York for the former (or indeed a mock-futuristic version of the same in *Sleeper*, 1973), a generic contemporary Britain for the later. A further and final example of the continuation of this comic genre tradition is provided by a French comedy of 1981 starring Gérard Depardieu and Pierre Richard, *La Chèvre* (dir. Francis Veber). This film is especially resonant for our discussion because it is explicitly tied to the notion of 'unluck' in its concept and plot, and because it replays in negative the exact pattern we saw above of unexplained, magical, hyperbolic incarnations of luck played out through specific characters and situations.

The title, *La Chèvre*, is colloquial French that roughly translates as 'the klutz' (the film was marketed in English as *Knock on Wood*, and later remade in English as *Pure Luck*, dir. Nadia Tass, 1991). It tells a convoluted story of a buddy couple sent from Paris on a mad mission to rescue a magnate's daughter (Corinne Charbit) who has gone missing in Mexico. The luck conceit is nothing if not forced: both the missing daughter and Pierre Richard's character Perrin are cursed with bad luck, both endlessly accident-prone and ridiculously clumsy and bumbling (an echo of the Clouseau films, perhaps). The somewhat tenuous plot trigger is the idea that, if Richard follows exactly in the daughter's tracks, the same unlucky things will happen to him as to her and so he will be inevitably led to find her. Depardieu is the hard-bitten detective, Campana, sent to babysit them both, who travels a familiar comic arc from contempt for the loser Perrin to a kind of love for him as the picaresque story follows its path.[42] Critic David Denby, reviewing the film in *New York Magazine* on its American release, made the key links both to the problematic of bad luck that is at the heart of the film and to the subset of 'unlucky' narratives we have been examining, and indeed back to silent comedy:

> What if bad luck, as folk wisdom has always insisted, is really a state of being? And if it is, then might not the unlucky be linked in some way to people with powers and dispensations – the saintly, the magical, the clairvoyant? The unlucky person might be suffering from the inadvertence of God; he could be a holy innocent. That is the certainly one of the reigning assumptions of silent comedy. A hero like Buster Keaton, dogged by all of nature, and by all of man's machinery, too, manages to persevere, through sweet patience, until he attains his goal. Unless we believed, at some level, in ill luck as a state of grace, silent comedy would be impossible.[43]

The hapless losers of silent film comedy and their progeny have long been acknowledged not only as formative influences on cinema, film stardom and the *longue durée* evolution of modern comedy, but also as influences on and close kin to some of the tragicomic, hapless and often picaresque anti-heroes of high modernism, from Joyce's Bloom in *Ulysses* to Italo Svevo's Zeno in *Zeno's Conscience* to Beckett's Vladimir and Estragon in *Waiting for Godot* (the latter portrayed variously by Beckett and later directors as tramps or clowns or both, their bowler hats quite likely derived directly from Laurel and Hardy).[44] But in the crossover between the two genres and modes, there is also a thread of connection in which the shadows of unluck loom larger than the light touch and the broad brush of slapstick, in which unexplained misfortune is more relentless and more disconcertingly without cause, and the comedy, if it is still there at all, turns bitter. Here the figures of the hapless point us also or instead to Kafka and his put-upon protagonists, who are variously absurd losers, cursed and entrapped not so much by accident as by an ungiving, deterministic and utterly impenetrable higher system of law (in works such as *The Trial, The Castle*, 'Before the law' or even 'Metamorphosis'). Similarly, but in even more abject form, Imre Kertesz included in his remarkable 1975 work of Holocaust testimony *Fateless* a nameless minor character whom the autobiographical protagonist and narrator Gyuri encounters in the concentration camps, known simply as 'the man with bad luck' ('*a balszerencses embert*').[45] He is a figure first of awkwardness and ridicule, whining and importuning those around him in the camps, but as he reappears over weeks and months to Gyuri, in Auschwitz and other camps, the man with bad luck seems both ever more abject, and somehow ever more of a mirror for Gyuri and for us all, until his final appearance as a corpse covered in rags. This extreme modern figure of the unluckiest man, drawn into literature from the darkest site of modern history, points us towards another mythical origin, in stark contrast to the divinely protected Achilles posited above as the progenitor of the modern man with all the luck. Instead, both Kertesz and Kafka suggest, we should perhaps look for the emblem of the modern self and its relation to luck to the Old Testament figure of Job.[46] Job's devastating suffering is brought down upon him by God on high and so hardly seems an apt figure for the indeterminate, 'fateless' modern loser.[47] But, on reflection, Job's bad luck, his incessant, cursed agony which is a by-product of a nihilistic bet between God and Satan, and his remarkable perseverance in the face of it all, feel to the modern reader like something quite detached from all divine or moral cause, a test of the existence of evil and injustice, for sure, but also a test of the workings of relentless, meaningless misfortune.

Notes

1. There is a regular pattern of intersection between luck stories and conspiracy stories that *Intacto*, among other works we will touch on, taps into, reflecting something of a key epistemological tension that is pervasive in the contemporary: surface coincidences, chance events, or slips and errors seem from one perspective like signals of pure luck, but they can just as easily seem, from another, 'paranoid' perspective, like a signal of a hidden cause, a secret determination, a coded or rigged system of control, of a conspiracy. This pattern has run like a seam through modern history and literature, from the *Protocols of the Elders of Zion* to the JFK assassination to postmodern fiction. One example of the latter is Umberto Eco's novel *Foucault's Pendulum* (1988), which playfully taps into a hidden universe of conspiracy theorists, mystics, Kabbalists and secret sects, which in the end collapses like a house of cards: its heroes have decoded a cryptic message about all these dark forces controlling the world from what was in fact a laundry list (Umberto Eco, *Foucault's Pendulum*, trans. William Weaver (London: Secker and Warburg, 1988)).
2. The motif has its origin in Mary Shelley's *The Last Man* (1826) and has had a sustained influence on dystopian, apocalyptic, and more recently climate-crisis fiction: see for example Sian MacArthur, *Gothic Science Fiction: 1818 to the present* (Basingstoke: Palgrave Macmillan, 2015), pp. 49–70.
3. On Achilles in modern literature, see Marta González González, *Achilles* (London: Routledge, 2018), pp. 127–37. There is a link to be explored here between this kind of immunity from harm or misfortune and the concept of immunity and self-immunity in contemporary biopolitical theory, for example as deployed by Robert Esposito, who posits immunity and community as a pair of mutually defining opposites that are constitutive of modern biopolitics: see for example Roberto Esposito, 'The immunization paradigm', *Diacritics*, 36.2 (Summer, 2006): 23–48; and cf. Timothy Campbell, *'Bios*, immunity, life: The thought of Roberto Esposito', *Diacritics*, 36.2 (Summer, 2006): 2–22. Esposito has made the link himself, in *Living Thought: The origins and actuality of Italian philosophy*, trans. Zakiya Hanafi (Stanford, CA: Stanford University Press, 2012), and in 'Fortuna e politica all'origine della filosofia italiana', *California Italian Studies*, 2.1 (2011), at http://escholarship.org/uc/item/5ht7n7p4.
4. See for example Wendy Haslem, Angela Ndalianis and Chris Mackie, eds, *Super/heroes: From Hercules to Superman* (Washington, DC: New Academia Publishing, 2007).
5. See C. J. Mackie, 'Men of darkness', in Haslem et al., *Super/heroes*, pp. 83–95, which attempts a transversal four-way reading between Achilles, Odysseus, Superman and Batman.
6. Michel Pastoureau, author of a series of fascinating books on the cultural histories and meanings of colour, explains how it is that green has been conventionally associated with good luck and with the goddess Fortuna, and is a 'symbol of life, luck and hope', but that at times it has been associated with danger, instability and therefore also bad luck (in Michel Pastoureau, *Green: The history of a color*, trans. Jody Gladding (Princeton, NJ: Princeton University Press, 2014), pp. 7, 84).
7. On Lady Luck, see the Wikipedia entry and its associated references: 'Lady Luck (comics)', at https://en.wikipedia.org/wiki/Lady_Luck_(comics).
8. The full title was *Stan Lee's Lucky Man* (Sky 1, seasons 1–3, 2016–18).
9. See for example 'Every time I go to a comic-book convention, at least one fan will ask me, "What is the greatest superpower of all?" I always say that luck is the greatest superpower, because if you have good luck then everything goes your way' (Stan Lee, quoted in Adam Tanswell, 'Meet Stan Lee, the amazing comic man', *Radio Times*, 22 January 2016, at https://www.radiotimes.com/tv/sci-fi/meet-stan-lee-the-amazing-comic-man/).
10. Cf. the discussion of *Intacto* and note 1 above on links to conspiracy and paranoid thinking.
11. Arthur Miller, 'Tragedy and the common man', *New York Times*, 27 February 1949.
12. Arthur Miller, *The Man Who Had All the Luck*, in *Plays* (London: Methuen, 1994), vol. 4, pp. 97–194.
13. This 'curse' looks forward to the discussion of 'survivor guilt' in Chapter 6.
14. See Miller, 'Introduction', in *Plays*, vol. 4, p. x.
15. Miller, 'Introduction', in *Plays* 4, p. ix. In the original version of the work, drafted as a novel, David and Amos were not brothers (see Christopher Bigsby, 'Afterword', in Miller, *Plays* 4, p. 263).
16. Miller, *The Man*, pp. 106–7.
17. Miller, *The Man*, p. 120.

18 Miller, *The Man*, pp. 109–10 (emphasis in original).
19 Miller, *The Man*, p. 157.
20 Miller, *The Man*, p. 167.
21 Miller, *The Man*, p. 103.
22 The association of luck with fertility is both ancient (the mystery of pregnancy and childbirth and the economic necessity of reproduction) and modern. See for example Philip K. Dick's science-fiction novel of 1963, *The Game-Players of Titan*, which we will touch on in Chapter 8, in which a post-apocalyptic scenario leads to fertility becoming a precious commodity (in this not unlike Margaret Atwood's *The Handmaid's Tale*, 1985). Cf. Giovanni da Col, 'Natural philosophies of fortune: Luck, vitality, and uncontrolled relatedness', in da Col and Humphrey (eds), *Cosmologies*, pp. 1–23 (pp. 1–2, 13).
23 Miller, *The Man*, p. 108.
24 Miller, *The Man*, p. 108.
25 Miller, *The Man*, p. 144.
26 Miller, *The Man*, p. 143.
27 Miller, *The Man*, p. 149.
28 Miller, *The Man*, pp. 165–6.
29 On 'moral luck', see Bernard Williams, *Moral Luck: Philosophical papers, 1973–1980* (Cambridge: Cambridge University Press, 1981) and further discussion in Chapter 6.
30 Miller, *The Man*, p. 154.
31 Miller, *The Man*, pp. 175, 176, 178.
32 Miller, *The Man*, p. 193.
33 See Lears, 'Gambling for grace' in *Something*, pp. 1–25, and *passim*.
34 Miller, *The Man*, pp. 177–8.
35 On Miller's larger themes of morality and the individual, see for example Stephen Barker's summary of his position: 'To be properly self-conscious is to come to understand the dialectic of choice, commitment, responsibility, conscience, morality, ethics, and, finally, tragic failure. Indeed, it is just these pulls and pushes of the critical enterprise that ostensibly make us successful (or unsuccessful) beings, and the appropriate subjects of serious drama' (Stephen Barker, 'Critic, criticism, critics', in Christopher Bigsby, ed., *The Cambridge Companion to Arthur Miller* (Cambridge: Cambridge University Press, 2011), pp. 259–72 (p. 265)).
36 Well before the 1990s, Hollywood genre films had regularly tapped into the spectrum of luck clichés as a device for drawing in audiences: an excellent example is the Doris Day and Phil Silvers vehicle, *Lucky Me* (dir. Jack Donohue, 1954). The trailer offers a colourful canvas of those clichés: see '*Lucky Me* (official trailer)', at https://www.youtube.com/watch?v=AQgRGpughz8.
37 See for example films ranging from *The Treasure of Sierra Madre* (dir. John Huston, 1948), which includes a lottery win alongside its central motif of greed in the California gold rush, to the discovery of a suitcase of money in *Shallow Grave* (dir. Danny Boyle, 1994), to the Italian comedy about failing to submit a winning lottery ticket, *Baciati dalla fortuna* (Kissed by luck) (dir. Paolo Costella, 2011). Freud himself developed an essentially Oedipal character-type out of related mechanisms, a type he called 'Those wrecked by success' (Sigmund Freud, 'Some character-types met with in psycho-analytic work' (1916), in *On the History of the Psycho-Analytic Movement, Papers on Metapsychology and Other Works*, trans. James Strachey, vol. 14 of *The Standard Edition of the Complete Psychological Works of Sigmund Freud* (London: Vintage, 2001), pp. 309–33). We will return to lotteries in Chapter 6.
38 Tom Gunning, 'The cinema of attractions: Early film, its spectator and the avant-garde', in Thomas Elsaesser, ed., *Early Cinema: Space, frame, narrative* (London: British Film Institute, 1990), pp. 56–63; and cf. on Gunning in relation to slapstick and gags Donald Crafton, 'Pie and chase: Gag, spectacle and narrative in slapstick comedy', in Wanda Strauven, ed., *The Cinema of Attractions Reloaded* (Amsterdam: Amsterdam University Press, 2006), pp. 355–64. (Strauven's volume also reproduces Gunning's article, pp. 381–8.)
39 The tradition of slapstick and farce has been revived with spectacular success in the twenty-first-century theatre by the *Goes Wrong* series and franchise, launched with *The Play That Goes Wrong* in London in 2012 by Mischief Theatre and subsequently performed worldwide, adapted into several alternative pieces (*Peter Pan Goes Wrong*, *Magic Goes Wrong*, etc.) and into a television series (*The Goes Wrong Show*).
40 Coincidentally, the very first film in which Stan and Ollie played together was entitled *The Lucky Dog* (dir. Jess Robbins, 1921).

41 See Wisse, *The Schlemiel*. On the evolution of this figure through to the 1990s American sitcom *Seinfeld* (1989–98), see Carla Johnson, 'The schlemiel and the schlimazl in *Seinfeld*', *Journal of Popular Film and Television*, 22.3 (1994): 116–24. Other contemporary figurations of the loser or fool, bound up with chance, operate in distinct cultural fields. Cf. for example two characteristically provincial English types of the mid- to late twentieth century: Kingsley Amis's Jim Dixon, weak and hapless protagonist of his 1954 novel *Lucky Jim* (the title comes from an old popular song whose opening is quoted in the epigraph, 'Oh, lucky Jim, / How I envy him. / Oh, lucky Jim, / How I envy him' (*Lucky Jim*, London: Penguin, 2000, p. 5), which wryly tells of two rivals in love, one lucky, one unlucky, until the former dies and the latter marries his widow, a sequence loosely echoed in the novel's plot), and the miserable, post-adolescent failure evoked in several songs by the Manchester band The Smiths in the 1980s (e.g. 'See, the luck I've had / Can make a good man turn bad', in 'Please, please, please, let me get what I want', 1984; thanks to Vittorio Montemaggi for the reference). We might recall also the more metaphysical, quasi-spiritual wisdom of the naive holy fool, hero of Jerzy Kosiński's *Being There* (1970; adapted for cinema in 1979, dir. Hal Ashby), named 'Chauncey Gardiner' or 'Chance, the gardener'. Chance was played in the film by Peter Sellers in his last role.

42 As an aside, it is worth noting an affinity between a certain kind of strung-out luck story as in *La Chèvre* and the genre of the picaresque, made explicit for instance in the title of William Thackeray's 1844 picaresque novel, *The Luck of Barry Lyndon* (adapted for cinema as *Barry Lyndon*, dir. Stanley Kubrick, 1975), where luck stands for all the incidents and accidents of the unreliable hero's tale.

43 David Denby, 'The luck of the French', *New York Magazine*, 12 August 1985, pp. 56–7.

44 On silent comedy and modernism, especially Chaplin, see David Trotter, *Cinema and Modernism* (Oxford: Blackwell Publishing, 2007). On Laurel and Hardy in *Waiting for Godot*, see Svetozar Poštic, 'Stan Laurel, Oliver Hardy and the concept of laughing through tears in Beckett's *Waiting for Godot*', in Biljana Čubrović, ed., *BELLS90 Proceedings*, vol. 2 (Belgrade: Faculty of Philology, University of Belgrade, 2020), pp. 51–65.

45 Imre Kertész, *Sorstalanság* (1975), in English as *Fateless*, trans. Tim Wilkinson (London: Harvill, 2005). The Hungarian term for 'luck', 'szerencse' is of Slavic origin and is another luck term that also connotes happiness (see Chapter 2).

46 On Job and his legacy in modern literature, see Leora Betnitzky and Ilana Pardes, eds, *The Book of Job: Aesthetics, ethics, hermeneutics* (Berlin: De Gruyter, 2015); Mark Larrimore, *The Book of Job: A biography* (Princeton, NJ: Princeton University Press, 2013).

47 Northrop Frye notably described the work of Kafka 'as a series of commentaries on the Book of Job' and terms *The Trial* 'a kind of Midrash' (Northrop Frye, *The Great Code: The Bible and literature* (London: Routledge & Kegan Paul, 1982), p. 195, quoted in Vivian Liska, 'Kafka's other Job', in Betnitzky and Pardes, *Book*, pp. 123–45 (p. 123)). Damon Runyon, a figure we will return to in Chapter 7, rewrote the Book of Job as a story of bad luck, using his inimitable style, in one of his last pieces, entitled 'Why me?': '"There is no one like Job," remarked the Lord to Satan. "He is a perfect and upright man. He fears God and eschews evil." "Well, why not?" said Satan. "You have fixed him up so he is sitting pretty in every way. But you just let a spell of bad luck hit him and see what happens. He will curse you to your face." "You think so?" said the Lord.' (Damon Runyon, 'Why me?', in *Written in Sickness* (1954), now collected in 'Runyon from First to Last', at https://gutenberg.net.au/ebooks18/1800711h.html).

6
Moral luck and the survivor

Luck stories are often comedies or fantasies, fables with happy endings, tales of troubles overcome. A Yiddish proverb, chosen by Primo Levi as the epigraph to his 1975 autobiography *The Periodic Table*, reads: '*Ibergekumene tsores iz gut tsu dertseyln*', 'Troubles overcome are good to tell'.[1] Literary historian Corrado Bologna has studied the ancient tradition of the nymph and its modern manifestation in the acrobat-clown, the *saltimbanque*, as a lesser-known figure for Fortuna, jumping, dancing, defying gravity, grabbing its chances and leaping free from danger and misfortune.[2] These are figures of luck as a force of light, in the dual sense of that word, of brightness or happiness, but also of what Italo Calvino called *leggerezza*, lightness, a quality of pleasurable weightlessness in event and language.[3] But there is an equally powerful, countervailing pattern in luck stories, one source of their compelling fascination, in an emphasis on heaviness, on the 'troubles' as much as on the 'overcoming', on 'slings and arrows' as much as on 'fortune', on the exciting if dangerous possibility of the acrobat's fall. To note this is in part simply a useful if banal corrective, a reminder that luck stories are *bad* luck stories just as often as *good* luck stories, and thus a reminder of an interesting conceptual and semantic bias, found in English and in numerous other languages, that means that 'luck' as a term on its own more naturally connotes good luck than bad. But above and beyond this binary and its biases, there is another aspect to this pattern to pay attention to here, one steeped in difficult questions of morality. What it suggests is that struggle and suffering are intimately bound up with, necessary partners of and preconditional to the upbeat side of the luck equation, and indeed that sometimes the struggle and the suffering are the very purpose and prime focus of the story. Luck stories, that is, are often – perhaps necessarily – mired in situations of danger and violence, in the everyday but stretching also to take in the awful extremes of war and death. Indeed, looking back over long traditions of imaginings of Fortuna, we find it is constantly reimagined and re-experienced through metaphors that reflect uncertain, fluid, dangerous, violent times: Boccaccio's *Decameron* repeatedly offers us, among its one hundred witty tales, instances of the vagaries of fortune, but the whole is framed by the terrible story of the Black Death of the 1340s as it devastated nearby Florence. Brutus in *Julius Caesar* declaims the metaphor of the 'tide' of fortune as he tries to persuade Cassius to seize the day against Octavius and Antony as Rome's civil war comes to a head. Hamlet's Elsinore is in a state of chaos in the aftermath of regicide, much as the chaos of Machiavelli's Italy in the early sixteenth century prompted his cynical reconceptualization of fortune and its dangers in *The Prince*. Plague, civil war, regicide, political chaos: Fortuna surges to the fore, is forcibly reprised and reimagined whenever extreme violence and disorder erupt into our world and threaten our very being and sense of value. Catastrophe breeds – among many other things – new thoughts, new stories, new obsessions about luck. And, given the nature of modern warfare and modern technology, and their related catastrophes over the course of the long twentieth century, it is perhaps unsurprising that modern luck stories have frequently evoked some of the darkest corners of modernity itself.[4] This chapter explores this looming constellation of luck and disaster through a singular and uncannily compelling figure in both modern narrative as a whole and modern luck stories more specifically, the figure of the survivor.

We have encountered generic modern situations of danger and figures of survival in previous chapters. We saw in Chapter 2 how the etymology and meaning of 'accident' intersect with the lexicon of luck, and in Chapter 5 how this quality of the 'accidental' was literalized in the figure of Max, the unlikely survivor of a plane crash in the film *Fearless*. The emblematic, shocking event of the crash – the car, train or plane crash – is linked to a specifically modern and newly dangerous form of the accident generated by modernity's mechanized technologies, and the crash survivor who tells its tale or lives its consequences thus becomes an emblem of both the improbable luck of the survivor and the modernity of the experience. A connection in literary history suggests itself here, since the same nexus between modern technology and danger generated a fascination with the crash in modernist and later experimental literature, linked to their ideological and at times erotic fascination with speed and mobility. A genealogy might trace this nexus back to one of the founding moments in European modernism, the first Futurist manifesto of 1909 by Filippo Tommaso Marinetti, which declares the palingenetic birth of the Futurist movement by telling the euphoric tale of Marinetti and his friends crashing their car into a roadside ditch, spinning and overturning and emerging energized into a new Futurist sensibility.[5] A morphed version of the same sensibility emerges in the erotics of speed, metal and the car crash in J. G. Ballard's *Crash* (1973) (and in cinema too, from the adaptation of Ballard's novel directed by David Cronenberg (*Crash*, 1996) to 2021's *Titane* (dir. Julia Ducournau)). Setting aside the specifically mechanical modernity of these crash narratives, there is a deeper analogy and genealogy, since these modern crash survivors are figural descendants of the ancient and early modern exemplars of Fortuna, of the storm and the shipwrecked sailor, the lucky survivor of an accident at sea, who is lucky but also cursed (much like certain configurations of the luckiest man). And furthermore, the shipwrecked sailor in the early modern imagination is one of the leading motifs of the broader modern category of the individual, who emerges in this period as a subject of power, colonization, trade and speculation, a self-sufficient creature who is nevertheless subject to the vagaries of circumstantial fortune, to literal and figural shipwreck and rescue, as emblematically embodied by Defoe's *Robinson Crusoe* (1719).[6]

All these survivors are subject to a deep, strange, at times magical fascination, as they are almost literally travellers returned from beyond the grave, ghosts, orphic figures who seem to have tricked death itself. (The famous scene of the knight playing chess with Death in Bergman's *The Seventh Seal* (1957), mentioned in Chapter 3, replays some of these tropes, the game suggesting the challenge is shaded by luck as well as fate.) But the most powerful modern narrative trope that binds luck to survival is to be found in individual life stories, rooted in historical forms of violence and assault on the person, lived out in the soul and on the body, often bound up with divisions of race and gender, assaults that once overcome take on essential, emblematic force.

Such is the case, for example, with the highly disturbing and ambivalent intersection of violence, survival and luck in Alice Sebold's 1999 memoir *Lucky*, which is an account of the author's rape and assault as a teenager, and its long-lasting traumatic legacies. The title word is threaded through Sebold's narrative, taking on a heavy weight of plural meanings both literal and relative, starting with the epigraph, even before the first chapter begins: 'In the tunnel where I was raped, [...] a girl had been murdered and dismembered. I was told this story by the police. In comparison, they said, I was lucky.'[7] Sebold accepts the label but also comes to understand that it relies on a terrible relativism – I was lucky compared to others who have suffered more – and moral irony, as she explained in a 2017 afterword: 'I chose the title *Lucky* both because I had indeed been truly lucky, but also because the ironies of how we define luck never seem to stop.'[8] And she acknowledges that this kind of luck can easily become bound up with the very essence of an identity, or sense of self, forged in disaster, accident, violence, misfortune:

> And then there was this: 'I'm glad it happened because I wouldn't be who I am now if it hadn't.' This last one is said by people who have survived war, cancer, been orphaned by natural disaster, become paralysed in a road accident. It was, for a very long time, said by me.'[9]

At the other end of the chronological spectrum we are working with here, we find a parallel conjunction of luck, trauma and unlikely survival, and storytelling, in Solomon Northup's remarkable 1853 autobiography, *Twelve Years a Slave* – in a sense, a variant on the picaresque narrative form – which opens with a deceptively generic nod to 'fortune':

> Having been born a freeman, and for more than thirty years enjoyed the blessings of liberty in a free State – and having at the end of that time been kidnapped and sold into Slavery, where I remained, until happily rescued in the month of January, 1853, after a bondage of twelve years – it has been suggested that an account of my life and fortunes would not be uninteresting to the public.[10]

The pattern recurs in other slave narratives, including Harriet Jacobs's *Incidents in the Life of a Slave Girl, written by herself* (1861), where the key term of the title, 'incidents', already flags up the serial 'adventure' shape of the narrative; several of the pivotal turns in the book are presented as turns of fortune, often paradoxically so in the face of danger and suffering, such as her description in the opening chapter of her childhood until the age of six, happily unaware that she was a slave ('Such were the unusually fortunate circumstances of my early childhood'), and that of her precarious hiding place after her escape, suffering from a grim snake or lizard bite ('I went to sleep that night with the feeling that I was for the present the most fortunate slave in town').[11]

There is a comparable figure from the mid-twentieth century, an iteration of the survivor topos, played out in both lived history and in narrative, that has seemed at times to stand as an essence of all the others and has thereby taken on near-talismanic cultural value for what we call modernity. This figure emerges as a consequence of the almost inconceivably improbable circumstances of their survival, from an 'accidental' encounter with what for many is the very darkest moment in modern history. The figure is that of the Holocaust survivor.[12]

The disturbing and difficult bond between luck and the Holocaust survivor has seeped across the field of modern narrative in varied fictional modes and genres, often as an incidental element of backstory as much as a central focus of interest, and this is in itself a sure signal of its familiarity and cultural purchase. Take as an example a typically sensitive and probing short story by Alice Munro, entitled 'Simon's luck', first published in 1978.[13] Actress Rose meets Simon at a party, where he saves her from an awkward situation. She ends up sleeping with him, falling for him, but then, losing faith in him, or rather in herself, she runs away, never to see him again. Later she learns he has died. Towards the middle of the story, in a manner that seems at once incidental but also touchingly entwined with turns in Rose's life, she learns Simon's backstory, his luck: he was once a Polish-Jewish child refugee in occupied France, escaping on a train towards Lyons. German guards search the train, but they somehow miss him, his sister and their friend:

> Simon said that when he realized they were safe he suddenly felt they would get through, that nothing could happen to them now, that they were particularly blessed and lucky. He took what happened as a lucky sign.[14]

In fact, a Holocaust survival story not dissimilar to Simon's – a story of survival through omission, through the unlikely luck of not being captured and taken to die – was already in place in another work we have encountered, the Spanish film *Intacto*. We saw in Chapter 5 how the plot of *Intacto* played games, literally, with a panoply of figures of luck, including plane crashes, car crashes and accidents of the most abstruse kind. And we saw how the fantastical sect it imagined was overseen by Max von Sydow's Sam (von Sydow was, of course, famous for playing the knight in *The Seventh Seal*). Crucially, Sam is Jewish – indeed, he is nicknamed '*el judío*', the Jew – and, what is more, we learn that he too was a child survivor of the Shoah. We see the number tattooed on Sam's arm early on in the film, a stock visual metonym for the genocide, and, perversely but not entirely implausibly, this is offered as a token of his good luck. Indeed, it is this that makes him 'the luckiest man in the world', or rather proves this to be the case. Holocaust survival, in other words, trumps any and every other imaginary, magical, innate instance of good luck that the film can stage. Sam is largely a silent character in the film, as befits his mysterious, all-powerful status. But in a climactic four-minute sequence staged outdoors with the young hero Tomás towards the end of the film, as he intuits and welcomes the fact that his last challenge is nearing, and the burden of always surviving, the curse of good luck, is about to be lifted, Sam speaks at length about the camps, about his parents, his sister, his companion and his guards, and about his survival by pure chance, as all those around him are taken out and murdered one by one, until he is left alone waiting for his turn as the last to die. Absurdly, inexplicably, causelessly, he explains, 'The next time the door opened, the uniforms had changed.'

Intacto searches out clichés, extreme incarnations of random, meaningless luck, to populate its fantasy world, and it is striking that it cannot imagine a higher instance of luck than the Holocaust survivor. This is the ultimate good luck. The film is of course no historically sensitive study in the history or meaning of the Shoah; indeed, its melodramatic tale could hardly be further from the horrific reality of deportation or survival. But its facile gathering of all the clichés is an indicator of something powerful precisely because it taps into the flow of vividly contemporary shared imaginaries.[15] It suggests how a historical reality and its legacy in popular culture can forge new constructs, which we then use to tell stories about and encapsulate something essential and generalizable about our selves. In the case of the Holocaust, any number of stock images and commonplaces have come down to us – the tattoos, the barbed wire, the very number 6 million, words such as 'Auschwitz' and indeed 'genocide' – and we might add to this list the voice of the single survivor, the witness that carries such remarkable force in our shared narrative consciousness and memory.[16]

Another disturbing work that taps into the emergence of the Holocaust as an obsessive, at times excessive, focus of cultural energy in the late twentieth and early twenty-first centuries, and also one that plays with tropes of luck, is Gil Hofman's 2007 film *The Memory Thief*. Hofman's film, set in contemporary California, follows its young, disaffected non-Jewish protagonist, Lukas, as he becomes more and more deeply obsessed with the Holocaust, and specifically with concentration camp survivors and their video testimonies. Lukas sinks into his obsession, staring at multiple television screens, imitating survivors in their gestures and accents, shaving his head and coming to believe he is himself the last of the survivors, berating strangers and telling them that they are lucky to be alive. A crucial turning point in his descent into psychosis and fantasy is marked when he begins to buy lottery tickets that match the numbers of the *Lager* tattoos of the victims he has seen on film, thus grotesquely crashing one key visual metonym and topos of the genocide against another longstanding topos of luck.

Any process of cultural evolution into cliché, however, has roots in historical reality. In the case of the Holocaust survivor and the association with luck, there is powerful evidence of its relevance in documented and first-hand stories of the genocide. Within the concentration camp universe, within a system of total violence such as Auschwitz (and indeed other genocides or other totalitarian systems), survival is indeed essentially possible by luck alone, by pure accident, rather than by way of any specific, predictable or controllable cause. Survival does not occur for any decipherable reason, at least not for those experiencing such persecution first-hand. To quote Primo Levi again, 'There is no why here' (*'Hier ist kein warum'*).[17] This is partly the result of the vast scale and the methods of murder – when millions are dying, any single survivor is an anomaly, a glitch in the system – and partly a result of the play of perspective and loss of agency; when you are reduced to abjection, on the bottom rung of a hideous hierarchy of persecution, how could you possibly grasp the higher 'causes' and 'rules' at play, however perverse, that might 'explain' your suffering? (Seen from the perspective of the perpetrators, of course, the Nazi project of involuntary euthanasia, ethnic cleansing and genocide, from the efficient planning and foresight of Aktion T4 or the Wannsee Conference and Eichmann's train timetables, the Shoah was one of the most planned, predicted and precisely 'caused', least 'accidental', of macro-historical events of modern history.)

This low-level, pervasive presence and perception of luck is borne out across the wide field of Holocaust testimony and Holocaust literature. Holocaust survivors repeatedly, anxiously put their survival down to luck. Almost every written or oral testimony repeats the awful pattern, taking trouble to explain how close to death the subject came and how often, how so many others around them died, how the most minimal, apparently inconsequential, often absurd shift in sequence or circumstance would have made their survival impossible. And many place luck itself as a term at the centre of their witnessing. We can illustrate the point through an array of 'ordinary' witness documents, with no pretension to writerly status nor to the self-conscious construction of figures and metaphors, as these set the tenor for a 'common sense' in the field, a shared vocabulary and frame of reference. And we see in them a broad tendency to tell survival tales that combine vivid luck storytelling, often drawn from worlds far away from the camps, with the experience of the horrors of the camps, how they got there and how they came out alive.

One magazine interviewee, Jack Polak, for example, speaking in New Jersey in 2008 at the age of 95, puts it lucidly and bluntly, using rough numbers to get his point across: '[it was] 97% luck and 3% willpower'.[18] A similar calculus is to be found in a self-help bestseller that somewhat crassly uses, among many other sources, stories of the Holocaust and Holocaust survival as part of its self-improvement programme: *The Survivors Club*, by Ben Sherwood (tagline: 'Discover how to become the kind of person who survives and thrives').[19] Sherwood uses the beguiling tools of (pseudo-)etymology to make his point:

> The Hebrew word for 'luck' – *mazal* – is an acronym composed of three different words. *Makom* means 'the place'; *zman* means 'the time'; and *la'asot* means 'the deed'. Combined, *mazal* consists of the right place, the right time, and the right action. [...] [W]hen you ask Holocaust survivors how they made it out alive, most answer that it was *mazal*, plain and simple. You can put forward all the theories in the world, but in the end, they were lucky. They were in the right place at the right time and they did the right things. Sure, some of them were able to go on because of personal qualities like tenacity and resolve. But given the magnitude of the murder and mayhem, most believe their survival was a matter of chance. In one survey, 74 percent of Holocaust survivors said luck was the main factor in staying alive.[20]

A similar point is made in a review essay by child survivor and psychoanalyst Sophia Richman, linked to a larger intuition about disaster and survival:

> Every survivor of a disaster, whether natural or man-made[,] feels lucky. Those of us who survived the Holocaust are only too aware that luck played a crucial role in our survival. It may have helped to be smart, resourceful, courageous and well connected, but more than any other factor, it is to luck that we owe our life.[21]

A cluster of published survivor memoirs underscores the point further, using luck in a variety of different storytelling registers and tropes. Michael Benanav tells the story of his grandparents, from Transnistria and Hungary, who lived through a series of devastating events and astonishing coincidences that brought them together and led them to the *Lager*, in his book *The Luck of the Jews: An incredible story of loss, love and survival in the Holocaust*.[22] The title alone plays many games with the tropes of luck, from the bold irony (including a nod to anti-Semitic tropes) of describing the Jews as lucky, in a Holocaust memoir of all places, to the mock-epic subtitle ('An incredible story ...'), to its play on stock romance and melodrama ('loss, love …'). Another survivor, Thomas Buergenthal, entitles his memoir *A Lucky Child: A memoir of surviving Auschwitz as a young boy*, and frames his survival narrative with a fairy-tale element. He recalls how a fortune-teller in Katowice in Poland told his mother that her child was '*ein Glückskind*', a lucky child, hence the book's title.[23] And most vividly of all, perhaps, French survivor Pierre Berg relates his deportation from Drancy, near Paris, to Auschwitz and Dora where he spent a total of 18 grim months, in his book *Scheisshaus* ['Shithouse'] *Luck: Surviving the unspeakable in Auschwitz and Dora*. Berg opens his book with a candid explanation of his title:

> If you're seeking a Holocaust survivor's memoir with a profound philosophical or poetic statement on the reasons six million Jews and many millions of other unlucky souls were slaughtered and why a person like myself survived the Nazi camps, you've opened the wrong book. I'd be lying if I said I knew the reason why or if I even believed there is a reason I'm still alive. As far as I'm concerned it was all shithouse luck, which is to say – inelegantly – that I kept landing on the right side of the randomness of life.[24]

Indeed, survivor's luck seems frequently to come accompanied with this baggage of irony or even comedy, at times acid and grotesque, at others melancholic and shadowed by loss, to signal that it is bound up with ambivalence.[25] The same frame, and the same ironic register or mix of registers, recur across the work of survivor-writers who sustain their reflections on the Holocaust over decades of writing, in testimony, essays and fiction, and have thereby become essential voices for the understanding and transmission of Holocaust memory. We can return here to two remarkable writers we have already encountered, Imre Kertesz and Primo Levi. We commented in Chapter 5 on one doomed character in Kertesz's autobiographical novel *Fateless*, the 'man with bad luck'. But the central character and the central concept of this work, declared in its title, 'fatelessness' (a literal translation of the original Hungarian title), address the very same conjunction of fate, luck and dark irony.

Fateless is narrated from the point of view, and in the quirky and perplexed voice, of its fourteen-year-old autobiographical protagonist, Gyuri, as he navigates the streets of Budapest, until first his father and then Gyuri himself are rounded up and deported. We follow Gyuri to Auschwitz, then to Buchenwald, and from there to a series of other, minor concentration and labour camps, before he is somehow able to make his way back to Budapest, a rare 'lucky' survivor. At the very end of the book, a disoriented Gyuri contemplates his survival and determines to struggle against the sense of randomness and chance, through a deliberately contorted sequence of thought as resistance against the void. Against the 'fateless' blind fortune and pure error that 'determined' both his deportation and his return, he paradoxically embraces his status as victim and survivor, *as if* he had been chosen, as if it were 'fate', and indeed his own fate,[26] and determines thereby to 'do something with it' and reclaim his singularity and his freedom:

> I now needed to start doing something with that fate, needed to connect it to somewhere or to something; after all, I could no longer be satisfied with the notion that it had all been a mistake, blind fortune, some kind of blunder. [... If] there is such a thing as freedom, then there is no fate; [...] that is to say, then we ourselves are fate.[27]

Gyuri and Kertesz are grappling here with the double bind of the lucky survivor, a bind that betokens itself a further, perhaps deeper form of irony: on the one hand, such luck is pointless, absurd, meaningless in the face of the scale and horror of death; on the other hand, if the luck is to be somehow reclaimed for meaning, then that meaning itself carries with it great dangers, as assigning any meaning to genocide is fraught with risk. Primo Levi, another great Holocaust survivor-writer, probed just such paradoxes and dangers of the nexus of luck and survival in equal, if not even greater, depth.

Levi was, among many other things, one of the great chroniclers of the oppressive binaries and zero-sum games, almost a forking-path algebra of suffering that he and his fellow victims were put through. Two poems help make the point. The first is the epigraph to his great work of testimony, *If This Is a Man* (1947), which lays out with stark clarity the boundary between the human and the non-human that the Nazi shoved him and his fellows across, as it does the archetypal binary enacted by the notorious 'selections' carried out periodically at Auschwitz, when a nod to the left or a nod to the right from a presiding officer of the SS (quite often the infamous Josef Mengele) would condemn prisoners to life or death:

> Consider if this is a man
>   Who works in the mud
>   Who does not know peace
>   Who fights for a scrap of bread
>   *Who dies because of a yes or a no*
> Consider if this is a woman [...] [28]

The second poem, from 1984, entitled precisely 'The survivor', as if to underline the archetypal force of the figure of the survivor, takes that binary of the yes and the no, of death and life, and projects onto it a terrible, self-harming, zero-sum calculus of shame, of survivor guilt. If I survived, its anxious thinking goes, if I was lucky, does that mean someone else died, someone else was unlucky in my place? (*Intacto*, again, plays this same game with its fantasy of 'winning' or 'stealing' other people's luck.)

> Stand back, leave me alone, submerged people,
> Go away. I haven't dispossessed anyone,
> Haven't usurped anyone's bread.
> No one died in my place. No one.
> Go back into your mist.
> It's not my fault [*colpa*] if I live and breathe,
> Eat, drink, sleep and put on clothes.[29]

The nightmarish anxiety of survivor guilt is shown here to be a sort of shadow- or counter-trope to that throwaway, 'shithouse', luck of survival by pure useless chance. If you did not survive for purely random reasons, through luck, if you survived for a reason, any reason, through any act of your own making, then you perhaps survived 'in someone's place', you are a usurper. The same anxiety, the same danger of meaning governs Levi's uncharacteristically furious response when a friend suggests his survival must have been providential, for a purpose, precisely in order that he might bear witness to the dead and to the crime that cause their death:

> After my return from imprisonment I was visited by a friend older than myself, mild and intransigent, the cultivator of a personal religion, which, however, always seemed to me severe and serious. He was glad to find me alive and basically unhurt, perhaps matured and fortified, certainly enriched. He told me that my having survived could not be the work of chance, of an accumulation of fortunate circumstances (as I did then and still do maintain) but rather of Providence. I bore the mark, I was an elect: I, the non-believer, and even less of a believer after the season of Auschwitz, was a person touched by Grace, a saved man. And why me? It is impossible to know, he answered. Perhaps because I had to write, and by writing bear witness. Wasn't I in fact then, in 1946, writing a book about my imprisonment?

Such an opinion seemed monstrous to me. It pained me as when one touches an exposed nerve, and kindled the doubt I spoke of before: I might be alive in the place of another, at the expense of another; I might have usurped, that is, in fact, killed. [...]

We survivors are not only an exiguous but also an anomalous minority: we are those who by their prevarications or abilities of good luck did not touch bottom. Those who did so, those who saw the Gorgon, have not returned to tell about it or have returned mute [...]. They are the rule, we are the exception.[30]

Levi's emphasis here on luck as a counter to Providence, to purpose and meaning, is no isolated moment. His wider oeuvre is shot through with reflections and narrative refractions of the problematics of luck for the Holocaust survivor.

The very first words of the preface of *If This Is a Man* strike a note of risky irony and insight by using the terminology of fortune: 'It was my good fortune to be deported to Auschwitz [...]'.[31] The continuation of the passage makes lucid sense of this apparently insouciant declaration, revealing it to be a typically sober act of historical precision and drawing of distinctions on Levi's part, showing how every individual's fate and circumstance was different, even among the indifferent system and the mass of millions caught up in the genocide: 'It was my good fortune to be deported to Auschwitz only in 1944, that is, after the German Government had decided, owing to the growing scarcity of labour, to lengthen the average lifespan of the prisoners destined for elimination; it conceded noticeable improvements in the camp routine and temporarily suspended killings at the whim of individuals.'[32]

Levi's survival itself, his work shows, was down to a series of contingencies, of circumstances that were in fact not purely down to empty, blind chance: for example, he worked the obscure rules of the camp system on occasion to find some extra food or a moment's shelter; he managed to parlay his education in chemistry to be assigned to an indoor, so-called 'laboratory', work detail, avoiding for a few weeks at least slave labour in the Polish winter and thus near-certain degradation and death. But the story of his very last days in Auschwitz, before his liberation by the Soviet Red Army in January 1945, is retold as an archetypal luck story, a story of forking paths (see Chapter 4), of exceptions to the norm, and of infinitesimally small causes of life-and-death effects. The story is vividly recounted, not in *If This is a Man*, but in a later essay-cum-short story entitled 'War pipette'.

'War pipette' tells the story of Levi's survival through a doubling, that is through his own story told in parallel with the story of the death of his closest friend in the *Lager* and his alter ego, fellow Italian prisoner Alberto. Alberto is so close to Primo in appearance and in origin, and they are so close in friendship, that they are treated like interchangeable twins by other prisoners. They therefore become dual variants in a controlled experiment on the workings of destiny and luck against the backdrop of the extreme reality of the camps:

> Alberto was my age, had the same build, temperament, and profession as I, and we slept in the same bunk. We even looked somewhat alike. [...] We were interchangeable, so to speak, and anyone would have predicted for us two the same fate: we would both go under or both survive.[33]

But a minimal, paradoxical and perverse irony of momentary small causes and chance hurtles them towards entirely opposite fates. In the early days of 1945, Primo and Alberto share half a bowl of contaminated soup, paid for with the stolen pipettes of the story's title. Levi falls seriously ill with scarlet fever, a death sentence at any other point in the history of Auschwitz. Unable to walk, he is left behind by the Nazis as they evacuate the Auschwitz concentration camp complex in the face of the rapidly advancing Soviet army, inexplicably neglecting to kill off him and others like him before they flee. Alberto in contrast is immune to scarlet fever because of a banal childhood bout of the illness, and so he is taken with thousands of other prisoners on the infamous Nazi 'death marches' towards Germany:

> But it was just at this point that the switch-pointer came into play, *the small cause with the determining effects*: Alberto had had scarlet fever as a child and was immune; I was not.[34]

No record of Alberto survives thereafter: he never returned. Earlier in the piece, Levi captures the awful, paradoxical complexity of this intervention of absurd luck by knowingly evoking older stories and older vocabularies of Fortune – Pascal's quip on love and Cleopatra's nose ('had it been shorter the whole aspect of the world would have been altered') and Providence – once again not because he believes in them, but because they evoke deeply resonant traditions of myth and storytelling to link to this affair of luck, the Holocaust and survival:

I was saved in the most *unpredictable* way by that business of the stolen pipettes, which gave me a *providential* sickness exactly at the moment when, paradoxically, not being able to walk was a godsend [*fortuna*].[35]

*

The line of connection from luck to the survivor is awkward, uncomfortable and deadly serious. It raises profound questions of a historical and political nature, about power, persecution and totalitarian violence, so that a system built on torture and systematic murder, degradation and death leaves room only for random glitches, momentary flaws, perverse combinations of chance as possible routes to resistance and survival, a bare minimum margin of uncertainty within a system of death. The system and the connection – as well as what the connection leaves unsaid – also assault the individual survivor at the level of psychology and subjectivity. The survivor is laden both with a miraculous aura and authority – so unlikely is their continuing presence – and with a strange sense of guilt that disturbs our deepest senses of action and agency, identity and morality.[36] Both Levi and Kertesz variously reflect on and struggle with this burden, searching for a new moral grounding that acknowledges their bond to their good luck, without using it to throw away any residual sense of morality and meaning, and responsibility to the unfortunate, to the dead. In their testimonies, their survivor stories, and by extension also their fiction, they struggle to accommodate morality to luck and vice versa, and in this they approach, if from an oblique angle, a series of highly delicate and important questions that are debated in contemporary philosophy under the heading of 'moral luck'.

The moral luck debate was born in an exchange in the late 1970s between Bernard Williams and Thomas Nagel, which posed the question of what remains of our sense of moral responsibility and agency, if and when we fully recognize the role of luck in determining our actions, our character and their consequences.[37] If, as we might intuitively assume, moral responsibility requires agency, control over our actions, and if it can be shown that some or all our actions are heavily determined by luck – whether that be a random turn of events, or something that goes all the way back to the 'luck' of being born with a certain character or disposition, or being caught up by chance in a specific historical moment or condition – then what forms of moral responsibility remain?[38]

The compelling relevance of the moral luck debate is well illustrated by a recent study of the question of meritocracy, that is, the idea or the ideal that it should be possible to strive and develop one's talents in a modern democracy, and thereby achieve success, through merit, not through privilege, wealth or any other instrument of structural inequality.[39] Michael Sandel's *The Tyranny of Merit* is an eloquent critique of meritocracy and of the notion that it is an ally of liberal ideals of equity and social justice. And at the core of Sandel's critique lies a 'moral luck' argument, a notion that the meritocratic ideal wilfully ignores the structural inequalities and straight prejudices inherent in any given society – and in particular for Sandel the society of modern America with its riven inequalities of wealth, gender and race – thereby blaming the already underprivileged for not 'striving' hard enough for a success that is in theory easily to hand. Sandel's is, in other words, a concerted critique of the mythology of the American dream that we encountered in Part I, which required not much more than an openness to luck and the immigrant's native wit and energy (as in *Hamilton*). Indeed, the terminology of luck – often couched in narrative tropes that we are familiar with, of games, winners and losers, lots, falls, accidents, and all the stories that go with them – is a powerful tool for Sandel to take down what he calls 'meritocratic hubris'.[40] Crucially, for Sandel, a heightened awareness of the moral and circumstantial force of luck is a conduit towards a kind of deeper communitarian sensibility, possibly even towards democracy itself, as the opposite of tyranny:

> Meritocratic hubris reflects the tendency of winners to inhale too deeply of their success, to *forget the luck and good fortune that helped them on their way*. It is the smug conviction of those who land on top that they deserve their fate, and that those on the bottom deserve theirs, too. This attitude is the moral companion of technocratic politics.
>
> A lively sense of the contingency of our lot conduces to a certain humility: 'There, *but for the grace of God, or the accident of fortune*, go I.' But a perfect meritocracy banishes all sense of gift or grace. It diminishes our capacity to see ourselves as sharing a common fate. It leaves little room for the solidarity that can arise when we reflect on the contingency of our talents and fortunes. This is what makes merit a kind of tyranny.[41]

Sandel, like Williams and Nagel, considers the luck of birth or its determinants, in terms of position, or indeed of innate talents that luckily coincide with what a given society at a given moment in its history prizes and rewards, as well as circumstances of poverty of money, education, culture and the like. In the exchange between Williams and Nagel, the latter had noted that if we follow the moral luck line of argument too rigidly to its logical endpoint, the potential for moral judgement disappears altogether into what he calls an 'extensionless point'.[42] But moral value cannot as a result be left as somehow 'immune' to luck, as Kant might have it, so that luck can be set to one side in reflections on morality: on the contrary, morality and ethics must take luck into account, even put luck at the centre, precisely because of its destabilizing effects. We need to retain an idea and a system of moral judgement and value, even or especially in a world that we do not control, in other words, in a luck-saturated world.

Crucially for our purposes – and as is typical of a certain kind of moral philosophy – Williams, Nagel and Sandel all have regular recourse to stories as moral thought experiments. And it is interesting to note that the best-known example in the field, posited by Williams in his original essay on the topic, takes us back to the scene of an accident, a crash. Williams invites us to consider the fictional case of a lorry driver who accidentally, 'through no fault of his, runs over a child'.[43] The driver bears no guilt or responsibility whatsoever, but nevertheless feels remorse. It is useless, even insane, Williams says, to point out to the driver that this feeling is irrational, to tell him he is not culpable, it was just bad luck, and leave it at that. Morality must take into account and allow for the driver's guilt – in the double sense of both affect and responsibility – as it must his inculpable lack of control and overarching bad luck. A further disturbing but illuminating gloss on Williams's story is offered by Derek Stanovsky, linking the case to Freud's reflections on 'ill-luck' in *Civilization and its Discontents* (1930) as always somehow an expression of a prior unspoken guilt, thus never allowing moral character to step aside from luck: 'Consider', Stanovsky suggests, 'what happens if we assume that the child killed in the accident was the truck driver's own.'[44] One ambiguity falls always instantly in this terrible circumstance: the driver's horrific sense of guilt and remorse becomes an inevitable consequence rather than a queried state. But the challenge to morality, and indeed the burden placed on luck and its meanings in this story, are if anything made heavier still.

The Holocaust survivor's guilt is radically different to the fictional case in Williams's story and variations on it, and yet it is of a comparable order – a feeling of guilt without fault – and it sets in analogous relation luck, responsibility and loss of control ('It's not my fault if I live and breathe / Eat, drink, sleep and put on clothes', as Levi's poem had it). Strangely, a certain conception of moral luck, one that acknowledges the profound ambiguity, and yet necessity, of making moral judgements in the face of chance, applies not only to the Holocaust victim and survivor, but also, with all due distinction, to the Holocaust perpetrator and collaborator. In reflecting on this odd fellowship also, Levi was once again extremely acute and careful in his thinking, on the one hand writing about the ambiguous 'grey zone' of complicity that all prisoners of the concentration camp universe were plunged into, and on the other hand acknowledging the overwhelmingly grave constraints that bound even the most venal and compromised of collaborators.[45] He was, for example, both horrified and fascinated by the case of Chaim Rumkowski, one of the leaders of the Jewish ghetto councils, the so-called *Judenräte*, in occupied Eastern Europe during the Nazi occupation, who accepted or were forced – were morally obliged? – to work with the Nazis and ultimately to manage the deportation of thousands of their fellow Jews to their deaths: 'The condition of the offended does not exclude culpability, which is often objectively serious, but I know of no human tribunal to which one could delegate the judgment.'[46]

Levi has no wish to abandon the categories of guilt and innocence altogether, but he pulls away from a justice system of courtrooms or tribunals that deal in such simple binaries. Moral luck, then, is bound up with the impossible complexities of the survivor figure, as it is with the collaborator, the perpetrator and the bystander. It challenges categories of agency across the board, indeed not only in matters of morality. Wider public spheres of justice, democracy, social equality and politics all feel the challenge posed by the ambiguities of moral luck, as Sandel powerfully argues, and once again it is in stories that these ambiguities and complexities, ironies and paradoxes are mostly vividly teased out. We can look, finally, at a handful of narratives in which one key topos in the luck tradition works as a formal device to stress-test these public or civic systems, in a dim echo of what was at work in the infernal systems of Nazi power. The figure in question is that of the lottery.

That the lottery was a key influence on the development of modern gambling, mathematics and thinking about probability, through sparkling figures such as Gerolamo Cardano or Giacomo Casanova, and also Pascal and Leibniz, is well documented,[47] and the same can be said of the parallel history of its uses in modern literature. In the twentieth century, the lottery motif frequently took an experimental and dark turn, deployed as a device for capturing the complexity and danger of modernity. Two of the most renowned short stories of the canon of twentieth-century literature are lottery stories in this vein: Jorge Luis Borges's 'The lottery in Babylon' (1941) and Shirley Jackson's 'The lottery' (1948). Borges's story recounts a mysterious history that saw the lottery, from rudimentary beginnings, expand to occupy every corner and phenomenon of life in Babylon, overseen by the ever more complex and arcane decisions of 'the Company', which eventually comes to exist as part totalitarian government, part secret sect and part divine entity.[48] Jackson's story exists in a very different world from Borges's Babylon, a small village of 300 inhabitants in rural America. But here too a strange, arcane lottery, one whose origins are lost in the mists of time, rules the civic life of the village. And in Jackson's story also, the lottery is steeped in ritual. But if Borges's story turns towards ever more arcane complexity and mystery, Jackson's takes a single, horrific turn towards civic violence, as it is revealed that the annual lottery and the civic governance of the village – and indeed of all surrounding villages – is centred on child sacrifice, stoning and scapegoating.

The lottery motif proves equally malleable and unpredictable in its capacity to tease out institutional and political questions in two lesser-known but fascinating post-war novels, one French and one American, both first published in 1954. Both in their different ways are works of genre science fiction[49] and both reimagine state institutions (respectively, of justice and government), precisely through a reinvention of ancient practices of the lottery or sortition: Jacques Charpentier's *Justice 65* and Philip K. Dick's *Solar Lottery*.[50]

Charpentier was French lawyer of high standing, a former anti-Nazi Resistance activist, and before that a leading legal functionary under the wartime Vichy regime.[51] In 1955, he made a rare, pointed foray into fiction with *Justice 65*, a satirical parable in the form of a near-future dystopian fantasy. In the book, his lawyer protagonist awakes in 1965, disoriented and confused, following a Rip Van Winkle-style 10-year sleep, only to find the places and practices of the august legal system of which he had been a native and citizen gone to ruin: the Law Faculty is abandoned and the 'Palais de Justice' is deserted and dusty, except for one hall that has been converted into a swimming pool. He happens upon a lecture on legal history that is intent on demonstrating the absurd inequities of the old and discredited legal system: its political and religious biases, its caprices and corruptions, its arbitrary dependence on individuals, whether judges or lawyers, on their talents, moods and inattentions, on their daily tribulations. A revolution has overthrown the old system while our narrator has been asleep and replaced it with a purely mechanical system of so-called 'justice machines', which churn out verdicts based entirely on chance (although not quite, as it turns out that the machines are programmed to produce a certain percentage of guilty and innocent verdicts overall, for the sake of keeping the peace and the illusion of arbitration). The human imperfections of man-made law are, in other words, replaced by the perfectly neutral workings of 'Alea, pure, impartial, absolute and for this reason fair'.[52] Luck is blind, just as Justice is, or should be, and thus one allies with and serves the other, and Charpentier's parable is therefore a rare instance of these two ancient forms of blindness converging into a single modern figural myth.[53]

Charpentier's substitution of due legal processes with luck is a hybrid, in part semi-serious, since it revives an ancient tradition of justice by sortition and alludes to longstanding debates in legal philosophy on so-called 'random justice',[54] and in part a mocking critique of the decay and venality of modern justice, its loss of balance and transparency and its standing as a metonymy for a general sense of modern power corrupted. In this sense it echoes from afar Kafka's legal parables and fictions, mentioned in Chapter 5. It is in this latter sense that luck could be said to stress-test the working of the law, pushing at its fragility through a fantastical *reductio ad absurdum*.

Dick's novel *Solar Lottery* plays parallel games with luck, in this case applying the paradoxes of randomness and the lottery principle not to jurisprudence but rather to state governance, totalitarian political power and the conflicting principles of freedom and control.[55] It is set in the year 2203, in a interplanetary state entity ruled over by an all-powerful 'Quizmaster' – games and governance literally merged into one – who is selected at random by a quantum-indeterminate machine known as 'the bottle', which turns or 'twitches' at unpredictable intervals of time. At each twitch of the bottle, a random citizen is selected to become the next Quizmaster. At the same time, however, another random lottery process selects another citizen as an assassin, whose sole duty and purpose is to penetrate the defences of the state's telepathic militia guard (the 'teeps') and kill the new Quizmaster. This elaborate dual, random sortition system is designed to create a temporary equilibrium between total power for the ruler on the one hand and the imminent danger of their overthrow on the other, which can last for days or for years, until eventually either an assassination or a new twitch triggers another crisis and transition of power.

Against this contorted backdrop, the plot of *Solar Lottery* weaves a noirish parable of deceit and betrayal. After an exceptionally long period of 10 years as Quizmaster, Reese Verrick – in equal parts brutally authoritarian and innately lucky ('Luck leaks out of his pores')[56] – is deposed by a twitch and replaced by a nobody called Cartwright.[57] Verrick, desperate to regain power, rigs the assassin lottery so that a remotely controlled android designed by his subordinates is selected.

Tricking the 'teeps' by bypassing their telepathy, Verrick's android goes after the unprotected, naive Cartwright, who seems doomed. But through a series of elaborate plot twists and turns of the lottery machinery, both Verrick and Cartwright are ousted, and our apparently unassuming narrator ends up as Quizmaster.

Solar Lottery creates a cosmos in which the fate and freedom of billions of citizens across the interplanetary society are determined by a strange play of lotteries and twitches. And so it is unsurprising that Dick imagines their world as luck-obsessed, peppering the novel with a bricolage of old junk motifs – more ancient–modern hybrids – such as fortune-tellers, lucky charms, quack theories, harbingers and eccentric astro-cosmologies, as citizens search for hidden clues, tricks, rituals and talismans to get lucky. At the same time, conversely, the society they live in is rigidly ordered, controlled by rituals of fealty and by strict hierarchies beneath the total but fragile power of the Quizmaster. Both Charpentier and Dick go round in circles in their futuristic imaginings to show how the purely mechanical or technological application of luck is most often a chimera, a game always open to being rigged and predetermined, or at the very least subject to its own flaws or glitches. As we saw also in Chapter 3, a structure or system of luck, randomness, chance, is in effect a contradiction in terms. Moral luck, legal luck, political luck: all the grave dimensions of luck and its stories that this chapter has explored suggest ways in which luck is an integral element of our collective systems, the opposite of empty, blind, 'dumb' in the sense of useless and meaningless ('mere' luck). But, they suggest, it circulates as an irritant, a space of exception, a residue, a stress-tester of systems rather than as a foundation of the system itself. To return to the figure with which we started this chapter, the survivor too, the lucky survivor – unsure of why they have survived and deeply unsure of their role in the world 'after' the disaster they have survived – is burdened with a similar kind of awkwardness and unease.

Notes

1   Primo Levi, *Il sistema periodico* (1975), in English as *The Periodic Table*, trans. Raymond Rosenthal (New York: Schocken, 1984), p. 2.
2   See Corrado Bologna, 'Immagini di fortuna, fortuna delle immagini', in Silvia Zoppi Garampi, ed., *Fortuna: Atti del quinto colloquio internazionale di letteratura italiana, Napoli 2–3 maggio 2013* (Rome: Salerno, 2016), pp. 13–36; and 'Picasso, Apollinaire e la Fortuna', in *I pensieri dell'istante: Scritti per Jacqueline Risset* (Rome: Riuniti, 2012), pp. 70–85, which examines in particular Picasso's *Saltimbanques* series (1904–5) and Apollinaire's 1909 poem 'Les Saltimbanques'.

3 Italo Calvino, 'Lightness', *Six Memos for the Next Millennium*, trans. Patrick Creagh (London: Penguin, 2002), pp. 3–30. This figure can be linked to another metaphorical field tied to bad and good luck: the stickiness and entanglement of the unlucky circumstance, as opposed to the slipperiness, the non-stick, 'Teflon' quality of the lucky person (the trademark term 'Teflon' was originally borrowed to describe the happy-go-lucky political persona of President Ronald Regan in 1980s America, who seemed to glide his way through all political storms). In contrast, however, as we saw in Chapter 2, 'jammy' in British English slang associates sticky sweetness with good luck.
4 This picture of modern warfare as having particular characteristics that tie it in new ways to luck and chance is borne out in many of the classic loci of modern war literature, for example in the chaotic, on-the-ground depictions of war in Stendhal and Tolstoy, and in the great nineteenth-century theorist of war von Clausewitz, who commented in *On War* (1832) on the 'trinity' of factors that determined the prosecution of modern warfare: violence, politics and chance; cf. Gallagher, *Telling*, pp. 39–47.
5 Filippo Tommaso Marinetti, 'The founding and manifesto of Futurism' (1909), at https://www.italianfuturism.org/manifestos/foundingmanifesto/. On the genealogy of the figure of the crash, see Jeffrey Schnapp, 'Crash (speed as engine of individuation)', *Modernism/Modernity*, 6.1 (1999): 1–49; Karen Beckman, *Crash: Cinema and the politics of speed and stasis* (Durham, NC: Duke University Press, 2010).
6 On the figure of Robinson Crusoe as an emblem of the modern 'bourgeois', capitalist and colonialist individual, shaped by forces of 'adventure', 'enterprise' and *'fortuna'*, see Franco Moretti, *The Bourgeois: Between history and literature* (London: Verso, 2013), pp. 25–9, 52; on Crusoe as a figure for 'improbability' in the context of the emergence of probability in early modern philosophy and literature see Rüdiger Campe, 'Defoe's *Robinson Crusoe*, or, The improbability of survival', in *The Game of Probability: Literature and calculation from Pascal to Kleist*, trans. Ellwood H. Wiggins, Jr (Stanford, CA: Stanford University Press, 2013), pp. 172–91.
7 Alice Sebold, *Lucky* (London: Picador, 2019), [p. xiii].
8 Sebold, *Lucky*, p. 255.
9 Sebold, *Lucky*, p. 257.
10 Solomon Northup, *Twelve Years a Slave* (Auburn, NY: Derby and Miller, 1853), p. 17; available at https://www.gutenberg.org/files/45631/45631-h/45631-h.htm.
11 Harriet Jacobs, *Incidents in the Life of a Slave Girl, Written by Herself* (Boston, MA: Published for the author, 1861), pp. 14, 154; available at https://www.gutenberg.org/files/11030/11030-h/11030-h.htm.
12 There is a vast field of scholarship on the aftermath of the Holocaust and on the role played by witnesses and survivors in the evolution of its memory. For a recent study of the specific figure of the survivor, see Arlene Stein, *Reluctant Witnesses: Survivors, their children, and the rise of Holocaust consciousness* (Oxford: Oxford University Press, 2014).
13 The story first appeared as 'Emily', and then as 'Simon's luck' in the collection *Who Do You Think You Are?* (1978), published outside Canada as *The Beggar Maid*.
14 Alice Munro, 'Simon's luck', in *The Beggar Maid* (London: Vintage, 2004), p. 164. Munro has also written stories centred on car and train accidents: one, titled 'Accident', pivots on the death of a child hit by a car as his father and the story's protagonist are having an illicit affair (in a typically subtle inversion by Munro, this 'clearly dividing moment' ends up cementing their love); another, 'Chance', turns not on an accidental death, but on a deliberate suicide on a train journey, which however accidentally intersects with and changes the life of the timid protagonist Juliet ('Accident' in Alice Munro, *The Moons of Jupiter* (London: Vintage, 2007), pp. 77–109 (p. 107); 'Chance', in Alice Munro, *Runaway* (London: Vintage, 2006), pp. 48–86).
15 The notion of a gathering or 'anthology' of the clichés as a mode of kitsch imperfection is advanced by Umberto Eco, in *'Casablanca*: Cult movies and intertextual collage', in *Travels in Hyperreality: Essays*, trans. William Weaver (New York: Harcourt Brace Jovanovich, 1986), pp. 197–211 (e.g. 'Two clichés make us laugh. A hundred clichés move us,' p. 209). On *Casablanca*, see Chapters 3 and 4.
16 On Holocaust clichés and mass culture, see Anne Rothe, *Popular Trauma Culture: Selling the pain of others in the mass media* (New Brunswick, NJ: Rutgers University Press, 2011), in particular pp. 9–21.
17 This was the brutal response given to Levi by a guard shortly after his arrival in Auschwitz in early 1944, after the guard had snatched away an icicle Levi was hoping to use to slake his desperate thirst. '"*Warum?*" I asked him in my poor German. "*Hier ist kein warum*"' (*If This Is a*

     Man; and The Truce, trans. Stuart Woolf (London: Abacus, 1987), p. 35, from Primo Levi, *Se questo è un uomo* (1947)).
18   Debra Rubin, 'Survivors share tale of love and luck', *New Jersey Jewish News*, 18 November 2008. The number game here picks up, consciously or otherwise, on the old cliché about genius, often attributed to Thomas Edison, being 'one per cent inspiration and ninety-nine per cent perspiration' (see Chapter 3).
19   Ben Sherwood, *The Survivors Club: The secrets and science that could save your life* (New York: Grand Central, 2009).
20   Sherwood, *Survivors Club*, p. 172. The etymology is surely false, but, as we saw in Chapter 2, none the less suggestive for that.
21   Sophia Richman, 'Lucky in misfortune: A review essay', *Division / Review*, 27.1 (2007): 40–3, at https://www.apadivisions.org/division-39/publications/reviews/eyes. See further Carolyn Ellis and Jerry Rawicki, 'More than mazel? Luck and agency in surviving the Holocaust', *Journal of Loss and Trauma*, 19.2 (2014): 99–120.
22   Michael Benanav, *The Luck of the Jews: An incredible story of loss, love and survival in the Holocaust* (2014), originally published as *Joshua & Isadora: A true tale of loss and love in the Holocaust* (Guilford, CT: Lyons Press, 2008).
23   Thomas Buergenthal, *A Lucky Child: A memoir of surviving Auschwitz as a young boy* (New York: Little, Brown, 2009).
24   Pierre Berg, *Scheisshaus Luck: Surviving the unspeakable in Auschwitz and Dora* (New York: AMACOM, 2008), p. xi.
25   By extension, the very act of juxtaposing luck with a Jewish life in the twentieth century has come to seem at times an instant marker of paradox, irony, or at least exception: see for instance the autobiography of Dan Vittorio Segre, *Memoirs of a Fortunate Jew: An Italian story* (London: Halban, 1987) which tells a story of anti-Semitic persecution in the 1930s, followed by exile to Israel, enrolment in the British army and a subsequent career in the Israeli diplomatic corps.
26   The 'as if' formulation recalls the conjunction between luck stories and counterfactuals flagged in Chapter 4.
27   Kertesz, *Fateless*, pp. 259, 260.
28   Levi, *If This Is a Man*, p. 12 (emphasis added).
29   Primo Levi, 'Il superstite' (1984), in English as 'The survivor', in *Collected Poems*, trans. Ruth Feldman and Brian Swan (London: Faber and Faber, 1988), p. 64.
30   Primo Levi, *I sommersi e i salvati* (1986), in English as *The Drowned and the Saved*, trans. Raymond Rosenthal (New York: Simon and Schuster, 1988), pp. 68, 70.
31   Levi, *If This Is a Man*, p. 3.
32   Levi, *If This Is a Man*, p. 3.
33   Primo Levi, *Moments of Reprieve*, trans. Ruth Feldman (New York: Simon and Schuster, 1986), p. 89.
34   Levi, *Moments*, p. 89 (emphasis added).
35   Levi, *Moments*, p. 91 (emphasis added).
36   On survivor guilt, see among many others Ruth Leys, *From Guilt to Shame: Auschwitz and after* (Princeton, NJ: Princeton University Press, 2007), esp. pp. 17–90.
37   See Williams, *Moral Luck*; Thomas Nagel, 'Moral luck' in *Mortal Questions* (Cambridge: Cambridge University Press, 1979), pp. 24–38. On the general problem of luck in philosophy, and moral luck in particular, see: Fernando Broncano-Berrocal, 'Luck', in *Internet Encyclopedia of Philosophy*, at https://iep.utm.edu/luck/; Dana K. Nelkin, 'Moral luck' (2013), in Edward N. Zalta, ed., *The Stanford Encyclopedia of Philosophy*, at https://plato.stanford.edu/archives/win2013/entries/moral-luck/.
38   Samuel Butler, in his satirical utopian novel *Erewhon* (1872), plays with this notion of luck and responsibility by imagining Erewhon as a place where the unlucky are blamed and even punished for their misfortune ('Ill luck of any kind, or even ill treatment at the hands of others, is considered an offence against society, inasmuch as it makes people uncomfortable to hear of it. Loss of fortune, therefore, or loss of some dear friend on whom another was much dependent, is punished hardly less severely than physical delinquency', *Erewhon*, chapter X, at https://www.gutenberg.org/files/1906/1906-h/1906-h.htm (accessed 20 September 2022)). I'm grateful to Simone Ghelli for the reference.
39   Michael Sandel, *The Tyranny of Merit: What became of the common good?* (London: Penguin, 2020). Cf. an interesting discussion of luck, law and redress in Richard A. Epstein, 'Luck', *Social Philosophy and Policy* 6.1 (1988): 17–38.

40   Sandel, *Tyranny*, p. 14.
41   Sandel, *Tyranny*, p. 25 (emphasis added).
42   Nagel, 'Moral luck', p. 35.
43   Williams, *Moral Luck*, p. 28. He also uses art and literature extensively to elaborate on his discussion, referring to Paul Gauguin and Tolstoy's *Anna Karenina* among others. In this vein it is worth noting both Martha Nussbaum's dialogue with Williams and the wider debate on moral luck, and the prominent role played by literature, in the major study by Nussbaum, *The Fragility of Goodness: Luck and ethics in Greek tragedy and philosophy* (Cambridge: Cambridge University Press, 1986), which has been profoundly influential well beyond its specialist field.
44   Derek Stanovsky, 'Stealing guilt: Freud, Twain, Augustine and the question of moral luck', *American Imago*, 63.4 (2006): 445–61 (p. 451). Cf. the 2016 film *Manchester by the Sea* (dir. Kenneth Lonergan), whose plot turns out to centre on the secret of the accidental killing in a house fire by a father of his children. The film and several comparable real-life situations are explored in Alice Gregory, 'The sorrow and the shame of the accidental killer', *The New Yorker*, 18 September 2017.
45   See the essay 'The gray zone', in Levi, *Drowned*, pp. 31–71.
46   Levi, *Drowned*, p. 33.
47   See for example Leonard Mlodinow, *The Drunkard's Walk: How randomness rules our lives* (New York: Pantheon Books, 2008); Rescher, *Luck*, p. 116.
48   Jorge Luis Borges, 'La lotería en Babilonia' (1941), in English as 'The lottery in Babylon', in Borges, *Collected Fictions*, pp. 101–6; Shirley Jackson, 'The lottery', *The New Yorker*, 26 June 1948. Another Argentinian writer published a key example of modern lottery literature a number of years later: Julio Cortázar, *Los premios* (1960), in English as *The Winners*, trans. Elaine Kerrigan (London: Souvenir Press, 1965).
49   On science fiction and luck, see Boris Eizykman, 'Chance and science fiction: SF as stochastic fiction', trans. Will Straw, *Science Fiction Studies*, 10.1 (1983): 24–34. Another major figure in science fiction, Stanislaw Lem, was obsessed with the role of chance as a principle in his own life and in his philosophy of science and literature: see for example Stanislaw Lem, 'Chance and order', *The New Yorker*, 30 January 1984.
50   Jacques Charpentier, *Justice 65* (Paris: Hautes Chaumes, 1954); Philip K. Dick, *Solar Lottery* (London: Gollancz, 2003). (I am grateful to Guido Vitiello, editor and translator of the Italian edition of Charpentier's work – *Justice Machines* (Macerata: Liberilibri, 2015) – for alerting me to it.)
51   On Charpentier, see Yves Ozanam, 'De Vichy à la Résistance: Le bâtonnier Jacques Charpentier', *Histoire de la Justice*, 18.1 (2008): 153–69. He was also the author of a study of the role of chance in history, like Levi departing from the myth of Cleopatra's nose: Jacques Charpentier, *Le Nez de Cléopâtre ou Le sens de l'histoire* (Paris: Berger-Levrault, 1967).
52   Charpentier, *Justice*, p. 27 (my translation from the Italian edition).
53   On the mythical motif of blindness that is shared by justice, fortune and love, see Raymond B. Waddington, 'Blind gods: Fortune, Justice, and Cupid in the *Merchant of Venice*', *ELH*, 44.3 (Autumn 1977): 458–77.
54   See Neil Duxbury, *Random Justice: On lotteries and legal decision-making* (Oxford: Oxford University Press, 1999).
55   There is a clear affinity with Borges's 'Lottery in Babylon' in aspects of Dick's lottery, and with Orwell's *1984*, originally published between the two in 1948, amid urgent debates on totalitarianism, linked also to early responses to the Holocaust and genocide.
56   Dick, *Solar*, p. 9.
57   As this summary suggests, Verrick and Cartwright (or indeed the narrator) could be read as further examples of the figures of 'the luckiest man' and 'the loser' explored in Chapter 5.

7
Luck and the low life

In 2011/12, HBO premiered a gold-plated, high-prestige drama series, called simply *Luck*. It starred Dustin Hoffman, appearing in his first major television role in his mid-70s, was directed for its pilot episode by leading neo-noir director Michael Mann, and was produced and created by renowned TV writer David Milch. *Luck* was a complicated, layered story of power and revenge, of plays, deceptions and betrayals, with all the sophistication in plot and production values characteristic of early twenty-first-century American television drama.[1] But what gave the series its distinctive resonance and energy – and made immediate sense of its title – was its setting in and around the Santa Anita Park racetrack in California, peopled with all its hangers-on, from Hoffman's 'Ace' Bernstein, recently released from prison and looking for payback, to mafia criminals, casino investors and poker players, two-bit hustlers, horse trainers and owners, jockeys and agents, dopers and bookies. This vivid world of the racetrack is opaque, dangerous and immediately recognizable as a site of danger, of risk, of high stakes and low crime, and because of all this as a neat microcosm of modern society. We have already visited a racetrack in Chapter 3, where it was the stage for Derren Brown's experiment in luck numerology. The world of HBO's *Luck* reminds us that there is also a very particular sociology to modern luck stories and that it is one that tends to pull us down low.

Luck stories tend by their very nature to be both 'on edge' and 'on the edge': on edge, because they are often anxious, steeped in risk, driven by all-or-nothing gambles, on the brink of catastrophe, and 'on the edge', because they tend to be staged at the margins and in the shadows, below or beside (or hidden within) the respectable, rational, controlled institutions and arenas of states, institutions and modern society. So although luck may be a 'human universal', as we noted in Chapter 1, at stake in the lives of everyone from emperors to paupers and slaves, in our imagination it seems to get dragged down low by some inherent force of gravity. We might say that luck stories are 'demotic', in both place and register, inhabiting those low-life settings and rundown, shady corners, from the racetrack to the gambling den, from underworlds to peripheries. This also means they open up spaces for stories of race, of the subaltern and the excluded trying to catch a break, as in a vein of African-American literature centred on 'numbers' rackets and other gambles.[2] These are messy, dirty tales, sharing something of the quality of dirt, impurity, as, in Mary Douglas's influential formulation, 'matter out of place'.[3] This chapter explores the strange affinity between luck and the low life, and the forms that demotic places and their voices take in modern luck stories.

A good place to start looking for combined stories of the low life and of modernity is the New York that was evoked in Chapter 1, specifically Manhattan and even more narrowly a few streets and bars in and around Broadway in the early twentieth century. Damon Runyon made his name as a writer by building a vivid storyworld and a vernacular language around these louche streets, in dozens of short stories set in 1920s–1940s New York, during Prohibition and after.[4] Runyon's is a world of hustlers and hoods, of chancers and their 'dolls' or 'dames', street characters who turn up across many different stories, living on the edge, often through long nights of drinking and gambling, betting on crapshoots, pool tables or horses. It is a world stuck in a few streets off Broadway, often starting in or recounted from hangouts like Mindy's restaurant, opening out onto a canvas of tales from a wider American landscape as characters swap their stories about forays to Miami or California, Boston or Texas.[5] It is inherently a world of luck and chancing (very much the gerund, not the abstract noun 'chance'), one in which luck is spun and strung out as a vital (life and narrative) force, a code for much that is venal, violent, empty but somehow also propulsively energetic, so that it spills over from its material presences in the stories, in the form of dice or wagers or markers of debt, into a governing (a)moral principle with its own anthropological rules and habits.

One story of many we might choose to pick out is an early piece called 'Lillian' (1931; DRO), named after a black cat who is in turn named after an actress called Lillian Withington, who has brutally ditched the story's drunken hero, singer Wilbur Willard. The story plays around with relish with 'cats', black cats, leopards, 'dames' and the two Lillians; and it opens with a riff on luck:

> What I always say is that Wilbur Willard is nothing but a very lucky guy, because what is it but luck that has been teetering along

Forty-ninth Street one cold snowy morning when Lillian is merowing [*sic*] around the sidewalk looking for her mamma?

And what is it but luck that has Wilbur Willard all mulled up to a million, what with him having been sitting out a few seidels of Scotch with a friend by the name of Haggerty in an apartment over in Fifty-ninth Street? Because if Wilbur Willard is not mulled up he will see Lillian as nothing but a little black cat, and give her plenty of room, for everybody knows that black cats are terribly bad luck, even when they are only kittens.

Wilbur befriends a stray cat, names her Lillian, and becomes strangely attached to her, even when 'she' turns out to be a 'he'. The cat, like the lady, turns out to be fickle, prone to scavenging and betrayal, altogether 'bad luck' for Wilbur, until, that is, in a typically unlikely Runyonesque twist, a drunken Wilbur's luck turns. He blunders into a burning building and saves both the cat and a small child who has been kidnapped by his father, and becomes a hero. Runyon's mock happy ending ties up the threads:

> About a year later it comes out that he marries his old doll, Lillian Withington-Harmon, and falls into a lot of dough, and what is more he cuts out the liquor and becomes quite a useful citizen one way and another. So everybody has to admit that black cats are not always bad luck, although I say Wilbur's case is a little exceptional because he does not start out knowing Lillian is a black cat, but thinking she is a leopard.[6]

The moral of the tale twists one last time when Wilbur reveals that the cat had in fact been looking for the Scotch in his milk, not for the kid, when it ran into the burning building.

'Lillian' is useful as a story because it offers a baroque transposition or translation of the old superstition about black cats and bad luck, projecting it in a play of unlikely twists onto the giddy, dirty-modern world of Runyon's Broadway, as seen through the narrator's arch detachment and Wilbur's drunken haze (he literally sees Lillian as a leopard when he's drunk, just as he walks nonchalantly into burning buildings). The story self-consciously points to the old superstition, riffing on it so that it takes on the language and association of the guys' patter:

> 'Cats are like women, and women are like cats. They are both very ungrateful.'

> 'They are both generally bad luck,' Big N*,⁷ the crap shooter, says. 'Especially cats, and most especially black cats.'
>
> Many other guys tell Wilbur about black cats being bad luck, and advise him to slip Lillian into the North River some night with a sinker on her, but Wilbur claims he already has all the bad luck in the world when he loses Lillian Withington, and that Lillian, the cat, cannot make it any worse.

'Lillian' was first published in book-form in a 1931 collection, Runyon's first, called *Guys and Dolls*.⁸ The same title was, famously, borrowed for the great post-war stage musical, first performed on Broadway in 1950, with music by Frank Loesser, and adapted for the cinema in 1955, directed by Joseph Mankiewicz and starring Frank Sinatra, Marlon Brando and Jean Simmons. *Guys and Dolls* the musical was based largely on a 1933 story, 'The idyll of Miss Sarah Brown' (DRFL), with elements drawn from a handful of others, including 'Blood pressure' (DRO), about a terrifying night spent with a thug called Rusty Charley and a problem with high blood pressure, and 'Pick the winner' (DRO), about a crystal ball, a small-time hustle on a racetrack in Miami and a Princeton professor.

'The idyll of Miss Sarah Brown' tells the story of Obadiah 'The Sky' Masterson, a street-smart inveterate cardplayer who travels from Colorado to Cincinnati to St Louis, New Orleans, Chicago and LA – 'and wherever else there is any action in the way of card-playing, or crap-shooting, or horse-racing, or betting on the baseball games' – before ending up in New York. Sky will bet on anything, from throwing a peanut to catching a rat (literally), and when he falls for the mission worker Sarah Brown, he starts laying bets at Nathan Detroit's craps game on the soul of unlucky Brandy Bottle Bates, in order to drum up business for Miss Brown's struggling mission:

> 'Well, Brandy,' The Sky says, 'I will make you a proposition. I will lay you a G note Big N* does not get his six. I will lay you a G note against nothing but your soul,' he says. 'I mean if Big N* does not get his six, you are to turn square and join Miss Sarah Brown's mission for six months.'

It doesn't go so well for The Sky, however, as Brandy just keeps on winning, until Miss Brown herself turns up:

> 'Good evening,' The Sky says. 'It is a nice evening,' he says. 'I am trying to win a few souls for you around here, but,' he says, 'I seem to be about half out of luck.'

'Well,' Miss Sarah Brown says, looking at The Sky most severely out of her hundred-per-cent eyes, 'you are taking too much upon yourself. I can win any souls I need myself. You better be thinking of your own soul. By the way,' she says, 'are you risking your own soul, or just your money?'

Sarah bets herself and so wins The Sky's soul, who declares his love and joins the mission: Miss Brown become 'Mrs Sky'. But the story ends with a kick: the dice she threw were Brandy Bottle's loaded dice, the miracle or the lucky run just a dirty trick and an illusion, just like the whole high-stakes microcosm of Nathan's crapshoot.

Transposed into the musical, The Sky becomes Sky, the twists are somewhat smoothed out and lightened, and Nathan Detroit's story, along with that of his long-suffering fiancée Adelaide, is fleshed out from other Runyon stories (their endlessly postponed marriage is an element borrowed from 'Pick the winner', for example), in order to balance out Sky's and Miss Brown's. But the heady mix of luck and salvation, of love, the street and the crapshoot, is preserved, and the play in Frank Loesser's song lyrics does some of the work of capturing and translating Runyon's strange, vibrant demotic. Thus, the show-stopping number towards the end of the play, 'Sit down, you're rockin' the boat', led by the character Nicely-Nicely Johnson with a chorus of gambler-sinners, is a phantasmagorical nightmare of death and salvation, the sinners heading for hell or paradise on a boat of souls, pleading with Nicely to give up his bottle, his sharp suit and his dice before he takes them all down to damnation.

Most telling of all, for its imitation and extension of Runyon's universe of luck stories, is Sky's signature number, sung as he lays his crazy bet to recruit the crapshooters for Sarah's mission, 'Luck be a lady'.[9] Loesser's song is a remarkable conflation of ancient and 'hip' language, of high and low, of love, eros, money and a certain desperation, even violence (all of a piece with the luck tradition). Indeed, 'Lady Luck' is a tradition and a stock phrase that comes down to us directly from the ancient myth of the goddess Fortuna, always gendered and always caught between absolute dominion over us and the possibility of control of her through our force (Machiavelli's topos of submission of Fortune through violence), our subjection, and also our love. The OED gives us instances in Middle French (*Dame Fortune*) and Golden Age Spanish (*señora Fortuna*), and an instance from the sixteenth century, but suggests that the alliterative English formula 'Lady Luck' is 'rare before 20th century'. Indeed, the first modern instance quoted in the OED, from 1919, is already down with the dice, and strikingly close in register and location to the Runyonesque vernacular: '1919. H. Wiley in F. van Wyck Mason *Fighting American* (1943) 707. "Gimme dem dice!... Lady Luck, I aims to run yo' ragged!"'[10]

'Luck be a lady' takes that new low (or lower) collocation and plays around with it with all the verve of the American musical songbook. In the lyrics, Luck is Sky's lady, his date for the evening, his lover, mistress, whore, even a she-devil; Sky needs her but she might give him 'the brush' at any time. The song is built on an elaborate mock contrast in class, between on the one hand the lady's good manners and decency that he came in with (his good luck), who will stay faithful and true to him, who will be 'polite', have 'manners', a heart and a soul, and on the other the risk she might turn out fickle, turn on him to favour others ('flirt with strangers'), not be a lady at all ('if you've ever been a lady to begin with'). The song is simply constructed on this and similar binaries that are worked and reworked, but the high–low binaries are blurred by the comic paradox of who's singing and where, of Sky Masterson giving lessons in sexual and social etiquette, at Nathan Detroit's dank craps game. But this is all part of the thrust of low-life luck stories. There is meaning, even salvation, to be found, even here. In fact, there is a quiet residue of *Fortuna*'s god-like status, as Sky sings that all he can do is 'pray' that Luck stays a lady, but this is as much as anything a reminder of Miss Sarah Brown, the mission and the salvation that awaits them all, mock or otherwise. Indeed, there is a careful parallel set up between Sky's Lady Luck and Sarah herself, whom Sky has indeed taken on a date, to Havana of all places, in Act I, and Sarah is indeed Sky's 'luck', since she promises him love and happiness. There is also a quiet, but still quite scandalous erotic side to Lady Luck in the song, which evokes everything that Sarah is not ('A lady doesn't wander all over the room, and blow on some other guy's dice,' giving us luck magic and sex rolled into one.) Sky, then, is grappling with two spinning models of luck and his future, as he plays around and sings around the highs and lows of a game of craps, just like the gambling addict he is, and hopes the dice fall his way. He knows very well there is more at stake here, though, as he sings, 'I've got my life on this roll'.

The existential resonance of the roll of the dice, if anything enhanced by the disreputable setting of the gamblers' den, is a nexus that was by no means invented in *Guys and Dolls,* nor by Runyon. In fact, it has its roots in one of the key threads for the whole aspect of modern luck we are exploring in this chapter, the literature of the modern casino, the roulette table as a site of moral fall, of loss of self and world. To trace the conjunction of modern gambling to the crisis of the modern self and morality, we have to travel back a few decades into the nineteenth century to a fictional spa town called Roulettenberg and to the casino at its heart, the setting of Fyodor Dostoevsky's 1866 novella *The Gambler*.[11]

Dostoevsky's Roulettenberg is a long way from Runyon's Broadway and is apparently the very opposite of the latter's low-life world of petty crime and street violence: it is populated by the cream of Europe's aristocracy and their retinues, from Russia, England, France and Germany. But this apparent haughty bearing – literally a 'ladylike' world – is 'low' in another sense, since Dostoevsky relentlessly probes its turbid, hypocritical and corrupt moral depths, tying money to sex, greed and envy, and gambling to prostitution, from the literal kind to the veiled kind tied to alliances and marriages. Even 'lower' still, the novel probes the sickness of addiction to gambling, establishing an affinity between the euphoria of giving oneself over to luck, again and again, losing (almost) every time, and a loss of self and of health that this and many other modernist works of literature were drawn to, for some as a kind of catastrophe, for others as a kind of redemption.[12]

The hero of the novel, Alexei Ivanovich, is torn between his obsessive love for Polina and his addictive love for the roulette table. Both Alexei and Polina, like the swirl of other characters around them, are further torn between the winnings and losings at the table, and the play of possible inheritances and marriage contracts, all flowing seemingly from the much-awaited death of the elderly matriarch, the Grandmother, a mysterious, ghostly figure until she suddenly turns up alive and well and herself plunges into roulette, winning and losing vast sums before just as suddenly leaving again. The game of luck for the gambler is both a chance to leap free from the tyranny of all this money and privilege (Roulettenberg is a microcosm of all the workings of capital and power, of the trade of *homo economicus*, as the novel itself hints more than once), and a prison-house where luck is everywhere and inescapable, a poison to all higher thought and emotion. In one of the key scenes of the novel, Alexei declares that his love for Polina is so great that he will willingly hurl himself off a nearby peak if she only gives the word, in a high romantic gesture that also evokes the figure of chance as a fall, a 'throw' of the dice. But, instead, Polina mockingly demands of Alexei a form of social fall or humiliation (she dares him to insult some acquaintances at the spa), something much closer to the emptiness and venality of the casino.

Just as in 'Luck be a lady', luck is gendered and sexualized for both Alexei and Polina. Alexei's moments of winning at the roulette table are, as one critic describes them, 'intoxicated, orgiastic'.[13] He rushes to show his gold to Polina, dizzy and as if reborn:

I felt only some sort of dreadful enjoyment of success, victory, power […] but I already scarcely remember what she has said to me a little while before and why I had gone, and all those sensations that there had recently been only an hour and a half before already seemed to me now something long past, revised, obsolete – about which we would no longer remember, because now everything would begin anew.[14]

But again, the combination of the erotics of winning and his desire for Polina will prove incompatible and Alexei, the empty modern anti-hero, will disastrously choose the former, or rather the delusion of the former.

Almost 50 years after *The Gambler,* Luigi Pirandello set a key early sequence of his 1904 novel *The Late Mattia Pascal* at the casino in Monte Carlo, another apparently luxury setting for a scene of low human venality and loss of self.[15] As the eponymous Mattia returns home from Monte Carlo by train, he will read a notice of his own suicide in a newspaper, thus transforming his life and propelling the bulk of the rest of the novel along its paradoxical, modernist path. Mattia will attempt – and fail – to reinvent his entire self and existence from scratch, freed by his own 'death'. The two sites of epiphany – at Monte Carlo and on the train – are profoundly linked by Pirandello, twin instances of transformation and of danger, both governed by luck and both, in a sense, out-of-body experiences.

At Monte Carlo, Mattia enters a microcosmic world of risk and luck at the casino. His absurd, hopelessly dysfunctional private life has impelled him to flee and he ends up at the tawdry, faux-glamorous roulette table, where he is witness to all the same euphoria and degradation that Dostoevsky had portrayed in *The Gambler.*

Monte Carlo occupies the entirety of chapter 6 of the novel, entitled 'Click, click, click' for the sound of the roulette ball jumping on the wheel.[16] It opens with dozens of players hanging on the spinning, tapping, ivory ball, praying to it as to the goddess of fortune or lady luck. Mattia looks on, for now ironically detached, a product of chance: 'I happened there, at Monte Carlo, by chance.'[17] Tellingly, he happens there as an alternative to a failed project to embark on the great modern adventure of emigration. His first fantasy had been to escape to Marseille and from there to America. But, feeling too weary for such a risky venture, he chances upon a shop-front display about roulette that tempts him instead to the casino. There, he finds a community of obsessives devoted to elaborating personal theorems on money, numbers and the spinning of the wheel, desperate to tame chance and wrench back control over their own destinies. Thus, one player is in love with 'his' number, others work on their formulae and systems to break the bank, as Mattia looks wryly on (or remembers doing so as narrator):

> Usually, those sofas [at the casino] are occupied by poor wretches whose passion for gambling has affected their brains in a singular way: they sit there studying the so-called balance of probability, and they seriously ponder the coups they are going to try, a whole architecture of gambling, based on the various ups and downs of the numbers. They want, in short, to extract a logic from chance, which is like saying, blood from stones; and they are convinced they'll succeed, today or at the latest, tomorrow.[18]

Initially cynical and immune to the allure of risk, like Alexei, Mattia's sudden and quite random success at the tables leads him to return for 12 days in a row, astonishing his fellows by winning for nine, before his luck turns bad. He acquires as a result an aura of tawdry charisma: other players start to cling to his magical, materialized luck (they touch him, chase him, ply him with offers of deals). The deluded air of excitement is shattered only by the corpse of a suicide, whose bloody, shattered face witnessed outside the casino grimly fascinates Mattia and his fellow gamblers, as they mirror themselves and their own future in him.

Suicide, indeed, permeates the whole novel (as it did *The Gambler*), in all its desperation and all its randomness, its futile gesturing against the tyranny of misfortune. The Monte Carlo suicide of a nameless dandy echoes the earlier suicide of a Liverpool merchant mixed up in a card game who, according to scurrilous rumour back at home, had been the source of Mattia's father's fortune, which Mattia has now lost. It foreshadows the presumed suicide of Mattia himself, reported in the newspaper that he glimpses on the train home, under the headline 'Suicide' (p. 69). And, finally, it looks forward to the carefully staged, fake, second 'suicide' in the Tiber in Rome of the man Mattia will reinvent himself as, thus setting the seal on the failure of his attempt to construct a new life for himself, a new 'self' for himself, out of the absurd turns of chance he has experienced.

Dostoevsky and Pirandello, in their intertwined works set up the roulette table as the emblematic site of 'low-life' modern, or even modernist, luck, in their different ways pitching it in a tragicomic register, their heroes or anti-heroes hopelessly weak, ridiculous, buffeted by good and bad luck, seduced by it, epitomes of a modern sensibility.[19] The same affinity of low anti-heroism and luck runs through modernist literature like a seam: the meandering choices of Italo Svevo's Zeno in *Zeno's Conscience* (1923), who proposes to a sequence of sisters whose names all begin with the letter A, as if one might randomly be substituted for the other; or the wanderings of Joyce's Leopold Bloom in *Ulysses* (1922) (modelled by Joyce in part on Svevo, whom he knew in Trieste), whose Dublin is a pit of low-life settings, from pubs to boxing rings to brothels, and whose sequencing is, or seems to be, the epitome of chance and empty cause.[20]

We could stretch this to the louche locales of Weimar Berlin as it has been forged in the cultural imagination – contemporary with Runyon's Broadway, of course – where the link of the chance encounter to decadent sexual promiscuity and polymorphous variety suggests a certain 'queering' quality in low-life luck stories, in direct contrast to the 'high' romance of the heterosexual couple, stably destined for love. Indeed, another Broadway musical, this time with its roots in Berlin city literature rather than Runyon's New York, makes the link: *Cabaret* (1966, by John Kander and Fred Ebb, from John Van Druten's 1951 play *I Am a Camera*, based on Christopher Isherwood's novel *Goodbye to Berlin*, 1939). *Cabaret* is set in early-1930s Berlin, in the Kit Kat Klub with its troupe of louche performers and clients who stand as a wholesale allegory for the decadence of Weimar as it collapses into Nazism. In the play, Herr Schultz, a minor character who is Jewish, encapsulates the turn from optimism to dark catastrophe in his repeated use of the Yiddish term for 'good luck', *mazel*, first as a bright greeting and ultimately as a forlorn farewell to the central character Cliff, as he (Schulz) is carried off by the Nazis:

> CLIFF: Goodbye, Herr Schultz. I wish you mazel.
> HERR SCHULZ: Mazel. That is what we all need.[21]

Such instances suggest that we should pay close attention to the political dimension of low-life luck stories, since the recourse to luck and gambling is often a last resort for the marginalized, for those outside systems of control, marginalized politically, but also economically, socially or sexually, holding to safety by only a fragile grip, a hand-to-mouth existence on the edge of catastrophe. And these places and such gambles are good for telling stories for precisely this reason of proximity to a fall. This perhaps further explains the particular fascination within low-life luck stories not only of the low *as such*, but often also of the rubbing up against each other of low and high, of the respectable and the disreputable, and the concomitant risk it brings of a fall that is as old as the image of the turn of the wheel of fortune, bringing the high down low, or the reputable into disrepute. This symmetrical patterning and its potential for moral and political allegory is played out with crafted comic skill in the role-swap film *Trading Places* (dir. John Landis, 1983), in which a simple bet between two wealthy brothers propels in opposite directions up and down the social ladder an obnoxious wealthy white man (Dan Aykroyd) and a poor black man (Eddie Murphy). In Chapter 6, Woody Allen was mentioned for the ways in which his early films played with comic traditions and the figure of the loser. In his mature work, Allen took an open interest in this more morally charged strand of luck narrative, centred on reputation, responsibility, choice and luck. A film in this vein is *Crimes and Misdemeanors* (1989), whose title is itself a nod to Dostoevsky. The plot is constructed around the quandaries of Judah (Martin Landau), a respectable, wealthy ophthalmologist who decides he needs to 'get rid' of his troublesome lover Dolores (Anjelica Huston). To do so, Judah turns reluctantly but in desperation to his low-life, criminal brother Jack (Jerry Orbach), who arranges for the dark deed to be done. Judah's hypocrisy lies in his gamble: his reputation against the bet that his and Jack's worlds, the respectable and the criminal, are so far apart that they will never meet and he will never be suspected. (It is a variation on the motif of the chance encounter and the perfect murder forged in *Strangers on a Train*, and all these point back in some sense to Dostoevsky's Raskolnikov.) To make this moral, criminal gamble, to take the desperate roll of the dice, Judah crosses over to the mirror-image, low-life world of his brother. And the film's boldest step is simply to watch him get away with it: no-one catches him, the crime is never solved, the gamble pays off, the moral jeopardy fades.[22]

One last aspect of the sociology of luck stories is worth flagging up, a somewhat different narrative pattern from the vivid idiolects of Hoffman's *Luck* or Runyon's Broadway, or the moral dramas of Dostoevsky and Pirandello, but one which perhaps subtends them all in their fascination with the 'low'. This aspect is rooted not so much in the grotesquery or vivid vernacular of the underworld, in the exceptional or the unfamiliar, but rather in its opposite facet, in the banal anonymity, invisibility and insignificance of the 'low'. Luck, after all, as we have repeatedly noted, is universal and therefore banal, often hardly worth a mention, a persistent part of any life ever lived. Luck is also 'low' in this sense, of being commonplace and so apparently unworthy of attention. But narrative in its modern forms, in literature and other arts, began at a certain point to pay close attention to precisely this kind of banal story, so that it became a leading feature of twentieth-century narrative to lay claim to labels such as realism, reportage, storytelling 'from below'. An iconic example of this turn to the ordinary was the 1948 film *Bicycle Thieves* (dir. Vittorio de Sica), one of the great films of the mid-century movement known as neo-realism.

In *Bicycle Thieves*, a man's bike is stolen and as a result his life falls apart. As French film critic André Bazin put it, in celebration of the film, 'nothing happens in *Bicycle Thieves*'; or rather, 'nothing happens in *Bicycle Thieves* that might just as well not have happened'.[23] This was Bazin's way of capturing neo-realism's narrative of pure contingency, and he glossed the point by linking this contingency both to the commonplace of the low and, crucially, to a certain kind of newspaper report: 'There is not enough material here even for a news item: the whole story would not deserve two lines in a stray-dog column.'[24] The film itself plays with this association: as the man reports the bicycle theft at a local police station, a journalist hovers around in the background looking for a juicy story: 'Anything new, brigadier?' he asks. 'No, nothing. Just a bicycle,' comes the policeman's reply.

In fact, this minor mode of storytelling, somehow beneath even a 'proper' news story, and the link to newspapers, has its own history and particular significance for our enquiry, since stray-dog columns, two-bit news items, gossipy, 'stranger-than-fiction' reportage of life's odd happenings, in other words ordinary stories of curiosity and coincidence, are themselves forms of modern storytelling that amount to low-level luck stories. This kind of incident, recounted in a few lines of newsprint for lightweight public consumption, was born with the modern newspaper itself, in particular in nineteenth-century France, and from there it filtered into the plotlines of the modern novel, as notably explained and analysed by Roland Barthes in a 1962 essay on the French term for this kind of event and its story, the *'fait divers'*.[25] An English term analogous to the *fait divers* might be the 'human interest story', or a phrase that is telling for its place in literary as well as journalistic history, 'a curious incident'. This phrase points us towards a well-known moment in Conan Doyle's Sherlock Holmes stories, the curious incident of the dog that does not bark, which becomes a clue for Holmes in the story 'Silver Blaze', reminding us that many *'faits divers'* and other low-life luck stories are also crime stories, that is, 'cases', as well as chance happenings (both *casi* in Italian, as we saw in Chapter 2). Modern crime stores, like *faits divers*, are full of incidental elements, on a low-level, microscopic scale, just like their constitutive feature, the clue, which triggers human curiosity and surprise, but also eventually a form of recognition or revelation.[26] Such luck stories are ordinary but also surprising, disturbances, exceptions and coincidences, often errors, that ripple almost invisibly across the surface of everyday life.

Several of the works we have looked at in this chapter contain hints of the *fait divers*, of the 'nothing' stories and their bond to minor forms of newspaper storytelling. We have seen the link made explicitly in *Bicycle Thieves*. Mattia Pascal reads of his own 'suicide' in a small local newspaper report and, years after the novel was published, Pirandello defended it against accusations of implausibility by digging up a real newspaper story in *Corriere della sera* from 27 March 1920, which almost precisely replicated the story of a man whose wife wrongly identified the body of an apparent suicide as his, following which the man eventually returned (in this case from prison).[27] And of course those misrecognitions and errors are, precisely, examples of odd errors that upturn lives and become 'stranger-than-fiction' narrative, in either tragicomic or melodramatic register. Runyon's stories too include several populated by reporters hanging out in Mindy's and other locales, part of the human fauna of his Broadway world. His label for these is 'newspaper scribes', and they have names like Waldo Winchester and Ambrose Hammer. And of course, the figure of the seedy reporter on the streets of New York and elsewhere is one that will become a topos and a cliché of modern narrative in its own right.[28] But besides the specifics of the newspaper connection, Runyon's world points us to a final label, another potential name for this genre of low-life luck stories that we have been exploring, one that captures both the throwaway contempt with which we are tempted to treat them, and the hardscrabble grit of the lives they narrate. Here is Runyon in a story called 'Hold 'em, Yale!':

> Well, naturally all this is commencing to sound to me like a *hardluck story* such as any doll is apt to tell, so I go on about my business because I figure she will next be trying to put the lug on me for a ducket, or maybe for her railroad fare back to Worcester, although generally dolls with *hard-luck stories* live in San Francisco.
>
> She keeps on standing there, and I notice she is now crying more than somewhat, and I get to thinking to myself that she is about as cute a little doll as I ever see, although too young for anybody to be bothering much about. Furthermore, I get to thinking that maybe she is on the level, at that, with her story. (DRO; emphasis added)

The 'hard luck story' is usually taken to mean a fake or exaggerated tale designed to elicit sympathy. Here, as can happen, it turns out to be a true 'hard luck' story of an innocent 'doll' (who turns out to be a wealthy heiress) being taken for a ride. Other writers have tapped into the quotidian reality of lived lives as all, in a sense, stories of struggle, risk and adversity, literally stories of hard luck. Alice Munro entitled one of her stories precisely thus, 'Hard-luck stories', which turns out to consist of not much more than the three protagonists, two women and a man, swapping tales of loves and love affairs gone wrong and the deceptions they entail.[29] Runyon's and Munro's stories share something of the dual aspect of the hard luck tale: they are tales of graft in at least two of its senses, hard work and trickery, tales of low-level turns of chance, fortune and misfortune, and of the impact these have on ordinary lives. And in these, as in the works by Dostoevsky and others we have looked at, it is precisely their intrusive, low moral uncertainties that offer up clues for a modern investigation of our deepest sense of self.

Notes

1 *Luck* was 'unfortunate', however, despite all the creative and financial resources poured into it. It ended up being cancelled by HBO after only one season because of worries about animal cruelty on set, after it was reported that three horses had died during production.
2 I'm grateful to an anonymous reader of the manuscript of this book who pointed me towards this affinity here, for example in two novels by Julian Mayfield, *The Hit* (1957) and *The Long Night* (1958). Of course, the very nomenclature of the 'numbers racket' takes us directly back to the 'lucky numbers' theme of Chapter 2.
3 Mary Douglas, *Purity and Danger: An analysis of concepts of pollution and taboo* (Abingdon: Routledge, 2002), p. 50. On mess, see David Trotter, *Cooking with Mud: The idea of mess in nineteenth-century art and fiction* (Oxford: Oxford University Press, 2000).
4 Runyon's stories during his life and since have been collected in a confusing array of overlapping collections. Many are available online in 'Damon Runyon From First to Last', https://gutenberg.net.au/ebooks18/1800711h.html, and 'Damon Runyon Omnibus', https://gutenberg.net.au/ebooks11/1100651h.html. Quotations below are taken from these sources, indicated respectively as DRFL and DRO.
5 For a study of Runyon's fictional world and its links to the real New York, see Daniel R. Schwarz, *Broadway Boogie Woogie: Damon Runyon and the making of New York City culture* (New York: Palgrave Macmillan, 2003).
6 The vernacular, picaresque comedy of Wilbur's bumbling good-luck ending is not dissimilar in register to the vignette contained in Bob Dylan's rambling song 'Idiot wind' (*Blood on the Tracks*, 1975), which plays around with a deliberately hyperbolic and generic sequence of unlikely events ('They say I shot a man named Gray / And took his wife to Italy. / She inherited a million bucks / And when she died it came to me. / I can't help it if I'm lucky'); cf. also the typically playful paradox of Dylan's turn of phrase in 'Pledging my time' (*Blonde on Blonde*, 1966): 'Somebody got lucky / But it was an accident.'
7 The full name of Runyon's character here has racist connotations and has been abbreviated.
8 Damon Runyon, 'Lillian', in *Guys and Dolls* (New York: Frederick A. Stokes, 1931), pp. 97–118.
9 See lyrics at https://www.stlyrics.com/lyrics/bestofbroadway-americanmusical/luckbealady.htm, and Brando's performance of the song at https://www.youtube.com/watch?v=BmEwtWBte84 (both accessed 1 August 2022).
10 OED, 'Lady', C2. 'Compounds with Lady', d. 'Lady Luck *n.*', at https://www.oed.com/view/Entry/105011 (accessed 30 March 2022). The modern figure of luck as a lady is also to be found in the origin story of one of the mythical figures of modern (British) masculinity, James

Bond: in the first Bond novel, *Casino Royale*, Ian Fleming describes Bond's attitude to luck as being in keeping with and coinciding with his attitude to women: 'Bond saw luck as a woman, to be softly wooed or brutally ravaged, never pandered to or pursued. But he was honest enough to admit that he had never yet been made to suffer by cards or by women. One day, and he accepted the fact, he would be brought to his knees by love or by luck' (Ian Fleming, *Casino Royale* (1953) (London: Pan, 1955), p. 48).

11 Fyodor Dostoevsky, *The Gambler* (1866), trans. Hugh Aplin (Richmond: Alma Classics, 2014). (In the light of the discussion of trains in Chapter 4, it is interesting to note that the casino in *The Gambler* is located in the railway station.)

12 For a recent study, see Peter Fifield, *Modernism and Physical Illness: Sick books* (Oxford: Oxford University Press, 2020).

13 Robert Louis Jackson, 'Polina and Lady Luck in Dostoevsky's *The Gambler*', in *Close Encounters: Essays on Russian literature* (Boston, MA: Academic Studies Press, 2013), pp. 45–70 (p. 64).

14 Dostoevsky, *The Gambler*, p. 134.

15 Luigi Pirandello, *Il fu Mattia Pascal* (1904), in English as *The Late Mattia Pascal*, trans. William Weaver (New York: New York Review Books, 2005).

16 Pirandello, *The Late Mattia Pascal*, pp. 48–64.

17 Pirandello, *The Late Mattia Pascal*, p. 48.

18 Pirandello, *The Late Mattia Pascal*, p. 51.

19 It worth noting here that there is another side to the depiction of gambling in *fin-de-siècle* Europe that is far more conservative and steeped in the valour of risk-taking, perhaps best encapsulated in some lines from Rudyard Kipling's 1895 poem 'If', about what it takes to 'be a man': 'If you can make one heap of all your winnings / And risk it on one turn of pitch-and-toss, / And lose, and start again at your beginnings / And never breathe a word about your loss' (ll. 17–20), in Rudyard Kipling, *Selected Poems*, ed. Peter Keating (London: Penguin, 1993), p. 134. Interestingly, Lindsay Anderson would borrow Kipling's title for his biting film satire of English education, class and empire, *If....* (1968); the sequel to *If....*, an allegory of capitalism and post-empire, was tellingly entitled *O Lucky Man!* (dir. Lindsay Anderson, 1973), with a title song that seems to be a direct, sarcastic riposte to Kipling, also structured around a series of ifs ('If you have a friend on whom you think you can rely you are a lucky man', and so on; see https://genius.com/Alan-price-o-lucky-man-lyrics (accessed 1 August 2022)).

20 See for example Derek Attridge, 'The postmodernity of Joyce: Chance, coincidence, and the reader', in *Joyce Effects: On language, theory, and history* (Cambridge: Cambridge University Press, 2000), pp. 117–25.

21 Joe Masteroff et al., *Cabaret: The illustrated book and lyrics* (New York: Newmarket Press, 1999), p. 96.

22 On *Crimes and Misdemeanors*, also in relation to the discussion in Chapter 6, see Ewa Mazierska, 'Moral luck in the films of Woody Allen', *Kinema* (November 2011), at https://openjournals.uwaterloo.ca/index.php/kinema/article/download/1235/1560?inline=1.

23 André Bazin, *What is Cinema?*, trans. Hugh Gray (Berkeley: University of California Press, 1971), vol. 2, p. 50. The conjunction with Vivian Mercier's quip on *Waiting for Godot*, quoted in Chapter 3 ('nothing happens, twice'), is interesting. A further variant on this 'realist' topos of stories where nothing much happens is suggested by Chloé Zhao's remarkable 2020 film *Nomadland*, in which the backstories of the various real-life and fictional characters on screen are left unsaid; they are rather the precondition of the wandering path the film takes. As critic Anthony Lane puts it, 'One of the things we learn from the films of Chloé Zhao is this: bad luck is the stuff that happens before a story begins' (Anthony Lane, 'Economic ruthlessness on the open road in *Nomadland*', *The New Yorker*, 27 November 2020).

24 Bazin, *What Is Cinema?*, vol. 2, p. 68.

25 Roland Barthes, 'Structure du fait divers' (1962), in English as 'Structure of the fait-divers', in *Critical Essays*, trans. Richard Howard (Evanston, IL: Northwestern University Press, 1972), pp. 185–95.

26 See Arthur Conan Doyle, 'Silver Blaze', in *The Memoirs of Sherlock Holmes* (1894) (Harmondsworth: Penguin, 1976), pp. 7–34 (p. 28). On the crucial significance of the Holmesian 'clue' as a paradigm for a modern form of epistemology, truth and evidence (and indeed of chance), see Carlo Ginzburg, 'Clues: Roots of an evidential paradigm' (1979), in *Clues, Myths, and the Historical Method*, trans. John and Anne C. Tedeschi (Baltimore, MD: Johns Hopkins University Press, 2013), pp. 87–113; and on Ginzburg see Chapter 1. On links between recognition, chance and plot contrivance, see Terence Cave, *Recognitions: A study in*

poetics (Oxford: Oxford University Press, 1990), p. 2; James, *Constraining*, pp. 70–4; and more generally on causality and modernity Stephen Kern, *A Cultural History of Causality: Science, murder novels and systems of thought* (Princeton, NJ: Princeton University Press, 2004); Richardson, *Unlikely Stories*.

27 See Pirandello's postface to later editions of the novel, 'A warning on the scruples of the imagination' (*The Late Mattia Pascal*, pp. 245–52).

28 See for example the 'Image of the Journalist in Popular Culture' project, USC Annenberg, at http://ijpc.org/index.html.

29 Alice Munro, 'Hard-luck stories', in *Moons*, pp. 181–97. The story was connected in its genesis to 'Simon's luck', discussed in Chapter 6.

8
Early style and child's play

In Chapter 7, we saw how modern luck stories have had a tendency to proliferate in and around the darker corners of the social field, at the margins of an often urban narrative space. This final chapter also looks at the draw of this thread of modern narrative to the margins, but it does so from a distinctly different angle, one rooted less in sociological and representational space than in literary form and the field of cultural production. It explores how luck stories might be said to cluster at the 'margins' of the modern literary field, in zones of what has been labelled the 'paraliterary'. This term has been deployed and understood in a number of ways, but it broadly indicates kinds of literature that sit beyond or to one side of the conventionally literary, construed as less developed, more naive, more one- or two-dimensional than the apparently more 'rounded' or 'deep' texts and products of the canon.[1] Paraliterary (or para-cultural) works emerge necessarily alongside and in close relation to a stable category of literature or the literary as such, which from the emerging modern literary market of the eighteenth century and after in Europe grew into an elaborate system of taxonomies and types of texts, each designed for a certain readership and each assigned a certain cultural value. In contrast to, or at the lower end of, this scale of value, the paraliterary exists in an eclectic range of other forms and genres, including popular literature, detective fiction, sci-fi and fantasy, and romance; analogous vertical structures of value emerge in other, new and emerging modern media and modes over this same period. The writer and critic Samuel Delany offers a list of the stuff of the paraliterary that includes '[c]omic books, mysteries, westerns, science fiction, pornography, greeting card verse, newspaper reports, academic criticism, advertising texts, movie and TV scripts, popular song lyrics'.[2] And Delany goes on to confirm that these apparently 'lesser' products are in fact integral to, even constitutive of, the wider and 'higher' field of modern literature and culture. Since it has been a core argument of this book that luck stories cut across cultural hierarchies and taxonomies through their sheer force of universal recognition, and that they flourish particularly at edges and margins, it is not surprising that this seems to hold also for a pervasive and lively presence of luck themes and motifs within the field of the paraliterary. Indeed, it is notable that a significant number of the modes of luck stories we have explored in Chapters 1 to 7 have been studiedly drawn from categories in Delany's list or in similar 'para-cultural' forms: from comics to science fiction, from silent-era slapstick comedy to the popular Hollywood comedy of the 1990s, from detective novels and newspaper *faits divers* to romances and musicals.

This marginal location of luck narratives within the cultural field, much like the wider category of paraliterature itself, has been one of the sources of a certain condescension towards luck that we have come across at several stages previously. Neither the category of luck nor its stories, whether old or new, have ever quite shaken off their origins in the realm of folklore and magic (understood by some, for some reason, as a limitation); at the same time, and because of this oblique and submerged quality, these stories have often demonstrated a certain de-canonizing energy and a hybridity, as we see luck turning up in richly unpredictable corners, taking on any number of different cultural shapes and forms. Somehow, in other words, luck has not quite settled into becoming one of the defining conceptual tools or tropes for reading modernity, and yet, as this book has set out to show, it is pervasive across that modern cultural field, permeating modernity and its cultural and narrative expression. Why and how that might be is a key question that this final chapter sets out to explore.

There is undoubtedly something jejune, something sophomoric, half-baked or middlebrow about the games played by modern luck stories, indeed perhaps about luck itself as a concept, as if it fascinates and attracts, for sure, but struggles to stand up to rigorous conceptual scrutiny or profound literary articulation.[3] It comes across at times perhaps as too forced or too constructed, too much of a bag of clever tricks, like an amateur magic show. Taken together, both the fascination and the limitation amount to a striking, even defining, facet of luck stories, deserving of careful attention, quite apart from the interferences of facile value judgements. We will see in this chapter how this is manifested in two intriguing and complementary ways: in a certain biographical marginalization apparent in a number of case studies we have already touched on, and in a corner of the paraliterary field we have not yet explored, children's literature.

A striking illustration of the somehow 'lesser' quality of luck stories, their 'para-' standing, lies in an apparently incidental connection between a substantial cluster of our key luck stories analysed in Part II and what was once called *juvenilia*, more neutrally labelled here as 'early style'. A conspicuous number of works in which we have seen luck come to the fore as a formal device, a pivotal theme, a governing idea or a materialized entity, appear chronologically in the early stages of their creators' careers, at a stage of development subsequently left behind for apparently more 'rounded', 'lofty' or 'mature' work. They are what we might call threshold or seedcorn works, and forms of luck are their seeding concept. They are early experiments in storytelling in which an attention to luck allows for a testing out, a stress-testing of nascent, tentative or intuitive ideas and voices, allowing a first articulation of character or concept that will evolve into that writer's, filmmaker's or artist's signature style. This holds true with a remarkable pattern of consistency in at least five of the major case studies undertaken in previous chapters (and more could be picked out): these are, in order of first appearance or publication, Miller's *The Man Who Had All the Luck*, Dick's *Solar Lottery*, Stoppard's *Rosencrantz and Guildenstern Are Dead*, Kieslowksi's *Blind Chance* and Haneke's *71 Fragments of a Chronology of Chance*.

Miller's play was the first of his to be performed in a professional theatre, and despite its initial failure it came shortly before and clearly informed the emergence of his streak of powerful mature dramas of the 1940s and early 1950s. In these latter works, as was noted in Chapter 5, profound questions of character and morality that the device of luck had levered open in *The Man Who Had All the Luck* moved to the structural and emotional centre of Miller's work, with forces of masculinity, family, work and money combining to create intense contradictions and tragic moral pressure. Dick's *Solar Lottery* was his first published novel, to be followed by over 40 more and an emerging reputation as a defining voice in genre science-fiction writing. Although it is impossible to encompass all the proliferating threads and ideas running through that later body of Dick's *oeuvre*, it is again plausible to point to how the luck motifs present in that first novel – themes linked to gameplay, number and determinism, political control, social hierarchy and chaos in the face of technology, divergent worlds and counterfactuals – also permeate the later *oeuvre*. One example of many we could look at would be the 1963 novel *The Game-Players of Titan*, where luck re-emerges as a key and plurally layered motif in a depiction of an etiolated post-apocalyptic future.[4]

Game-Players is set several centuries in the future, after a catastrophic planetary war that has wiped out much of humanity on

Earth and left most of its few hundred thousand survivors infertile. Only a handful of prized couples – in pairings that are unknown and unpredictable – are able to conceive and have children. An elite group of humans, known as 'Bindmen', play a planet-wide, *Monopoly*-like game called 'Bluff',[5] in which they exchange and gamble property deeds, but also, tellingly, prizes of marriage and copulation with each other, in a regulated attempt to search out those rare fertile couplings.

The double-gaming system of capital and sex in *Game-Players* points to a governing analogy in the novel between fertility, property and luck (not so alien to a comparable cluster of motifs we saw in *The Man Who Had All the Luck*). And luck lies at the very heart of the analogy, even linguistically as it is italicized in the book into a neologism that stands for both pregnancy and fertility in this barren futureworld:

> *Luck*, he thought, this late in my life. One hundred and fifty years. After so many tries; after the failure of so many, many combinations.
>
> 'Why'd they kill him?' Sharp asked quietly.
> 'Because of his *luck*,' the Doctor replied. 'His fertility.'[6]

Another crystal-clear example of luck and the early style is offered by Tom Stoppard, who was influenced by Miller, as well as by Beckett, Pirandello and others we have touched on in passing. *Rosencrantz and Guildenstern Are Dead*, performed first in 1966 at the Edinburgh Festival and shortly thereafter in London, represents one of the most remarkable stories in modern British theatre of the instant success of an unknown and the emergence of a 'great' new talent. The intellectual and formal games it plays had clearly brewed over formative years in Stoppard, since it was preceded by a shorter version of the play written during a stay in Germany (*Rosencrantz and Guildenstern Meet King Lear*) and, crucially, an even earlier student adaptation of Dostoevsky's *The Gambler*,[7] suggesting that luck games in particular fascinated him and seeded the brilliant inventions of *Rosencrantz*. In turn, *Rosencrantz* projects forward onto several of Stoppard's vibrant, ideas-driven and formally experimental intellectual dramas of the following decades. Indeed, although they are tonally very different, Stoppard shares with Kieślowski an intuition that chance and luck, and related quandaries of time and morality, can generate and be generated by rich formal patterns of narrative such as doublings, convergences and inversions, all in evidence in, for example, *Travesties* (1974), *Arcadia* (1993), and even the screenplay of *Shakespeare in Love* (dir. John Madden, 1998).

Finally, both the film directors mentioned above, Kieślowski and Haneke, offer powerful further cases in point. *Blind Chance*, a film made in 1981 but suppressed in Poland until 1987, was by no means Kieślowski's first, but it belongs to a relatively early phase of his career when he was largely unknown outside Poland, and it was certainly a threshold work, emerging in the late 1980s at a remarkable moment in his development. Its release shortly preceded the remarkable 10-film cycle of *Dekalog* (1989), followed by the international Francophone productions that cemented his reputation, *The Double Life of Veronique* (1991) and the *Three Colours* trilogy (1993–4). Across all these final five films (which are in reality 14 films), before his early death in 1996, the theme and structuring force of luck and its merging with an idea of fate that was found in *Blind Chance* can be seen sublimated into recurrent patterns that become incisive devices for moral enquiry, from doubles and coincidences, to unpredictable encounters and forking-path moments or choices, from spiritual questions to questions of justice, extending even to include specific motifs found also in *Blind Chance,* such as travel or sickness and medicine. Of course, the very structural principle of multi-stranded or parallel narrative structures – the Ten Commandments, the three colours, the double life – points us back to the threefold luck narrative of *Blind Chance*, and stands as a powerful formal token of the multiple possibilities that so many luck stories seem to stage.[8]

The sequence in Haneke's career seems to follow a strikingly similar path, when looked at from this one no doubt partial but nevertheless illuminating angle. His *71 Fragments* was an early, perhaps somewhat forced and experimental, piece, steeped in the random vagaries of luck and chance. It precedes, and surely lays some of the groundwork for, his rich and penetrating subsequent work that challenges both the private and the public politics of identity, violence, negotiation with the other and the ethics of filmmaking and looking. As Thomas Elsaesser put it, quoted in Chapter 4, *71 Fragments of a Chronology of Chance* is 'not so much a title as a program, a motto, albeit one to which Haneke is dedicating his creative life'.[9]

Edward Said's unfinished last book, picking up on an idea from Theodor Adorno, proposed a model for the 'late style' of certain composers and writers, a model which was something like the opposite of what conventional and classical models of the 'ages of man' might suggest. For Said, the late styles of, say, Mann, Genet, Lampedusa, Cavafy (among others) were far from wise and serene, or detached and conservative, but were rather defiant and unsettling, radical, untimely, 'against the grain'.[10] Perhaps we can suggest a similarly contrary model for these instances of 'early style', in the light of its strange affinity, in our cluster of modern writers and directors, with luck stories. A certain early style is no doubt immature and limited, as we might expect; but it can also be radically generative and this seems to be the case with our luck stories, in which luck as a device and an idea is not so much good to think with, as good to *start thinking* with, to start thinking in new ways. This is the 'seedcorn' energy that was posited above as a common element in all these works and it suggests that luck can be a sort of first step, an initial constraint and a signal of the potential to 'put aside childish things'. And yet, as we have seen, these writers and directors never quite forget entirely the challenging, early questions of first principle posed by luck. It is indeed perhaps no coincidence that the protagonists of all the five works revisited are, loosely speaking, young men (nor indeed that they are all men; the overwhelming gender biases of modern luck stories are deeply embedded in this field as one of its defining characteristics, as we have seen repeatedly).

The implications of this hypothesis about luck's affinity with an early style are not, however, to be limited to an interest in artists' biographies, in the cod psychology of personal development ('X only reached full artistic maturity following their early, naive efforts'). In fact, the pattern it suggests of limit and potential, of generative constraint, of complexity growing out of 'early' simplicity, points us in a number of analogous but distinct directions that help us to position the category of luck stories in their rather peculiar location in the modern cultural field. For instance, the combination of initial constraint and generative literary potential might well evoke the highly distinctive formal literary games played by the Parisian Oulipo group, founded in 1960, its remarkable members including Georges Perec, Raymond Queneau and Italo Calvino. As Alison James, among others, has argued compellingly, the 'potential literature' of Perec and Oulipo (the acronym stands for *Ouvroir de littérature potentielle*, 'Workshop of potential literature') – like a great deal of modern avant-garde art, from surrealist free association to John Cage and the Fluxus group – was built on the bond between constraint and chance, between random acts and indeterminacy.[11] Oulipo set formal, often numerical, limits on their works of creative literature, for example writing a novel without the letter 'e' or with the letter 'e' as the only vowel, or writing a set of 10 sonnets whose 14 lines can be read in any order and combination, producing 10^{14} sonnets.[12] The combinatorial or constrained potential for creation is immense and also immensely challenging, but the aesthetic is as much one of second-order chance juxtaposition as it is of ordered formulae (or rather the latter generates the former). As one device is constrained, random secondary elements, for example words chosen for their combination of vowels, are shoved into close proximity. These are not quite 'luck stories', then, but rather works created according to the formal properties of chance (in so far as this distinction between luck and chance holds tightly, which, as this book knows all too well, it does not).

This two-step between limit and potential is a dance between order and disorder, limit and proliferation, clarity and disorientation. And chance or luck can be said to stand on either side of this partnership or on both; this is no doubt one of the reasons why it persists as a fundamental and pervasive drive behind so many of our stories and our interrogations of the world. The same combination points us in yet another distinct direction, towards one final corner of the paraliterary field of storytelling to explore, and towards another prolific modern publishing genre and product, one where yet again luck stories seems to cluster with remarkably density and where luck as a motif poses and plays games with simple but profound questions; that is, towards children's writing.

Luck stories are everywhere in children's literature. In part, this is because of a shared genealogical link. As was noted in Chapter 1, there is a strong anthropological affinity between luck beliefs, magic and fable, and, as Marina Warner among others has explained, the modern genre of children's literature emerged in the West, especially from the nineteenth century onwards, out of the field of fable and folklore, gathered by pioneering collectors and editors, from Perrault to the Grimms and Andersen.[13] What folklore and children's stories have in common are their schematic, iterative and self-generative qualities, so that distilled questions, emotions, situations and stock characters can recur in endless variation on a limited number of themes (once again, that pattern of limit and proliferating potential). This is why the Russian formalists, such as Vladimir Propp in his *Morphology of the Folktale* (1928), were drawn to folk culture and fable, as they seemed to hold out the promise of a systemic clarity and a quantitative typology of all narrative. And one of the constant, structuring presences in both traditions is a situation of danger, of sudden change in fortune (or the magical dream or nightmare of the same), and the possibility or otherwise of surviving this. Children's stories, like their ancestors in fable, are in other words stories of adventure, of haps and mishaps, of luck at its most elemental.

Many have seen a simple didacticism in this aspect: children's stories are intended to 'educate' their young listeners into how to navigate the uncertainties of fortune and misfortune, among other things, and thus to grow into adults (and indeed, for more ideologically attuned critics of modern children's literature, into citizens of the nation, or subjects of capital and empire, especially in the quietly tamed and revised versions of folk traditions produced in the Victorian and Edwardian eras).[14] Contemporary, and perhaps especially feminist, readers, have seen something far more dynamic and subversive in the tradition, or at least less definite: the psychoanalyst Adam Phillips, for example, has plausibly proposed that things in children's stories are neither so linear nor so neat as all that, that fable and children's tales cannot be reduced to problem-solving exercises nor to stern warnings about dangers afoot and how to avoid them. For Phillips, these fables, and perhaps stories more generally,

> give us no real clue where help comes from; and might make us wonder [...] what else we might want from stories other than help. All we know is that the protagonists really want something and *they get lucky* [...]. The tales just give us instances of when wishing worked.[15]

This mode of storytelling, in other words, is no simplistic form of directed thinking nor of pedagogy. It rather recalls the corrective conception that we encountered in Chapter 1, in Gramsci's notion of folklore as a form of collective first philosophy, here carried out through shared storytelling.

Key founding works of the late nineteenth-century transition, which saw folk and fable traditions morph from gathered anthologies of oral tales into something closer to a modern conception of children's literature (as a form, but also as a publishing phenomenon), seem to confirm the link with luck in a number of ways. *Alice in Wonderland* is of course, in its full title, *Alice's Adventures in Wonderland* (1865), and her adventures are understood, structured and told as a sequence of random, chance episodes, starting from her very first, unlikely ('fortunate') decision to follow the White Rabbit down the rabbit hole: 'burning with curiosity, [Alice] ran across the field after it, and *fortunately* was just in time to see it pop down a large rabbit-hole under the hedge'.[16] All fairy tales and folk tales share this paratactic ('and then ...') and contingent quality, telling of a thing that happened and then another thing that happened, but might as well not have happened, and Carroll plays self-consciously with the absurdity and creative fertility of this random sequencing. Carlo Collodi's *Pinocchio* (1883) is also a tale of adventures in the same sense as *Alice*: its full original title was *Le avventure di Pinocchio: Storia di un burattino* ('The adventures of Pinocchio: story of a puppet')[17] and it too is steeped in an episodic, accidental and incidental storytelling principle of adventure – part mock-epic tale of heroic deeds, part serial sequence – as his puppet-hero stumbles into a series of fortunate and unfortunate events, of haps and mishaps, and simply reacts, usually in the most thoughtless, childish and foolish way possible.

Collodi's story of a poor, wilful wooden puppet who dreams of becoming a real boy was serial and episodic first of all because it was originally published in serial form between 1881 and 1883 in the *Giornale per i bambini* ('Newspaper for children') in Florence. But above and beyond its status and form as a product for a new market of child readers, it is saturated in a fluid vocabulary of luck and fortune which also pushes towards loose sequence and parataxis. We can spot the usage of a dozen or so luck terms in the book – including chance, disaster, ill fortune, venture and adventure (*caso, sciagura, sventura, ventura, avventura*) and more – but two particular terms stand out as densely recurrent, used well over 50 times throughout the book, almost but not quite a pairing of opposites: these are *fortuna*, fortune, and *disgrazia*, a term that takes in a spectrum of meanings from misfortune to disaster to disgrace. Between them, these terms quietly stake out a territory for luck in children's stories that is variegated, unpredictable and energizing, part absurd, part magical, part melancholy, and part self-consciously metaliterary. A handful of examples illustrate the point. First, Pinocchio's name itself, his baptism and his destiny (*nomen omen*, as the Latin adage has it), comes under a magical sign of good luck:

> 'What shall I call him?', [Geppetto, his maker] said to himself. 'I'd like to call him Pinocchio. It's a name that will bring him luck [*porterà fortuna*].'[18]

From here, the book runs on from strange turn to surprising encounter on waves of good and bad luck: 'in the end, by good fortune [*per buona fortuna*], a policeman came along'; 'and he would have had to stay even longer had it not been for a very lucky chance [*un caso fortunatissimo*, combining two terms for luck]'; 'the wood where he had the misfortune [*disgraziatamente*] to meet the Fox and the Cat'; and so on.[19] This is the seriality of luck events, turns of fortune this way or that that allow a story to evolve, not on an arc of crafted development, but along a messy, jumping line of stuff that happens. (Here the puppet and his story are somewhat like the *saltimbanques* referred to in Chapter 5, the leaping, tumbling figures associated with luck.) In this, as in the other ways linked to form and status already noted, fable and children's literature stand apart from canonical literature. More subtly, however, the play of fortune and misfortune in *Pinocchio* allows for a face-off between, on the one hand, morality and cause and effect, and, on the other, uncertainty, contingency and the embrace of a 'pure' present that is also an openness to change. The unruly puppet tries, half-heartedly, to learn to be a 'good boy' and to take up the lessons of morality:

> 'I'm sorry to say that I have been a bad boy, and the Talking Cricket was right to say that "disobedient children will not fare well in this world". And I've proved it to my cost, because such great misfortune [*dimolte disgrazie*] has befallen me.'[20]

But neither Pinocchio's actions nor the reader's emotions pay much heed to the trite (and sadly false) lesson of the Talking Cricket, that good behaviour leads to good fortune. Instead, this modern child-Prince intuitively lives in uncertainty, contingency and action, in immediate pleasure and forgetfulness, endlessly tricked, diverted and falling short of all rules and standards. In the end, it is this freewheeling spirit and narrative mode, not the regulated progress of a *Bildung*, that carries him on a wave (literally, in the later parts of the book) to his dream of self-transformation, of personhood:

> 'Don't you know about the great occasion? Don't you know about my good luck [*la fortuna che mi è toccata*]?'
> 'What's that?'
> 'Tomorrow I shan't be a puppet any more; I'm going to be a boy like you and all the others.'[21]

It is worth noting also, in case this breezy ending seems to seal an easy optimism around Pinocchio's luck, that the same unheeding play of *fortuna* and *disgrazia* led, literally, to Pinocchio's death, when he was hanged from an oak tree in an earlier chapter, written by Collodi as the ending of the very first serial version of the story, before he was forced into imagining a miraculous resurrection by market demand to keep the character going.[22] This too reminds us of the persistent presence of violence, danger and death, as well as of magical resolutions and happy-ever-after endings, in the luck stories of children's literature, a further powerful legacy shared with the fable and folk traditions.

If we now take a grand leap, acrobat-style, from Alice and Pinocchio in the nineteenth century to the late twentieth and early twenty-first, it is remarkable to see how commonplace and how playfully reworked the motif of luck is in contemporary children's writing.[23] One remarkable example, rooted in the traditions of fairy tale, the legacy of Carroll but also of Shakespearean wonder, is a novel created not for children but about children, family and fantasy, Angela Carter's *Wise Children* (1991).[24] Carter's last novel before her death in 1992, *Wise Children* is a phantasmagorical and openly carnivalesque work which is head-spinning in its turns of plot and its coincidences, and the underlying link to the realm of luck is heavily signalled in the playful names of the two overlapping and incestuously coupling families at its heart, the Chances (including the twins Dora and Nora Chance) and the Hazards (including the twins Melchior and Peregrine Hazard).

The presence of luck motifs in contemporary literature written *for* children is, if anything, even more persistent. It is almost as if (re)visiting the problems of luck were *de rigueur* for writers of children's stories, and, more importantly, for their young readers. Across the spectrum of children's literature – from picture books to early-years reading primers, from comic books and pre-teen serials to adolescent and young-adult (YA) fiction – luck finds its place, not necessarily as a dominant or even a primary feature, but as a recurrent, constantly reworked and revisited topos, something easily familiar and good for telling tales with.

Here are some examples, in rough order of reader age.[25] The *Mister Men* series was created by Roger Hargreaves in 1971 for pre-school children to huge success and it was followed in 1981 by the accompanying *Little Miss* series. Eighteenth in this latter series is *Little Miss Lucky*. Dr Seuss was over 30 books into his career as a children's rhyme and nonsense writer, which had already included tongue-twisting or nonsense masterpieces such as *Horton Hears a Who!* (1954), *The Cat in the Hat* (1957), *How the Grinch Stole Christmas* (1957) and *Green Eggs and Ham* (1960), when he published *Did I Ever Tell You How Lucky You Are?* (1973). A key niche in the pre-teen market that boomed in the early 2000s was illustrated or cartoon book series about naughty children, and the rough and tumble of good and bad luck repeatedly turns up as a motif in these, from *A Tiny Bit Lucky* (2014) in the 'Tom Gates' series by Liz Pichon, to *Hard Luck* (2013) in the *Diary of a Wimpy Kid* series by Jeff Kinney. For slightly older and more 'knowing' readers who like comic adventure as well as playing elaborate games with the tricks of storytelling itself (a metaliterary self-awareness present in Carroll, Collodi and indeed across the children's literature tradition), one remarkable series of mystery and adventure novels appeared in the early 2000s that mixed magic in with dark family histories and was explicitly created under the sign of fortune and misfortune: Lemony Snicket's *A Series of Unfortunate Events*

(1999–2006). J. K. Rowling's *Harry Potter* series (1997–2007) also maintained the old and familiar fantastical bond between magic and luck, with a passing nod to old traditions and lexicons, for example in one of Hogwarts' magical potions called Felix Felicis, 'liquid luck' (the cod Latin evoking the link we have seen regularly before between luck and happiness), which makes anyone who drinks it unerringly lucky and successful. And, finally, moving into the arena of YA fiction, there are powerful luck motifs in perhaps the single most successful, genre-defining phenomenon of the early 2000s, the fantasy-dystopian-sci-fi trilogy of novels, *The Hunger Games* (2008–10), created by Suzanne Collins. The dramatic essence – and the marketing, both fictional and real – of the Hunger Games phenomenon was encapsulated in the pregnant tagline of both the books and the film adaptations (2012–15), a slogan that was borrowed from the futuristic lottery and the game of survival that it generates, the hunger games, which are at once a substitute for war and a devious mechanism for populist totalitarian control. The slogan is a luck motif and a luck story all in one: 'May the odds be ever in your favor.'[26]

What can this rich but impossibly varied ragbag tell us about contemporary luck stories and the paraliterature of children's writing? A first aspect to note is how playfully complex even the simplest tales for the youngest readers are, suggesting that luck, far from being a simplistic motif, is a device for layered thinking, even in its most elemental form. Both *Little Miss Lucky* and *Did I Ever Tell You How Lucky You Are?* are strikingly alert to the shadow-play of luck, to the ways in which good luck constantly contains, and exists in relation to, its opposite, bad luck, and so to other, possible, imagined stories and lives. These stories are deftly aware of themselves as stories, little experiments in metanarrative that powerfully suggest something at the heart of the argument of this book also: that luck is bound up with storytelling, not incidentally but fundamentally and essentially. Little Miss Lucky, at home in Horseshoe House, seems to tumble from scare to disaster to loss: locked out of her house, blown into the air, dumped on a haystack, terrified by a talking tree, she, we and our avuncular narrator repeatedly ask as a refrain, 'I wonder why this story is called *Little Miss Lucky*?'[27] The answer – so simple and conventional as to amount to another playful 'meta' nod to both its parent and child readers – is that it was all a dream. Little Miss Lucky is lucky because when she wakes up she realizes that none of those feared things actually happened to her. Dr Seuss's tongue-twisting poem-story is not so dissimilar: the young narrator, perched atop a cactus, is taught a lesson by 'an old man in the Desert of Drize'[28] about what to do when things are going bad:

> Just tell yourself, Duckie,
> you're really quite lucky!
> Some people are much more …
> oh, ever so much more …
> oh, muchly much-much more
> unlucky than you![29]

Hardly the most altruistic of moral lessons, at least apparently, this notion nevertheless allows the old man to unleash a panoply of imagined, worse, alternative lives. Most of these alternatives are nonsense elaborations of typical mid-twentieth-century (Western) lives, work lives of repetitive drudgery, tough labour, pointless toil (e.g. Mr Potter, who is a 'T-crosser and I-dotter' in a 'I-and-T factory'[30]), or dealing with mad machines, snarled traffic and oddballs or loners (e.g. Harry Haddow, who has no shadow). Just one or two of the old man's imaginings veer into the metaphysical and the magical, for example conjuring up how lucky you are not to be a radish, or not to be a thing, especially a thing abandoned or forgotten ('thank goodness you're not something someone forgot […] like a rusty tin coat-hanger hanging in space').[31] Lucky is thus someone or something you are not, the life not lived, the counterfactual present or future (a pattern of thinking we have seen before); feeling lucky, understanding luck, the old man seems to suggest, means imagining other lives, projecting the stories and situations of all those who are worse off than you. Regarding the luck of others begins to look here like an ethical, even a political, position, akin to Sontag's 'regarding the pain of others',[32] at a minimum an act that opens up the possibility of an ethical understanding, the choice between selfish relief at one's own good luck and empathetic understanding of the 'unluckier' world around us, the forms varied and plural, human and non-human, that unluck can take. In Chapter 2, we referred to Jackson Lears's remarkable study, *Something for Nothing*, in which Lears bound up the story of luck in American history with an idea of 'grace', variously understood as in creole and slave religion as well as in institutional Christianity. Here again, luck seems to stand in for something like a (modern) notion of grace, even if degraded into its commonplace sense in the saying 'there but for the grace of God go I'.

This is all, admittedly, somewhat heavy-handed as exegesis of a nonsense poem and its colourful Heath Robinson-like illustrations, but that very mismatch suggests something important about how children's simple luck stories can conceal deeper facets of the wider uses and meanings of luck and its stories. Luck is drawn in to these paraliterary, apparently simpler forms and we too are drawn to their elemental familiarity also, and growing out from there, like a chrysalis, it contains and evolves into all its profound, and universal, complexity as a driver of human lives. This is not so different, as a pattern, from the progress from early style to later 'mature' work sketched out earlier in this chapter, and not a bad summation of the force and value of luck stories that this book has tried to capture throughout.

Pre-teen and teen fiction, if anything, play even more elaborate games with these and other tropes of luck, as we might expect from their far more sustained, and formally and psychologically more complex, stories and their reader-writer-protagonist empathies. Lemony Snicket plays constant winking games with his readers, for example providing an alternative book cover for one companion volume to his series, so that his young readers can hide the truth of what they are reading from prying parents and teachers: instead of *A Series of Unfortunate Events*, the fake cover reads 'The Pony Party! Book #1! of a series called *The Luckiest Kids in the World*'.[33] A further, rich illustration of the paratextual framing power of the cover is a 2016 book by Pseudonymous Bosch entitled *Bad Luck*.[34] Bosch (the pseudonym of Raphael Simon) is the author of two series of playful fantasy novels, of which *Bad Luck* is the second of the second series. (The others are *Bad Magic*, 2014, and *Bad News*, 2017; both magic and news are categories we have seen rubbing up against luck themes in previous chapters, as we have seen also with the epithet 'bad'.) Throughout both series, a central conceit and play, as with Lemony Snicket, is that the books are in some way secret and dangerous and that whoever decides to read them is taking their life in their hands: the very act of opening the books brings with it a frisson of excitement. And the back-cover blurb of *Bad Luck* underlines this vividly, while picking up on several tropes and patterns of children's luck stories that we are learning to recognize. It is packed with all the same metaliterary trickery, the play on positives and negatives, on facts and counterfactuals, as well as the familiar links to adventure, fantasy (dragons!), excitement and danger. The overall effect is to transmit a kind of compelling transgressive quality, that 'naughtiness' which is one of the dominant registers across swathes of this sector of contemporary children's writing:

> Reader, beware! This is a BAD book.
>
> A VERY BAD book that will bring you nothing but bad luck.
>
> Luckily no one would want to read it as it is extremely BORING and contains NO ADVENTURE whatsoever.

No magic. No betrayal. And NO DRAGONS.

No flying dragons. No fire-breathing dragons. No dragon hunters.

ABSOLUTELY NO DRAGONS.

The only reason anyone would DARE to read this book is if they are VERY BAD and never do what they're told.

And you always do what you're told. Don't you?[35]

Mechanisms of luck, along with magic, fantasy and danger, seem to be a force for protection and resistance for the young protagonists of many of these stories. But, crucially, their resistance against whatever confronts them is often set up as a civil war within the realm of luck: what confronts them, it seems, is a corrupt or controlled force that also taps into luck dynamics, whether that be the controlled, structured game of the *Hunger Games*, the bad magic of the dark forces in the *A Series of Unfortunate Events* or the *Harry Potter* cycles, or, more banally, the simply incomprehensible world of adults or school or friendship and the like in the *Tom Gates* or *The Diary of a Wimpy Kid* books. In the volume *Hard Luck* in the latter series, for example, we follow our hero Greg's miserable school year, in which he loses his best friend, is bullied and humiliated at school, and is forced to suffer through embarrassing family gatherings. Greg is saved when he turns himself into a kind of pre-teen 'Diceman' (see Chapter 5) and decides to let a roll of his toy 'Magic 8-ball', which he has found under a hedge by a remarkable stroke of luck, make all his decisions for him, freeing him up from his fretful over-thinking and his faltering sense of self-worth. One form of luck challenges and defeats another, or at least provides temporary, possibly illusory, respite from another, that is, from the governing, random chaos of the world and all those forces that lie above, beyond or hidden from our control. To stage this struggle in simple form, whether through the embryonic intuitions of the early style or through the accessible language of children's tales, is no mean feat. Luck stories allow us to do this.

Notes

1 The term's use in English is often traced to Rosalind Krauss, 'Poststructuralism and the "Paraliterary"', *October* 13 (1980): 36–40.
2 Samuel R. Delany, *Shorter Views: Queer thoughts and the politics of the paraliterary* (Hanover, NH: University Press of New England, 1999), p. 210. The inclusion in Delany's list of 'academic criticism' perhaps seems anomalous, but for Kraus also the rejection of 'theory' and the marginalization of the kind of academic discourse it attempted meant it was challenging

canons in its way. Other paraliterary fields that might be included here are the area of self-help and popular psychology, which as noted in Chapter 1 is a prominent area for publications on luck; and the non-literary, 'ordinary' or real-life biography or autobiography, where luck comes through frequently either as an everyday feature of lived life or as its underlying experiential current. A powerful chronicle of the 'fortunate' ordinary life (for which read humanly varied, enriching and enriched) is John Berger's *A Fortunate Man: The story of a country doctor* (1967), in which Berger and his collaborator, the photographer Jean Mohr, follow the devoted community labours of John Sassall, a provincial local doctor in southern England. (The theme was recently reprised by Polly Morland, with photographer Richard Baker, under the title *A Fortunate Woman: A country doctor's story* (2022).)

3 'Luck' as a term seems especially prone to this kind of condescension, but 'chance' too can seem all too banal to some: here is a reviewer commenting on Andrew Miller's book *On Not Being Someone Else*, cited in Chapter 4: 'Opening Miller's book, I braced myself for musings on the *gimmicky* film *Sliding Doors*. There was no need to worry, however, since Miller disarmingly *mentions his own embarrassment* in talking about the book's theme and turns the conversation toward literature that resists easy conclusions. *Trite speculations about the role of chance* are quickly put to rest by David Copperfield's conversation-stopper: "Suppose we had never been born!"' (Matthew Rubery, 'Stop reading like a critic', *Public Books* (14 January 2021), at https://www.publicbooks.org/stop-reading-like-a-critic/ (emphasis added)).

4 Philip K. Dick, *The Game-Players of Titan* (1963) (London: Voyager, 2008). The novel appeared in the year following his most celebrated novel, *The Man in the High Castle* (1962), an elaborate work of counterfactual (and indeed counter-counterfactual) fiction which is also steeped in the thematics of luck, not least through its use of the *I Ching* as a plot device.

5 See Chapter 2 on *Monopoly*.

6 Dick, *Game-Players,* pp. 106, 157 (emphasis in the original).

7 On these early phases of Stoppard's career, see Hermione Lee, *Tom Stoppard: A life* (London: Faber and Faber, 2020), pp. 101–27. Lee's biography and Stoppard's repeated assertion in interviews that he feels he has led a 'charmed life' point to a personal fascination with the problematic gift of luck (see for example *Tom Stoppard: A charmed life*, BBC documentary, 16 September 2021).

8 See Marek Haltof, *The Cinema of Krzysztof Kieślowsk:. Variations on destiny and chance* (New York: Wallflower, 2004); Yvonne Ng, 'Fate and choice in Kieślowski's *Blind Chance*', *Kinema* (Fall 2005), at https://openjournals.uwaterloo.ca/index.php/kinema/article/view/1088/1266.

9 Elsaesser, 'Performative', p. 67.

10 Edward Said, *On Late Style: Music and literature against the grain* (London: Bloomsbury, 2006).

11 See Alison James, *Constraining Chance: Georges Perec and the Oulipo* (Evanston, IL: Northwestern University Press, 2009); Motte, 'Clinamen redux'. For other formal avant-garde experiments with chance, see Iversen, *Chance*; Lejeune, *Radical*.

12 See respectively Georges Perec, *La Disparition* (1969), in English as *A Void*, trans. Gilbert Adair (London: Harvill, 1994); Georges Perec, *Les Revenentes* (1972), in English as *The Exeter Text: Jewels, secrets, texts*, trans. Ian Monk in *Three by Perec* (London: Harvill, 1996); Raymond Queneau, *Cent mille milliards de poèmes* (1961), in English as *One Hundred Million Million Poems*, trans. John Crombie (Paris: Kickshaws, 1983).

13 Marina Warner, *Once Upon a Time: A short history of the fairy tale* (Oxford: Oxford University Press, 2014).

14 On fairy tale, fable and children's literature as an educational tool, see Warner, *Once Upon a Time*, pp. 98, 108–9, 125–6.

15 Adam Phillips, 'Afterword', in *Great Fairytales. IV: Quests and Riddles*, supplement to *The Guardian* (October 2009), p. 34 (emphasis in the original).

16 Lewis Carroll, *Alice's Adventures in Wonderland* (1865), chapter 1 (full text available at Project Gutenberg, at https://www.gutenberg.org/files/11/11-h/11-h.htm).

17 Carlo Collodi, *Le avventure di Pinocchio: Storia di un burattino* (1883), in English as *The Adventures of Pinocchio*, trans. Ann Lawson Lucas (Oxford: Oxford University Press, 2000).

18 Collodi, *Pinocchio*, p. 7. (Quotations are from the Lawson Lucas translation.)

19 Collodi, *Pinocchio*, pp. 10, 66, 77.

20 Collodi, *Pinocchio*, p. 36.

21 Collodi, *Pinocchio*, p. 118.

22 On Collodi and the genesis of the book, see Ann Lawson Lucas, 'Introduction', in Collodi, *Pinocchio*, pp. vii–xlvii.
23 The leap to the near present should not be taken to imply there is any dearth of examples in the intervening period. On the contrary, the mid-twentieth century is just as steeped in instances of children's luck stories. A sample might include: the comics adventure strip *Tim Tyler's Luck*, created by Lyman Young in 1928 and still appearing in the 1990s; the lucky Disney character Gladstone Gander, created in 1948, cousin to the perennially bungling Donald Duck and another figure endowed with natural good luck; and the picture book for young readers by Isaac Bashevis Singer, a retelling of an old Yiddish tale, called *Mazel and Shlimazel, or, The Milk of a Lioness*, trans. Elizabeth Shub (New York: Farrar, Straus and Giroux, 1967).
24 Angela Carter, *Wise Children* (London: Chatto and Windus, 1991).
25 There is a strikingly large pool to draw on: as an illustration, an online search of books in the area of children's literature currently available on Amazon UK (summer 2021) merely with 'luck' or 'lucky' in the title gives well over 50 examples. As if to underline the point, just as this book was going to proofs, in August 2022, the Disney+ streaming channel released a new children's animation feature film called *Luck* (dir. Peggy Holmes). The film tells a fascinatingly convoluted tale of an unlucky young girl who, Alice-style, falls into a hidden fantasy realm, where good luck and bad luck are manufactured as materials and propelled back into the world of humans.
26 See Roger Hargreaves, *Little Miss Lucky* (London: Thurman, 1984); Dr Seuss, *Did I Ever Tell You How Lucky You Are?* (New York: Random House, 1973); Liz Pichon, *Tom Gates: A tiny bit lucky* (New York: Scholastic, 2014); Jeff Kinney, *Diary of a Wimpy Kid: Hard luck* (New York: Amulet, 2013); Lemony Snicket, *A Series of Unfortunate Events*, 13 vols (New York: HarperCollins, 1999–2006); J. K. Rowling, *Harry Potter*, 7 vols (London: Bloomsbury, 1997–2007) (for the 'liquid luck' potion, see *Harry Potter and the Half-Blood Prince* (London: Bloomsbury, 2005), pp. 177–83); Suzanne Collins, *The Hunger Games*, 3 vols (New York: Scholastic, 2008–10).
27 Luck turns up incidentally as a theme in a number of other *Mister Men* and *Little Miss* volumes, not least in the accident-prone *Mr Bump* (1971), or in a number of franchise follow-up stories written after Roger Hargreaves's death by his son Adam Hargreaves (e.g. *Little Miss Lucky and the Naughty Pixies*, 2008).
28 Dr Seuss, *Did I Ever*, p. 1.
29 Dr Seuss, *Did I Ever*, p. 3.
30 Dr Seuss, *Did I Ever*, p. 22.
31 Dr Seuss, *Did I Ever*, p. 45.
32 Susan Sontag, *Regarding the Pain of Others* (New York: Farrar, Straus and Giroux, 2003).
33 Lemony Snicket, *Lemony Snicket: The unauthorized autobiography* (New York: HarperCollins, 2002). On this trick and other ways these books and their child readers use them as a means to manage moral and psychological risk, see Margaret Mackey, 'Risk, safety, and control in young people's reading experiences', *School Libraries Worldwide*, 9.1 (2003): 50–63.
34 Pseudonymous Bosch, *Bad Luck* (New York: Little, Brown, 2016).
35 Bosch, *Bad Luck*, back-cover blurb (capitals in the original).

Afterword

The approach of this book to modernity and its multiple intersections with luck's fascinating fictions has been pitched somewhere between a panoramic study of millennial traditions in the modern and a localized analysis of luck beliefs at specific times and places in cultural history: somewhere between *longue durée* and *histoire événementielle*, as the Annales school of historiography might have termed it. Both perspectives are valid, indeed essential, but the pitch here has rather been somewhere on a middle path, intent on capturing a certain 'conjuncture' in images of luck that has sustained itself over a century and more, a conjuncture that has shaped luck stories and charged them with a keen potential energy, as ancient traditions and tropes were adapted to a dynamic, disorienting modernity. This modernity brought with it, variously and unevenly, a destabilizing loss of faith in God and a rise of new scientific paradigms, a fragmentation of the human subject and of notions of space and time (and space-time), the crystallization of the rational, controlling (at its extreme, totalitarian) power of the modern nation-state, a distortion of form, eye and voice in the dizzying forms of modern art, a displacement, if not a destruction, of the human by advancing technology, by expanding and collapsing global empires, and by an Anthropocenically damaged nature. And so on. All of these grand vectors of human history over the course of the long twentieth century have underpinned, fed into and fed on the patterns of how we have told stories about luck. Even if these stories often came with only the barest, intuitive grasp of such deep historical processes, they nonetheless manifested a profound sensitivity to the experience of human life under their aegis. Those patterns are what we have been intent on teasing out and tracking in this book, first through the origins, associations and meanings of the lexicon of luck, then through its characteristic numbers and places, figures and identities, values, experiences and cultural positionings, suggesting how all these have shaped the varicoloured spectrum of modern luck stories. Such stories have long been and continue to be operative devices for navigating the uncertainty of the (modern) world.

The luck conjuncture of the long twentieth century, like all such phenomena, is unstable but unlikely to come to any neat, abrupt endpoint (although it might look that way in retrospect to our successors). Luck rolls on along its human-universal path, figuring and reconfiguring itself as it goes. But we can perhaps point in closing to some signals of a new configuration, or rather a new mix of old and new, if we glance at some of the ways in which the digital contemporary is already reshaping our self-perceptions and our stories in relation to luck. And since we started this book with a focus on words, we can hang these final comments on the hook of three all too familiar neologisms that powerfully evoke the transformed world of the early twenty-first century: Google, Facebook and Covid.

For digital archaeologists, the brief timespan of the Age of the Internet already splits neatly in two: BG and AG, Before Google and After Google.[1] It is telling to note, then, that a constituent feature of the early Google interface (again, earliness seems pertinent), from its inception in 1998, was a mysterious option that sat alongside the standard 'Google Search' button on www.google.com, which read 'I'm feeling lucky'.[2] Clicking on 'I'm feeling lucky' took the user directly to a webpage that Google's algorithm had guessed would be the most useful to them, skipping the intermediary stage of a list of relevant sites and further laborious trawling and selecting. It thus seemed to offer all the virtues and potential energy of a lucky gamble, a spin of the wheel: speed, freedom and open access to the proliferating millions, soon to be billions, of online sites, data and connections (Google was of course named for the vast number 'googol', 10^{100}). It suggested an unpredictability that was all of a piece with optimistic, utopian ideals of the early web. The leap of faith into the divination of the 'I'm feeling lucky' button tied the experience of search to human affect ('feeling'), and the 'I' of the searcher to the higher knowledge of the algorithm, as well as to the joy of finding a single site in an instant, like an epiphany. John Durham Peters writes eloquently of the hybrid of old and new offered here, in a way that is precisely in line with the old–new mix of modern luck:

> At the Google search page, you stand on the threshold and knock. Two alternatives await you side by side: the ancient one of divination and the modern one of Google. The cultural resonance of the company comes in pairing its computerized claim to trawl the totality with I Ching-like mystery. Ancient, modern; God, Google – the continuities are clear.[3]

As with many of the luck-generating systems we have encountered, however, the seductions of Google's 'I'm feeling lucky' hid a darker side, a rigged, markedly non-random bias in the system. In practice, the feature was a loss-leader for the corporation: the halo of feeling and sheer fun it provided deprived Google of advertising revenue, since it skipped the results-list page, which from quite early on in the corporation's history began to include revenue-generating rankings and adverts linked to the search terms. Furthermore, the 'lucky' leap into a specific, unpredictable webpage result was in fact simply a link to the top page generated by the algorithm, which was increasingly determined by detailed tracking of the user's previous searches, channelling them towards a self-replicating sameness. This self-reinforcing bubble was what was being hidden by this little luck fantasy, a higher-order system determining every step of an apparently open choice of freedom, connoted by luck.[4]

The smoke and mirrors of Google's 'I'm feeling lucky' point us towards the wider dark turn in the workings of the web and the damage it does to civic society and the polity as diagnosed by critics such as Shoshana Zuboff through her notion of 'surveillance capitalism'.[5] From Google's tracking to Facebook likes to any number of other operators in the field who gather and monetize knowledge of their users in minute detail, there is a direct line towards a chilling new determinism, which – very like the providential determinism of monotheism or the mathematical determinism of positivism – dreams of total knowledge, a perfect grasp of cause and effect and thus of an elimination of all uncertainty, chance and the free play of luck. The more Facebook knows about you, the more it can detect and predict your likes and preferences, the more it can direct and control your choices, your field of vision, and in due course, in its most dystopian version, your very beliefs and existence. As Tim Wu put it, reviewing Zuboff,

> to know everything about someone is to create the power to control that person. We may not be there yet, but there is a theoretical point – call it the Skinnerlarity[6] – where enough data will be gathered about humanity to predict, with some reasonable reliability, what everyone on earth will do at any moment. That accomplishment would change the very structure of experience. As the legal scholar Jonathan Zittrain has said, it would make life 'a highly realistic but completely tailored video game where nothing happens by chance'.[7]

This challenge to luck is already underway, according to recent sociology of sex and love in the digital world. Cupid and Fortuna have long been sister deities, deeply intertwined in myth, motif and story: both love and luck are blind, both strike in an instant, both operate through a kind of magic (helped along by potions and philtres) and both lead to a fall (falling in love, the throw of the dice) that can also be a form of happiness. In the secular modern age of romance, at least, love and luck have conjoined through affect and encounter, through the chance meeting of two people who may or may not become soulmates. In this book, we have seen how this has been extended into modern love journeys and love encounters, which are also often modern luck stories, in films such as *Brief Encounter*, *Before Sunrise* and *Casablanca*. But the world of online twenty-first-century love, according to studies such as Marie Bergström's *The New Laws of Love*, is very different as an experience, and, we might add, has a starkly different narrative design.[8] Bergström's focus is on the privatization of the sphere of intimacy through online platforms, taken away from social and civic spheres such as school, work, family and friends where partners might have been found before now. Encounters today take place in the private digital space of dating sites and apps, in a controlled environment that is knowingly pre-populated, by user and algorithm in tandem, with chosen types and features, including an untroubled application of exclusions and prejudices (of ethnicity, colour, sexuality, ability, etc.). Love is thus no longer blind at all, in the romantic sense, nor even socialized and public as in the rituals of arranged marriage and matchmaking. It is concertedly cut off from the vagaries of luck, the heady experience of the chance encounter, the risk and thrill of rejection or taboo-breaking, and the myth of love at first sight. Much like the bait-and-switch trick of Google's 'I'm feeling lucky', an apparently ideal freedom of choice from an open field of vast possibility offered by the online universe is engineered into something close to its inverse, through the selective narrowing of options and the filtering power of algorithms. As Bergström puts it, 'far from pairing users at random, online dating is characterized by assortative matching'.[9] And we can take the term 'matching' here to stand both for the matchmaking of sexual partners and for a generic homogeneity, a matching of similar types, in contrast to a kind of luck in love that once valued variety and difference, and the myth of love as challenging boundaries and hierarchies.

Covid-19 also, in its disconcerting, destabilizing way, has forced us to confront our lack of agency, our confusion in the face of higher orders of data and bits, and thus our uneasy relationship to luck in these contemporary and confused times. If privatization and homogeneity have proven to be dangerous by-products of the new structures of digital space in the twenty-first century, constricting the unpredictable, draining the chances of stories of luck, the pandemic too has shut down the social spaces of encounter, reinforced hierarchies, collapsed the potential for self-making and self-discovery brought by adventure, journeying in the world, social interaction and all the spaces, lines and determinants of luck that we have explored in this book. Further, it has trained us all to become amateur statisticians and epidemiologists, while at the same time laying bare our struggle to contain an anxious sense of randomness, of the sheer good and bad luck of who falls victim to the disease. Covid has been a continual game of risk and chance, gambles played out by more or less competent state actors and governments, by medical experts and organizations, public health officials and pharma; and, crucially, by billions of individuals, each of us deciding on acceptable levels of risk versus reward, states of exception versus normality. If the science presented us with a crash course in the numbers of probability, exponential growth, population risk and the like, the stories of Covid, the states of being it has created within a kind of 'pandemic modernity', which feels like a suspended but also hyperbolic variant of the modernity we have been tracking in this book, have also in some sense recalibrated our sense of luck. We know more than ever, in the face of Covid and its after-effects, that luck is everywhere, that luck is all around us. Every time we leave our homes now, encounter family and friends, step onto a bus or train, take off or put on a mask, count the days since our last vaccine, we calculate a risk, assess our chances, give ourselves over to luck, more often than not improvising that familiar combination of old luck intuitions and new luck calculations. These scenes from countless stories of the Covid everyday in spring 2022 (as I write this Afterword) suggest perhaps that it is at the moment of stepping out of lockdown or zero Covid, in the transition to something after, that we will see the full force and complexity of our Covid luck calculations. The luck stories of the twenty-first century are likely to be found not so much in stories of a catastrophic pandemic modernity as in stories of a rumbling, troubling, messy and ever-present endemic luck.

Notes

1 See for example John Naughton, 'Platform power and responsibility in the attention economy', in Martin Moore and Damian Tambini, eds, *Digital Dominance: The power of Google, Amazon, Facebook, and Apple* (Oxford: Oxford University Press, 2018), pp. 371–95 (p. 385).
2 See illustrations at Version Museum, 'History of Google Search', at https://www.versionmuseum.com/history-of/google-search. Google has tried out variations on the theme, offering alternatives such as 'I'm feeling curious' and 'I'm feeling adventurous', terms and emotions we have seen linked to luck in this book. The feature is still there on some versions of

Google's homepage, but in practice it was rendered redundant after 2010 when Google added instant 'as you type' results to the search box, and also by the embedding of search-only boxes in browsers, which has led to a decline in the prominence of the Google homepage. The phrase itself is commonly assumed to be a echo of Harry Callahan's iconic catchphrase from the *Dirty Harry* films, 'Do I feel lucky?', discussed in Chapter 3.

3 John Durham Peters, 'God and Google' in *The Marvelous Clouds: Toward a philosophy of elemental media* (Chicago, IL: University of Chicago Press, 2015), pp. 315–76 (p. 332). Peters also notes the affective charge of the 'I', evoking the figure of the gambler, dear to Jackson Lears (*Something for Nothing*) and to several of the texts analysed in this book: 'this is me, the first person, entering the web, and also the cry of the gambler, muttering incantations over something he can't control' (p. 337).

4 Against this filter bubble, rival search engine 'DuckDuckGo' promised never to track users' histories to shape its search results, an offer it underlined by a parodic variant of Google's 'I'm feeling lucky' feature, called 'I'm feeling Ducky'.

5 Zuboff, *The Age of Surveillance Capitalism*.

6 Wu refers here to behaviourist B. F. Skinner, playing also on the notion of the AI 'singularity', the hypothetical point at which machine intelligence will outstrip human intelligence.

7 Tim Wu, 'Bigger Brother', *New York Review of Books*, 47.6 (9 April 2020): 18–19 (p. 19).

8 Marie Bergström, *The New Laws of Love: Online dating and the privatization of intimacy* (Cambridge: Polity, 2022).

9 Bergström, *The New Laws*, p. 102.

References

Abney, Wesley, *Random Destiny: How the Vietnam War draft lottery shaped a generation* (Wilmington, DE: Vernon Press, 2019).
'Aby Warburg Mnemosyne Atlas', at http://www.engramma.it/eOS/core/frontend/eos_atlas_index.php?lang=eng (accessed 2 August 2022).
Adams, James Truslow, *The Epic of America* (Garden City, NY: Blue Ribbon Books, 1931).
Alford, Steven E., 'Chance in contemporary narrative: The example of Paul Auster', *Lit: Literature Interpretation Theory*, 11.1 (2000): 59–82. https://doi.org/10.1080/10436920008580257.
Amis, Kingsley, *Lucky Jim* (1954) (London: Penguin, 2000).
Angier, Carole, *Speak, Silence: In search of W. G. Sebald* (London: Bloomsbury Circus, 2021).
Attridge, Derek, 'The postmodernity of Joyce: Chance, coincidence, and the reader', in *Joyce Effects: On language, theory, and history* (Cambridge: Cambridge University Press, 2000), pp. 117–25.
Augé, Marc, *Non-Places: Introduction to an anthropology of supermodernity*, trans. John Howe (London: Verso, 1995).
Augé, Marc, *Casablanca: Movies and memory*, trans. Tom Conley (Minneapolis: University of Minnesota Press, 2009).
Baciati dalla fortuna (dir. Paolo Costella, 2011).
Barker, Stephen, 'Critic, criticism, critics', in Christopher Bigsby, ed., *The Cambridge Companion to Arthur Miller* (Cambridge: Cambridge University Press, 2011), pp. 259–72.
Barry Lyndon (dir. Stanley Kubrick, 1975).
Barthes, Roland, 'Structure du fait divers' (1962), in English as 'Structure of the *fait-divers*', in *Critical Essays*, trans. Richard Howard, (Evanston, IL: Northwestern University Press, 1972), pp. 185–95.
Baudrillard, Jean, *L'Échange impossible* (1999), in English as *Impossible Exchange*, trans. Chris Turner (London: Verso, 2011).
Baulch, David M., 'Time, narrative, and the multiverse: Post-Newtonian narrative in Borges's "The garden of the forking paths" and Blake's *Vala or The Four Zoas*', *The Comparatist*, 27 (May 2003): 56–78. https://doi.org/10.1353/com.2003.0002.
Bazin, André, *What Is Cinema?*, 2 vols, trans. Hugh Gray (Berkeley: University of California Press, 1971).
Beck, Ulrich, *Risk Society: Towards a new modernity*, trans. Mark Ritter (London: Sage, 1992).
Beckman, Karen, *Crash: Cinema and the politics of speed and stasis* (Durham, NC: Duke University Press, 2010).
Before trilogy (dir. Richard Linklater: *Before Sunrise*, 1995; *Before Sunset*, 2004; *Before Midnight*, 2013).
Being There (dir. Hal Ashby, 1979).
Belletto, Steven, *No Accident, Comrade: Chance and design in Cold War American narratives* (Oxford: Oxford University Press, 2011).
Benanav, Michael, *The Luck of the Jews: An incredible story of loss, love and survival in the Holocaust* (2014), originally published as *Joshua & Isadora: A true tale of loss and love in the Holocaust* (Guilford, CT: Lyons Press, 2008).
Benjamin, Walter, *The Arcades Project*, trans. Howard Eiland and Kevin McLaughlin (Cambridge, MA: Belknap Press of Harvard University Press, 1999).
Berg, Pierre, *Scheisshaus Luck: Surviving the unspeakable in Auschwitz and Dora* (New York: AMACOM, 2008).
Berger, John, *A Fortunate Man: The story of a country doctor* (London: Allen Lane, 1967).

Bergström, Marie, *The New Laws of Love: Online dating and the privatization of intimacy* (Cambridge: Polity, 2022).
Bernstein, Peter L., *Against the Gods: The remarkable story of risk* (New York: John Wiley & Sons, 1998).
Betnitzky, Leora and Ilana Pardes, eds, *The Book of Job: Aesthetics, ethics, hermeneutics* (Berlin: De Gruyter, 2015).
Biard, Jean-Dominique, 'Chance encounters as a novelistic device', *Journal of European Studies*, 18.1 (March 1988): 21–35. https://doi.org/10.1177/004724418801800103.
Bicycle Thieves (dir. Vittorio De Sica, 1948).
Biel, Steven, 'The *Deer Hunter* debate: Artistic license and Vietnam War remembrance', *Bright Lights Film Journal*, 7 July 2016, at http://disq.us/p/2izosqx (accessed 3 August 2022).
Bigsby, Christopher, 'Afterword', in Arthur Miller, *Plays* (London: Methuen, 1994), vol. 4, pp. 251–75.
Biskind, Peter, 'The Vietnam Oscars', *Vanity Fair*, March 2008, at https://www.vanityfair.com/news/2008/03/warmovies200803 (accessed 3 August 2022).
Blastland, Michael and David Spiegelhalter, *The Norm Chronicles: Stories and numbers about danger* (London: Profile Books, 2014).
Blatchley, Barbara, *What Are the Chances? Why we believe in luck* (New York: Columbia University Press, 2021).
Blind Chance (dir. Krzysztof Kieślowski, 1987).
'Bodies across borders: Oral and visual memory in Europe and beyond' (ERC project, 2013–18), at https://cordis.europa.eu/project/id/295854 (accessed 3 August 2022).
Bologna, Corrado, 'Picasso, Apollinaire e la Fortuna', in *I pensieri dell'istante: Scritti per Jacqueline Risset* (Rome: Riuniti, 2012), pp. 70–85.
Bologna, Corrado, 'Immagini di fortuna, fortuna delle immagini', in Silvia Zoppi Garampi, ed., *Fortuna: Atti del quinto colloquio internazionale di letteratura italiana, Napoli 2–3 maggio 2013* (Rome: Salerno, 2016), pp. 13–36
Bordignon, Giulia et al., 'Fortuna during the Renaissance: A reading of Panel 48 of Aby Warburg's *Bilderatlas Mnemosyne*', *Engramma*, 137 (August 2016), at http://www.engramma.it/eOS/index.php?id_articolo=2975 (accessed 3 August 2022).
Bordwell, David, 'Film futures', *SubStance*, 31.1 (2002): 88–104. https://doi.org/10.2307/3685810.
Borges, Jorge Luis, 'El jardin de senderos que se bifurcan' (1941), in English as 'The garden of forking paths', in *Collected Fictions*, pp. 119–28.
Borges, Jorge Luis, 'Examen de la obra de Herbert Quain' (1941), in English as 'A survey of the works of Herbert Quain', in *Collected Fictions*, pp. 107–11.
Borges, Jorge Luis, 'La lotería en Babilonia' (1941), in English as 'The lottery in Babylon', in *Collected Fictions*, pp. 101–6.
Borges, Jorge Luis, *Collected Fictions*, trans. Andrew Hurley (London: Allen Lane, 1998).
Bosch, Pseudonymous, *Bad Luck* (New York: Little, Brown, 2016).
Branigan, Edward, 'Nearly true: Forking plots, forking interpretations: A response to David Bordwell's "Film futures"', *SubStance*, 31.1 (2002): 105–14. https://doi.org/10.2307/3685811.
Brendecke, Arndt and Peter Vogt, eds, *The End of Fortuna and the Rise of Modernity* (Berlin: De Gruyter, 2017).
Brenner, Reuven, Gabrielle Brenner and Aaron Brown, *A World of Chance: Betting on religion, games, Wall Street* (Cambridge: Cambridge University Press, 2008).
Brief Encounter (dir. David Lean, 1945).
Broncano-Berrocal, Fernando, 'Luck', in *Internet Encyclopedia of Philosophy*, at https://iep.utm.edu/luck/ (accessed 3 August 2022).
Brown, Donald E., *Human Universals* (New York: McGraw-Hill, 1991).
Bruno, Giuliana, *Atlas of Emotion: Journeys in art, architecture, and film* (London: Verso, 2002).
Bruzzi, Stella, *Men's Cinema: Masculinity and mise en scène in Hollywood* (Edinburgh: Edinburgh University Press, 2013).
Buergenthal, Thomas, *A Lucky Child: A memoir of surviving Auschwitz as a young boy* (New York: Little, Brown, 2009).
Busch, Christian, *The Serendipity Mindset: The art and science of creating good luck* (London: Penguin, 2020).
Calvino, Italo, *Il castello dei destini incrociati* (1973), in English as *The Castle of Crossed Destinies*, trans. William Weaver (New York: Harcourt Brace Jovanovich, 1979).
Calvino, Italo, 'Lightness', in *Six Memos for the Next Millennium*, trans. Patrick Creagh (London: Penguin, 2002), pp. 3–30.

Campbell, Timothy, 'Bios, immunity, life: The thought of Roberto Esposito', *Diacritics*, 36.2 (Summer 2006): 2–22. https://doi.org/10.1353/dia.2008.0009.

Campe, Rüdiger, 'Defoe's *Robinson Crusoe*, or, The improbability of survival', in The *Game of Probability: Literature and calculation from Pascal to Kleist*, trans. Ellwood H. Wiggins Jr (Stanford, CA: Stanford University Press, 2013), pp. 172–91.

Carrère, Emmanuel, 'Who is the real Dice Man? The elusive writer behind the disturbing cult novel', *The Guardian*, 7 November 2019.

Carroll, Lewis, *Alice's Adventures in Wonderland* (1865), at https://www.gutenberg.org/files/11/11-h/11-h.htm (accessed 3 August 2022).

Carter, Angela, *Wise Children* (London: Chatto and Windus, 1991).

Casablanca (dir. Michael Curtiz, 1942).

Castells, Manuel, *The Information Age: Economy, society and culture. Volume 1: The Rise of the Network Society* (Oxford: Blackwell, 1996).

Cavarero, Adriana, *Horrorism: Naming contemporary violence*, trans. William McCuaig (New York: Columbia University Press, 2011).

Cave, Terence, *Recognitions: A study in poetics* (Oxford: Oxford University Press, 1990).

Ceserani, Remo, *Treni di carta. L'immaginario in ferrovia: L'irruzione del treno nella letteratura moderna* (Genoa: Marietti, 1993).

Charpentier, Jacques, *Justice 65* (Paris: Hautes Chaumes, 1954), in Italian as *Justice Machines*, trans. Guido Vitiello (Macerata: Liberilibri, 2015).

Charpentier, Jacques, *Le Nez de Cléopâtre ou Le sens de l'histoire* (Paris: Berger-Levrault, 1967).

Clegg, Brian, *Dice World: Science and life in a random universe* (London: Icon Books, 2013).

Coffman, E. J., *Luck: Its nature and significance for human knowledge and agency* (New York: Palgrave Macmillan, 2015).

Collins, Suzanne, *The Hunger Games*, 3 vols (New York: Scholastic, 2008–10).

Collodi, Carlo, *Le avventure di Pinocchio: Storia di un burattino* (1883), in English as *The Adventures of Pinocchio*, trans. Ann Lawson Lucas (Oxford: Oxford University Press, 2000).

Conan Doyle, Arthur, 'Silver Blaze', in *The Memoirs of Sherlock Holmes* (1894) (Harmondsworth: Penguin, 1976), pp. 7–34.

Cortázar, Julio, *Los premios* (1960), in English as *The Winners*, trans. Elaine Kerrigan (London: Souvenir Press, 1965).

Crafton, Donald, 'Pie and chase: Gag, spectacle and narrative in slapstick comedy', in Wanda Strauven, ed., *The Cinema of Attractions Reloaded* (Amsterdam: Amsterdam University Press, 2006), pp. 355–64.

Crimes and Misdemeanors (dir. Woody Allen, 1989).

da Col, Giovanni, 'Introduction: Natural philosophies of fortune: Luck, vitality, and uncontrolled relatedness', in da Col and Humphrey, *Cosmologies*, pp. 1–23. https://doi.org/10.3167/sa.2012.560102.

da Col, Giovanni and Caroline Humphrey, eds, *Cosmologies of Fortune: Luck, vitality, and uncontrolled relatedness*, special issue, *Social Analysis*, 56.1 (2012).

da Col, Giovanni and Caroline Humphrey, eds, *Future and Fortune: Contingency, morality, and the anticipation of everyday life*, special issue, *Social Analysis*, 56.2 (2012).

Daniels, Inge Maria, 'Scooping, raking, beckoning luck: Luck, agency and the interdependence of people and things in Japan', *Journal of the Royal Anthropological Institute*, 9.4 (2003): 619–38. https://doi.org/10.1111/j.1467-9655.2003.00166.x.

Dante Alighieri, *Purgatorio*, trans. Robin Kirkpatrick (London: Penguin, 2007).

Deer Hunter, The (dir. Michael Cimino, 1978).

de Grazia, Victoria, *Irresistible Empire: America's advance through twentieth-century Europe* (Cambridge, MA: Belknap Press of Harvard University Press, 2005).

Dehaene, Stanislas, *The Number Sense: How the mind creates mathematics* (Oxford: Oxford University Press, 1997).

Delany, Samuel R., *Shorter Views: Queer thoughts and the politics of the paraliterary* (Hanover, NH: University Press of New England, 1999).

De Martino, Ernesto, *Magic: A theory from the south*, trans. Dorothy Louise Zinn (Chicago, IL: HAU Books, 2003).

Denby, David, 'The luck of the French', *New York Magazine*, 12 August 1985, pp. 56–7.

Derrida, Jacques, 'My chances / *Mes chances*: A rendezvous with some Epicurean stereophonies', trans. Irene Harvey and Avital Ronell, in *Psyche: Inventions of the other, vol. I* (Stanford, CA: Stanford University Press, 2007), pp. 344–76.

Deshaye, Joel, '"Do I feel lucky?" Moral luck, bluffing and the ethics of Eastwood's outlaw-lawman in *Coogan's Bluff* and the Dirty Harry films', *Film-Philosophy*, 21.1 (2017): 20–36. https://doi.org/10.3366/film.2017.0029.
Dick, Philip K., *Solar Lottery* (London: Gollancz, 2003).
Dick, Philip K., *The Game-Players of Titan* (London: Voyager, 2008).
Didi-Huberman, Georges, 'The surviving image: Aby Warburg and Tylorian anthropology', *Oxford Art Journal*, 25.1 (2002), pp. 59–69. https://doi.org/10.1093/oxartj/25.1.59.
Dirty Harry (dir. Don Siegel, 1971).
Doane, Mary Ann, *The Emergence of Cinematic Time: Modernity, contingency, the archive* (Cambridge, MA: Harvard University Press, 2002).
'Dollars' trilogy (dir. Sergio Leone: *A Fistful of Dollars*, 1964; *For a Few Dollars More*, 1965; *The Good, the Bad and the Ugly*, 1966).
Dostoevsky, Fyodor, *The Gambler* (1866), trans. Hugh Aplin (Richmond: Alma Classics, 2014).
Dotti, Marco, *Il calcolo dei dadi: Azzardo e vita quotidiana* (Milan: O barra O, 2013).
Douglas, Mary, *Purity and Danger: An analysis of concepts of pollution and taboo* (Abingdon: Routledge, 2002).
Dr Seuss, *Did I Ever Tell You How Lucky You Are?* (New York: Random House, 1973).
Duxbury, Neil, *Random Justice: On lotteries and legal decision-making* (Oxford: Oxford University Press, 1999).
Dyer, Richard, *Brief Encounter* (London: British Film Institute, 1993).
Dylan, Bob, 'Pledging my time' (*Blonde on Blonde*, 1966).
Dylan, Bob, 'Idiot wind' (*Blood on the Tracks*, 1975).
Eco, Umberto, '*Casablanca*: Cult movies and intertextual collage', in *Travels in Hyperreality: Essays*, trans. William Weaver (New York: Harcourt Brace Jovanovich, 1986), pp. 197–211.
Eco, Umberto, *Foucault's Pendulum*, trans. William Weaver (London: Secker and Warburg, 1988).
Eco, Umberto, *Serendipities: Language and lunacy*, trans. William Weaver (New York: Columbia University Press, 1998).
Edgerton, David, *The Shock of the Old: Technology and global history since 1900* (Oxford: Oxford University Press, 2007).
Edwardes, Tickner, *Lift-Luck on Southern Roads* (London: Methuen and Co., 1910).
Eizykman, Boris, 'Chance and science fiction: SF as stochastic fiction', trans. Will Straw, *Science Fiction Studies*, 10.1 (1983): 24–34. https://doi.org/10.2307/4239525.
Ellis, Carolyn and Jerry Rawicki, 'More than mazel? Luck and agency in surviving the Holocaust', *Journal of Loss and Trauma*, 19.2 (2014): 99–120. https://doi.org/10.1080/15325024.2012.738574.
Ellwood, David, *The Shock of America: Europe and the challenge of the century* (Oxford: Oxford University Press, 2016).
Elsaesser, Thomas, 'Performative self-contradictions: Michael Haneke's mind games', in Roy Grundmann, ed., *A Companion to Michael Haneke* (Chichester: Wiley-Blackwell, 2010), pp. 53–74.
Epstein, Richard A., 'Luck', *Social Philosophy and Policy*, 6.1 (1988): 17–38. https://doi.org/10.1017/S0265052500002661.
Esposito, Roberto, 'The immunization paradigm', *Diacritics*, 36.2 (Summer, 2006): 23–48. https://doi.org/10.1353/dia.2008.0015.
Esposito, Roberto, '*Fortuna* e politica all'origine della filosofia italiana', *California Italian Studies*, 2.1 (2011), at http://escholarship.org/uc/item/5ht7n7p4 (accessed 3 August 2022). https://doi.org/10.5070/C321008978.
Esposito, Roberto, *Living Thought: The origins and actuality of Italian philosophy*, trans. Zakiya Hanafi (Stanford, CA: Stanford University Press, 2012).
Farrell, Joseph, *Honour and the Sword: The culture of duelling* (Oxford: Signal Books, 2021).
Fearless (dir. Peter Weir, 1993).
Festen (dir. Thomas Vinterberg, 1998).
Fifield, Peter, *Modernism and Physical Illness: Sick books* (Oxford: Oxford University Press, 2020).
Fleming, Ian, *Casino Royale* (1953) (London: Pan, 1955).
Forgacs, David, ed., *The Gramsci Reader: Selected writings 1916–1935* (New York: New York University Press, 2000).
Freud, Sigmund, *The Psychopathology of Everyday Life* (1901), trans. James Strachey, vol. 6 of *The Standard Edition of the Complete Psychological Works of Sigmund Freud* (London: Vintage, 2001).

Freud, Sigmund, 'Some character-types met with in psycho-analytic work' (1916), in *On the History of the Psycho-Analytic Movement, Papers on Metapsychology and Other Works*, vol. 14 of *The Standard Edition of the Complete Psychological Works of Sigmund Freud* (London: Vintage, 2001), pp. 309–33.
Frost, Robert, *The Road Not Taken and Other Poems*, ed. David Orr (London: Penguin Books, 2015).
Frye, Northrop, *The Great Code: The Bible and literature* (London: Routledge & Kegan Paul, 1982).
Gallagher, Catherine, *Telling It Like It Wasn't: The counterfactual imagination in history and fiction* (Chicago, IL: University of Chicago Press, 2018).
Gawande, Atul, *Being Mortal: Illness, medicine and what matters in the end* (London: Profile Books, 2014).
Ginzburg, Carlo, 'Conversations with Orion', trans. Giovanni Zanalda, *Perspectives on History*, 45 (May 2005), at https://www.historians.org/publications-and-directories/perspectives-on-history/may-2005/conversations-with-orion (accessed 3 August 2022).
Ginzburg, Carlo, 'Clues: Roots of an evidential paradigm' (1979), in *Clues, Myths, and the Historical Method*, trans. John Tedeschi and Anne C. Tedeschi (Baltimore, MD: Johns Hopkins University Press, 2013), pp. 87–113.
Ginzburg, Carlo, 'A proposito di Nondimanco / Il caso, i casi', *Doppiozero*, 12 April 2019, at https://www.doppiozero.com/materiali/il-caso-i-casi (accessed 3 August 2022).
González García, José M., *La Diosa Fortuna: Metamorfosis de una metáfora política* (Madrid: Antonio Machado, 2006).
González González, Marta, *Achilles* (London: Routledge, 2018).
Gould, Stephen Jay, *Wonderful Life: The Burgess Shale and the nature of history* (New York: W. W. Norton, 1989).
Gould, Stephen Jay, 'Darwinian fundamentalism', *New York Review of Books*, 44.10 (12 June 1997): 34–7.
Gramsci, Antonio, 'Observations on folklore', in Forgacs, *Gramsci Reader*, pp. 360–2.
Greenblatt, Stephen, *The Swerve: How the world became modern* (New York: W. W. Norton, 2011).
Gregory, Alice, 'The sorrow and the shame of the accidental killer', *The New Yorker*, 18 September 2017.
Groundhog Day (dir. Harold Ramis, 1993).
Gunning, Tom, 'The cinema of attractions: Early film, its spectator and the avant-garde', in Thomas Elsaesser, ed., *Early Cinema: Space, frame, narrative* (London: British Film Institute, 1990), pp. 56–63.
Guys and Dolls (dir. Joseph Mankiewicz, 1955).
Hacking, Ian, *The Taming of Chance* (Cambridge: Cambridge University Press, 1990).
Hales, Steven D., *The Myth of Luck: Philosophy, fate, and fortune* (London: Bloomsbury Academic, 2020).
Haltof, Marek, *The Cinema of Krzysztof Kieślowski: Variations on destiny and chance* (New York: Wallflower, 2004).
Hamilton, Ross, *Accident: A philosophical and literary history* (Chicago, IL: University of Chicago Press, 2007).
Hardy, Thomas, *Selected Poetry*, ed. Samuel Hynes (Oxford: Oxford University Press, 1994).
Hargreaves, Roger, *Mr Bump* (London: Fabbri, 1971).
Hargreaves, Roger, *Little Miss Lucky* (London: Thurman, 1984).
Hargreaves, Roger, and Adam Hargreaves, *Little Miss Lucky and the Naughty Pixies* (London: Egmont, 2008).
Haslem, Wendy, Angela Ndalianis and Chris Mackie, eds, *Super/heroes: From Hercules to Superman* (Washington, DC: New Academia Publishing, 2007).
Heidbrink, Henriette, '1, 2, 3, 4 futures: Ludic forms in narrative films', *SubStance*, 42.1 (2013): 146–64. https://doi.org/10.1353/sub.2013.0010.
His Wooden Wedding (dir. Hal Roach, 1925).
Holland, Agnieszka, interview, 2003, on DVD / Blu-ray edition (New York, Criterion, 2015) of *Blind Chance* (dir. Krzysztof Kieślowski, 1987).
Hughes, Robert, *The Shock of the New* (London: BBC, 1980).
If.... (dir. Lindsay Anderson 1968).
'Image of the journalist in popular culture', USC Annenberg, at http://ijpc.org/index.html (accessed 4 August 2022).
Intacto (dir. Juan Carlos Fresnadillo, 2001).
Ipsen, Carl, *Fumo: Italy's love affair with the cigarette* (Stanford, CA: Stanford University Press, 2016).

Irwin, William, ed., 'The Matrix' and Philosophy: Welcome to the desert of the real (Chicago, IL: Open Court, 2002).
Irwin, William, ed., More 'Matrix' and Philosophy: 'Revolutions' and 'Reloaded' decoded (Chicago, IL: Open Court, 2005).
Iversen, Margaret, ed., Chance (London: Whitechapel Gallery, 2010).
Jackson, Robert Louis, 'Polina and Lady Luck in Dostoevsky's The Gambler', in Close Encounters: Essays on Russian literature (Boston, MA: Academic Studies Press, 2013), pp. 45–70.
Jackson, Shirley, 'The lottery', The New Yorker, 26 June 1948.
Jacobs, Harriet, Incidents in the Life of a Slave Girl: Written by Herself (Boston, MA: Published for the author, 1861), available at https://www.gutenberg.org/files/11030/11030-h/11030-h.htm (accessed 4 August 2022).
James, Alison, Constraining Chance: Georges Perec and the Oulipo (Evanston, IL: Northwestern University Press, 2009).
Jerome, M. K. and Jack Scholl Johnson, 'Knock on wood', in Casablanca (1942).
Johnson, Carla, 'The schlemiel and the schlimazl in Seinfeld', Journal of Popular Film and Television, 22.3 (1994): 116–24. https://doi.org/10.1080/01956051.1994.9943676.
Kahneman, Daniel, Thinking, Fast and Slow (New York: Farrar, Straus and Giroux, 2011).
Kahneman, Daniel, Olivier Sibony and Cass Sunstein, Noise: A flaw in human judgment (London: William Collins, 2021).
Kapuściński, Ryszard, Shah of Shahs, trans. William R. Brand and Katarzyna Mroczkowska-Brand (New York: Vintage, 1992).
Kavanagh, Thomas M., ed., Chance, Culture and the Literary Text (Ann Arbor: Department of Roman Languages, University of Michigan, 1994).
Kern, Stephen, A Cultural History of Causality: Science, murder novels and systems of thought (Princeton, NJ: Princeton University Press, 2004).
Kertész, Imre, Sorstalanság (1975), in English as Fateless, trans. Tim Wilkinson (London: Harvill, 2005).
Kinney, Jeff, Diary of a Wimpy Kid: Hard luck (New York: Amulet, 2013).
Kipling, Rudyard, Selected Poems, ed. Peter Keating (London: Penguin, 1993).
Klein, Richard, Cigarettes Are Sublime (Durham, NC: Duke University Press, 1994).
Kosiński, Jerzy, Being There (New York: Harcourt Brace Jovanovich, 1970).
Krauss, Rosalind, 'Poststructuralism and the "paraliterary"', October, 13 (1980): 36–40. https://doi.org/10.2307/3397700.
La Chèvre (dir. Francis Veber, 1981).
Lakoff, George and Mark Johnson, Metaphors We Live By (Chicago, IL: University of Chicago Press, 1980).
Landy, Joshua and Michael Saler, eds, The Re-enchantment of the World: Secular magic in a rational age (Stanford, CA: Stanford University Press, 2009).
Lane, Anthony, 'Economic ruthlessness on the open road in Nomadland', The New Yorker, 27 November 2020.
Larrimore, Mark, The Book of Job: A biography (Princeton: Princeton University Press, 2013).
Lawson Lucas, Ann, 'Introduction', in Collodi, Pinocchio, pp. vii–xlvi.
Lears, T. J. Jackson, Something for Nothing: Luck in America (London: Penguin, 2003).
Lee, Hermione, Tom Stoppard: A life (London: Faber and Faber, 2020).
Leigh, John, Touché: The duel in literature (Cambridge, MA: Harvard University Press, 2015).
Lejeune, Denis, The Radical Use of Chance in 20th Century Art (Amsterdam: Rodopi, 2012).
Lem, Stanislaw, 'Chance and order', The New Yorker, 30 January 1984.
Levi, Primo, Il sistema periodico (1975), in English as The Periodic Table, trans. Raymond Rosenthal (New York: Schocken, 1984).
Levi, Primo, Moments of Reprieve, trans. Ruth Feldman (New York: Simon and Schuster, 1986).
Levi, Primo, Se questo è un uomo (1947), in English as If This Is a Man, and The Truce, trans. by Stuart Woolf (London: Abacus, 1987).
Levi, Primo, 'Il superstite' (1984), in English as 'The survivor', in Collected Poems, trans. Ruth Feldman and Brian Swan (London: Faber and Faber, 1988), p. 64.
Levi, Primo, I sommersi e i salvati (1986), in English as The Drowned and the Saved, trans. Raymond Rosenthal (New York: Simon and Schuster, 1988).
Levine, George, Darwin and the Novelists: Patterns of science in Victorian fiction (Chicago, IL: University of Chicago Press, 1991).

Lewis, Geraint and Luke Barnes, *A Fortunate Universe: Life in a finely tuned cosmos* (Cambridge: Cambridge University Press, 2016).
Leys, Ruth, *From Guilt to Shame: Auschwitz and after* (Princeton, NJ: Princeton University Press, 2007).
Liska, Vivian, 'Kafka's other Job', in Betnitzky and Pardes, *The Book of Job*, pp. 123–45.
Loesser, Frank, 'Luck be a lady', in *Guys and Dolls* (stage première 1950).
Luce, Henry, 'The American century', *Life*, 17 February 1941.
Luck (HBO, Season 1, 2011–12).
Luck (dir. Peggy Holmes, 2022).
Lucky Dog, The (dir. Jess Robbins, 1921).
Lucky Me (dir. Jack Donohue, 1954).
Luperini, Romano, *L'incontro e il caso: Narrazioni moderne e destino dell'uomo occidentale* (Bari: Laterza, 2007).
MacArthur, Sian, *Gothic Science Fiction: 1818 to the present* (Basingstoke: Palgrave Macmillan, 2015).
Macdonald, Helen, *H is for Hawk* (London: Jonathan Cape, 2014).
Machiavelli, Niccolò, *The Prince*, trans. and ed. Russell Price and Quentin Skinner (Cambridge: Cambridge University Press, 2019).
Mackey, Margaret, 'Risk, safety, and control in young people's reading experiences', *School Libraries Worldwide*, 9.1 (2003): 50–63.
Mackie, C. J., 'Men of darkness', in Haslem et al., *Super/heroes*, pp. 83–95.
Manchester by the Sea (dir. Kenneth Lonergan, 2016).
Mann, Karen, 'Kieślowski's narrative conscience: Physical time and mental space', *Quarterly Review of Film and Video*, 19.4 (2002): 343–53. https://doi.org/10.1080/10509200214855.
Marinetti, Filippo Tommaso, 'The founding and manifesto of Futurism' (1909), at https://www.italianfuturism.org/manifestos/foundingmanifesto/ (accessed 5 August 2022).
Marr, Johnny and Morrissey, 'Please, please, please, let me get what I want', The Smiths, 1984.
Masteroff, Joe et al., *Cabaret: The illustrated book and lyrics* (New York: Newmarket Press, 1999).
Matrix, The (dir. the Wachowskis, 1999).
Mazierska, Ewa, 'Moral luck in the films of Woody Allen', *Kinema* (November 2011), at https://openjournals.uwaterloo.ca/index.php/kinema/article/download/1235/1560?inline=1 (accessed 5 August 2022).
Memory Thief, The (dir. Gil Kofman, 2007).
Menkman, Rosa, *The Glitch Moment(um)* (Amsterdam: Institute of Network Cultures, 2011).
Mercier, Vivian, 'The uneventful event', *Irish Times*, 18 February 1956.
Merlin, Francesca, 'Evolutionary chance mutation: A defense of the modern synthesis' consensus view', *Philosophy, Theory, and Practice in Biology*, 2.3 (September 2010), at https://quod.lib.umich.edu/cgi/t/text/text-idx?cc=ptb;c=ptb;c=ptbbio;idno=6959004.0002.003;view=text;rgn=main;xc=1;g=ptpbiog (accessed 5 August 2022). http://dx.doi.org/10.3998/ptb.6959004.0002.003.
Miller, Andrew, *On Not Being Someone Else: Tales of our unled lives* (Cambridge, MA: Harvard University Press, 2020).
Miller, Arthur, 'Tragedy and the common man', *New York Times*, 27 February 1949.
Miller, Arthur, 'Introduction', in Arthur Miller, *Plays* (London: Methuen, 1994), vol. 4, pp. vii–xii.
Miller, Arthur, *The Man Who Had All the Luck* (1944), in Arthur Miller, *Plays* (London: Methuen, 1994), vol. 4, pp. 97–194.
Miranda, Lin-Manuel, 'Alexander Hamilton', in *Hamilton: An American musical* (2015).
Mlodinow, Leonard, *The Drunkard's Walk: How randomness rules our lives* (New York: Pantheon, 2008).
Mogg, Ken, *The Alfred Hitchcock Story* (London: Titan, 1999).
[Mogg, Ken], 'What's a MacGuffin?' (2016), at https://hitchinfo.net/faqs.html (accessed 5 August 2022).
Monod, Jacques, *Chance and Necessity: An essay on the natural philosophy of modern biology*, trans. Austryn Wainhouse (New York: Alfred A. Knopf, 1971).
Moretti, Franco, *The Bourgeois: Between history and literature* (London: Verso, 2013).
Morland, Polly, *A Fortunate Woman: A country doctor's story* (London: Picador, 2022).
Motte, Warren F., 'Clinamen redux', *Comparative Literature Studies*, 23.4 (Winter 1986): 263–81.

Munro, Alice, 'Simon's luck', in *The Beggar Maid* (London: Vintage, 2004), pp. 156–77.
Munro, Alice, 'Chance', in *Runaway* (London: Vintage, 2006), pp. 48–86.
Munro, Alice, *The Moons of Jupiter* (London: Vintage, 2007)
Murakami, Haruki, *Colorless Tsukuru Tazaki and His Years of Pilgrimage*, trans. Philip Gabriel (London: Harvill Secker, 2014).
Murdock, George P., 'The common denominator of cultures', in Ralph Linton, ed., *The Science of Man in the World Crisis* (New York: Columbia University Press, 1945), pp. 123–42.
Music Box, The (dir. James Parrott, 1932).
Nagel, Thomas, 'Moral luck', in *Mortal Questions* (Cambridge: Cambridge University Press, 1979), pp. 24–38.
Naughton, John, 'Platform power and responsibility in the attention economy', in Martin Moore and Damian Tambini, eds, *Digital Dominance: The power of Google, Amazon, Facebook, and Apple* (Oxford: Oxford University Press, 2018), pp. 371–95.
Nelkin, Dana K., 'Moral luck' (2013), in Edward N. Zalta, ed., *The Stanford Encyclopedia of Philosophy*, at https://plato.stanford.edu/archives/win2013/entries/moral-luck/ (accessed 5 August 2022).
New Scientist, *Chance: The science and secrets of luck, randomness and probability* (London: John Murray, 2016).
Ng, Yvonne, 'Fate and choice in Kieślowski's *Blind Chance*', *Kinema* (Fall 2005), at https://openjournals.uwaterloo.ca/index.php/kinema/article/view/1088/1266 (accessed 5 August 2022).
Northup, Solomon, *Twelve Years a Slave* (Auburn, NY: Derby and Miller, 1853); available at https://www.gutenberg.org/files/45631/45631-h/45631-h.htm (accessed 5 August 2022).
Nussbaum, Martha, *The Fragility of Goodness: Luck and ethics in Greek tragedy and philosophy* (Cambridge: Cambridge University Press, 1986).
O Lucky Man! (dir. Lindsay Anderson, 1973).
Ortalli, Gherardo (ed.), *Lotteries, Lotto, Slot Machines: The luck of the draw: A history of games of chance* (Rome: Viella / Fondazione Benetton, 2019).
Ozanam, Yves, 'De Vichy à la Résistance: Le bâtonnier Jacques Charpentier', *Histoire de la Justice*, 18.1 (2008): 153–69.
Passerini, Luisa, ed., *Conversations on Visual Memory* (Florence: EUI, 2018), at https://cadmus.eui.eu/handle/1814/60164 (accessed 5 August 2022).
Pastoureau, Michel, *Green: The history of a color*, trans. Jody Gladding (Princeton, NJ: Princeton University Press, 2014).
Perec, Georges, *La Disparition* (1969), in English as *A Void*, trans. Gilbert Adair (London: Harvill, 1994).
Perec, Georges, *Les Revenentes* (1972), in English as *The Exeter Text: Jewels, secrets, texts*, trans. Ian Monk, in *Three by Perec* (London: Harvill, 1996).
Perec, Georges and Robert Bober, *Récits d'Ellis Island: Histoires d'errance et d'espoir* (Paris: P.O.L., 1994).
Peters, John Durham, 'God and Google', in *The Marvelous Clouds: Toward a philosophy of elemental media* (Chicago: University of Chicago Press, 2015), pp. 315–76.
Pettitt, Clare, *Serial Forms: The unfinished project of modernity, 1815–1848* (Oxford: Oxford University Press, 2020).
Phillips, Adam, 'Afterword', in *Great Fairytales. IV: Quests and Riddles*, supplement to *The Guardian* (October 2009).
Pichon, Liz, *Tom Gates: A tiny bit lucky* (New York: Scholastic, 2014).
Pievani, Telmo, *Serendipità: L'inatteso nella scienza* (Milan: Raffaello Cortina, 2021).
Pinker, Steven, *The Blank Slate: The modern denial of human nature* (New York: Penguin, 2002).
Pirandello, Luigi, *Uno, nessuno e centomila* (1926), in English as *One, None and a Hundred-Thousand*, trans. Samuel Putnam (New York: Dutton, 1933).
Pirandello, Luigi, *Six Characters in Search of an Author and Other Plays*, trans. Mark Musa (London: Penguin Books, 1995).
Pirandello, Luigi, *Il fu Mattia Pascal* (1904), in English as *The Late Mattia Pascal*, trans. William Weaver (New York: New York Review Books, 2005).
Popper, Karl, *The Logic of Scientific Discovery* (1934) (Abingdon: Routledge, 2002).

Poštic, Svetozar, 'Stan Laurel, Oliver Hardy and the concept of laughing through tears in Beckett's *Waiting for Godot*', in Biljana Čubrović, ed., *BELLS90 Proceedings*, vol. 2 (Belgrade: Faculty of Philology, University of Belgrade 2020), pp. 51–65.

Prendergast, Christopher, *Counterfactuals: Paths of the might have been* (London: Bloomsbury Academic, 2019).

Price, Alan, 'O lucky man!', in *O Lucky Man!*, 1973.

Queneau, Raymond, *Cent mille milliards de poèmes* (1961), in English as *One Hundred Million Million Poems*, trans. John Crombie (Paris: Kickshaws, 1983).

Raphals, Lisa Ann, 'Fate, fortune, chance, and luck in Chinese and Greek: A comparative semantic history', *Philosophy East and West*, 53.4 (October 2003): 537–74.

Récits d'Ellis Island (dir. Robert Bober, 1980).

Rescher, Nicholas, *Luck: The brilliant randomness of everyday life* (Pittsburgh: University of Pittsburgh Press, 2001).

Rhinehart, Luke, *The Dice Man* (1971) (London: HarperCollins, 1999).

Richardson, Brian, *Unlikely Stories: Causality and the nature of modern narrative* (Newark, DE: University of Delaware Press, 1997).

Richman, Sophia, 'Lucky in misfortune: A review essay', *Division / Review*, 27.1 (2007): 40–3, at https://www.apadivisions.org/division-39/publications/reviews/eyes (accessed 6 August 2022).

Rond, Mark de and Iain Morley, eds, *Serendipity: Fortune and the prepared mind* (Cambridge: Cambridge University Press, 2010).

Rothe, Anne, *Popular Trauma Culture: Selling the pain of others in the mass media* (New Brunswick, NJ: Rutgers University Press, 2011).

Rowling, J. K., *Harry Potter*, 7 vols (London: Bloomsbury, 1997–2007).

Rubery, Matthew, 'Stop reading like a critic', *Public Books* (14 April 2021), at https://www.publicbooks.org/stop-reading-like-a-critic/ (accessed 6 August 2022).

Rubin, Debra, 'Survivors share tale of love and luck', *New Jersey Jewish News*, 18 November 2008.

Run Lola Run (dir. Tom Tykwer, 1998).

Runyon, Damon, 'From First to Last', at https://gutenberg.net.au/ebooks18/1800711h.html (accessed 6 August 2022).

Runyon, Damon, 'Omnibus', at https://gutenberg.net.au/ebooks11/1100651h.html (accessed 6 August 2022).

Russo, Richard, *Chances Are …* (New York: Alfred A. Knopf, 2019).

Said, Edward, *On Late Style: Music and literature against the grain* (London: Bloomsbury, 2006).

Sandel, Michael, *The Tyranny of Merit: What became of the common good?* (London: Penguin, 2020).

Schatzki, Theodore R., 'Human universals and understanding a different socioculture', *Human Studies*, 26.1 (2003): 1–20. https://doi.org/10.1023/A:1022535817631.

Schivelbusch, Wolfgang, *The Railway Journey: The industrialization of time and space in the 19th century* (Berkeley: University of California Press, 1986).

Schnapp, Jeffrey, 'Crash (speed as engine of individuation)', *Modernism/Modernity*, 6.1 (1999): 1–49. https://doi.org/10.1353/mod.1999.0010.

Schwarz, Daniel R., *Broadway Boogie Woogie: Damon Runyon and the making of New York City culture* (New York: Palgrave Macmillan, 2003).

Sebald, W. G., *Austerlitz*, trans. Anthea Bell (London: Hamish Hamilton, 2001).

Sebold, Alice, *Lucky* (London: Picador, 2019).

Seelig, Tina, 'The little risks you can take to increase your luck', TED Talk, June 2018, at https://www.youtube.com/watch?v=PX61e3sAj5k (accessed 6 August 2022).

Segre, Dan Vittorio, *Memoirs of a Fortunate Jew: An Italian story* (London: Halban, 1987).

Senn, Stephen, *Dicing with Death: Chance, risk and health* (Cambridge: Cambridge University Press, 2003).

Seventh Seal, The (dir. Ingmar Bergman, 1957).

Seven Years Bad Luck (dir. Max Linder, 1921).

71 Fragments of a Chronology of Chance (dir. Michael Haneke, 1994).

Shallow Grave (dir. Danny Boyle, 1994).

Sherwood, Ben, *The Survivors Club: The secrets and science that could save your life* (New York: Grand Central, 2009).

Singer, Isaac Bashevis, *Mazel and Shlimazel, or, The Milk of a Lioness*, trans. Elizabeth Shub (New York: Farrar, Straus and Giroux, 1967).
Sliding Doors (dir. Peter Howitt, 1998).
Smith, Ed, *Luck: What it means and why it matters* (London: Bloomsbury, 2013).
Snicket, Lemony, *A Series of Unfortunate Events*, 13 vols (New York: HarperCollins, 1999–2006).
Snicket, Lemony, *Lemony Snicket: The unauthorized autobiography* (New York: HarperCollins, 2002).
Sontag, Susan, *Illness as Metaphor* (New York: Farrar, Straus and Giroux, 1978).
Sontag, Susan, *Regarding the Pain of Others* (New York: Farrar, Straus and Giroux, 2003).
Stan Lee's Lucky Man (Sky 1, seasons 1–3, 2016–18).
Stanovsky, Derek, 'Stealing guilt: Freud, Twain, Augustine and the question of moral luck', *American Imago*, 63.4 (2006): 445–61. https://doi.org/10.1353/aim.2007.0009.
Stein, Arlene, *Reluctant Witnesses: Survivors, their children, and the rise of Holocaust consciousness* (Oxford: Oxford University Press, 2014).
Stoppard, Tom, *Rosencrantz and Guildenstern Are Dead* (New York: Grove Press, 1967).
Succession (HBO, seasons 1–3, 2018–21).
Superstizione (dir. Michelangelo Antonioni, 1949).
Surdez, Georges, 'Russian roulette', *Collier's Illustrated Weekly*, 30 January 1937.
System, The (Channel 4, 1 February 2008).
Taleb, Nassim Nicholas, *Fooled by Randomness: The hidden role of chance in life and in the markets* (New York: Random House, 2005).
Taleb, Nassim Nicholas, *Black Swan: The impact of the highly improbable* (New York: Random House, 2007).
Tanswell, Adam, 'Meet Stan Lee, the amazing comic man', *Radio Times*, 22 January 2016, at https://www.radiotimes.com/tv/sci-fi/meet-stan-lee-the-amazing-comic-man/ (accessed 5 August 2022).
Tocqueville, Alexis de, *Democracy in America* (1835 and 1840), trans. G. Bevan (London: Penguin, 2003).
Tom Stoppard: A charmed life (BBC, 16 September 2021).
Trading Places (dir. John Landis, 1983).
Treasure of the Sierra Madre, The (dir. John Huston, 1948).
Trotter, David, *Cooking with Mud: The idea of mess in nineteenth-century art and fiction* (Oxford: Oxford University Press, 2000).
Trotter, David, *Cinema and Modernism* (Oxford: Blackwell Publishing, 2007).
Truman Show, The (dir. Peter Weir, 1998)
29th Street (dir. George Gallo, 1991).
Vyse, Stuart, *Superstition: A very short introduction* (Oxford: Oxford University Press, 2020).
Waddington, Raymond B., 'Blind gods: Fortune, Justice, and Cupid in the *Merchant of Venice*', *ELH*, 44.3 (Autumn 1977): 458–77. https://doi.org/10.2307/2872568.
Warner, Marina, *Once Upon a Time: A short history of the fairy tale* (Oxford: Oxford University Press, 2014).
White, E. B., *Here is New York* (New York: Little Bookroom, 1999).
Whitehead, Colson, *The Underground Railroad* (New York: Doubleday, 2016).
Williams, Bernard, *Moral Luck: Philosophical papers, 1973–1980* (Cambridge: Cambridge University Press, 1981).
Wiseman, Richard, *The Luck Factor: The scientific study of the lucky mind* (London: Arrow, 2003).
Wisse, Ruth, *The Schlemiel as Modern Hero* (Chicago, IL: University of Chicago Press, 1971).
Wright, Will, *Six Guns and Society: A structural study of the Western* (Berkeley: University of California Press, 1975).
Wu, Tim, 'Bigger Brother' (review of Shoshana Zuboff, *The Age of Surveillance Capitalism*), *New York Review of Books*, 47.6 (9 April 2020): 18–19.
Young, Kay, '"That fabric of times": A response to David Bordwell's "Film futures"', *SubStance*, 31.1 (2002): 115–18. https://doi.org/10.2307/3685812.
Žižek, Slavoj, 'Chance and repetition in Kieslowski's films', *Paragraph* 24.2 (July 2001): 23–39. https://www.jstor.org/stable/43263628.
Žižek, Slavoj, 'Run, Isolde, run', in Slavoj Zizek and Mladen Dolar, *Opera's Second Death* (London: Routledge, 2002), pp. 197–225.
Zuboff, Shoshana, *The Age of Surveillance Capitalism: The fight for the future at the new frontier of power* (London: Profile Books, 2019).

Index

'accidents' 17, 21, 26, 34n, 72, 83–4, 90, 98, 103, 111–12
Achilles, invulnerability of 79–80, 88–9, 93
Adams, James Truslow 15–16n
Adorno, Theodor 140
African-American literature 121
agency 67, 110, 113
 loss of 103
Aiello, Danny 89
Alda, Rutanya 48
Alice's Adventures in Wonderland 143, 145
Allen, Woody 13, 91
All My Sons 88
'American dream', way of life 10–11, 29–31, 43–4, 49–50, 88, 111
Amis, Kingsley 96n
Anderson, Lindsay 134n
Annales school 153
Annie Hall 91
anti-heroic figures 32
anti-Semitism 104
Atkinson, Kate 75n
Atkinson, Rowan 91
Augé, Marc 64
Auschwitz ix, 93, 103–9
Auster, Paul 76n
Aykroyd, Dan 130

Back to the Future (film series) 81
Bad Luck (book) 149
Ballard, J.G. 99
'banal anonymity' 130–1
Banks, Brenda 80
Barnett, Laura 75n
Barry, Lyndon 96n
Barthes, Roland 131
Baudrillard, Jean 56n, 75n
Bazin, André 131
Beck, Ulrich 35n
Beckett, Samuel 31, 93, 139
Before Sunrise 66, 156
Before trilogy (of films) 66
Being There 96n
Benanav, Michael 104
Benjamin, Walter 35–6n
Berg, Pierre 105
Berger, John 151n
Bergman, Ingmar 99
Bergman, Ingrid 40
Bergström, Marie 156
Bicycle Thieves 131–2

Black Death 98
Blind Chance 68–72, 138, 140
Boccaccio, Giovanni 63, 98
Bogart, Humphrey 40
Boguslaw, Linda 68
Bologna, Corrado 97
Bond, James 133–4n
Bordwell, David 69–72
Borges, Jorge Luis 12, 22, 67, 69, 113–14
Bosch, Pseudonymous 13, 149
Bridges, Jeff 89
Brief Encounter 65–6, 69, 156
Brown, Charlie 52
Brown, Derren 54, 120
Brown, Donald 3, 5
Brownian motion 23
Buchenwald concentration camp 105
Buergenthal, Thomas 105
Butler Samuel 118n

Cabaret (musical) 129
Calvino, Italo 63, 97, 141
The Canterbury Tales 63
capitalism 8, 9, 27, 30, 117n, 126, 134n, 155
Cardano, Gerolamo 113
Carroll, Lewis 143, 146
Carter, Angela 13, 146
Casablanca (film) 40–1, 58–64, 70, 156
Casanova, Giacomo 113
'case' 20, 34n, 68, 74n, 131
Casino Royale 134n
casinos and casino literature 60, 77, 120, 125–8
The Castle of Crossed Destinies 63–4
'casualty' 34n
catastrophe 26, 33, 88; economic 98, 120
chance (as term) 18–23, 142
Channel 4 television (UK) 53–4
Chaplin, Charlie 90
Charbit, Corinne 92
Charpentier, Jacques 114, 116
Chase, Charley 91
Chaucer, Geoffrey 20, 63
children's literature 137, 142–50
Christianity 24, 148
Cimino, Michael 46, 48
cinema, temporality of 66
clairvoyants 24
Clouseau film series 91–2
cognitive biases 9–10

Cold War 75n
Collier's (illustrated *magazine*) 43
Collins, Suzanne 147
Collodi, Carlo 12, 143–6
colloquial terms 27–8
colonialism 8, 117n
colour symbolism 80
Conan Doyle, Arthur 131
conspiracy 24, 61, 77, 94n
contingency, etymology of 2
Cortazar, Julio 118n
Covid-19 pandemic 33, 156–7
Coward, Noël 65
cowboy books and films 43
crash 71, 77, 89, 98–9
Crimes and Misdemeanors 130
Cronenberg, David 99
The Crucible 82
'cult' novels 50
cultural change 7–8
cursing 6, 83, 87–8
Curtiz, Michael 13

Dante 75n
Darwin, Charles 22, 34n
dating sites and apps 156
De Niro, Robert 44, 46–7
De Sica, Vittorio 13
'death marches' 109
Decameron 63, 98
Declaration of Independence, American 19
The Deer Hunter 44, 46–9
Defoe, Daniel 99
Dehaene, Stanislas 39
Dekalog film cycle 140
Delany, Samuel 136–7
Delpy, Julie 66
democracy 8, 10–11, 82, 111
Denby, David 92
Depardieu, Gérard 13, 92
Derrida, Jacques 34n
de Tocqueville, Alexis 16n
Diary of a Wimpy Kid (book series) 150
dice 2, 25–7, 49–53, 79, 124–5
The Dice Man 49–53, 79
Dick, Philip K. 12, 114–16, 138
digital technology 154
Dirty Harry 44, 46–8
disaster 21, 26, 88, 98, 100, 104, 116, 144
disenchantment 9
Doane, Mary Ann 66
Dostoevsky, Fyodor 12, 126–32, 139
The Double Life of Veronique 69, 140
Douglas, Mary 121
Ducournau, Julia 99
duels 43, 45, 47
Dylan, Bob 133n

'early style' 138–42
Eastwood, Clint 13, 44–5
Ebb, Fred 129
Eco, Umberto 35n, 94n, 117n
economics 5, 26–7, 29, 85–6
Edgerton, David 15n
Edwards, Blake 91
Eichmann, Adolf 103

Eisner, Will 80
Elsaesser, Thomas 73, 140
English language 17, 20–1
Enlightenment thought 9
epistemology 23
equilibrium, punctuated 7
Erewhon 118n
Esposito, Roberto 94n
ethnic cleansing 103
etymology 21–2, 26–8
euthanasia 103

Facebook 33, 155
fairy tales 145–6
fait divers 131–2
fast thinking (Kahneman) 9–10
Fateless 93, 105–6
Fearless 89, 98
fertility 80, 85–6, 139
Festen 67–8
Florence 98
folk psychology 70–2
folklore 6–7, 70–2, 142–3
forking-path narratives 22, 67–73, 108, 140
Fortuna 5–10, 20, 24, 26, 63, 79, 85, 97–9, 124–5, 155–6
Fox, Michael J. 81
free association 50
Fresnadillo, Juan-Carlos 77
Freud, Sigmund (and Freudian theory) 50, 95n, 112
Frost, Robert 67
Funny Games 73

Gallagher, Catherine 67
Gallo, George 89
The Gambler (novella) 126–8, 139
gambling 30, 33, 113, 125–6, 128
The Game-Players of Titan 95n, 138–9
de Gaulle, Charles 60
Gawande, Atul 57n
gender 11–12, 14n, 16n, 52, 78, 99, 111, 124, 128, 141
genocide 102–8
Ginzburg, Carlo 34n, 74n, 134n
glitch 43, 53, 81, 103, 110
Goes Wrong (theatre franchise) 95n
good life 5, 19
Google 33, 154–6
Goscinny, René 31
Gould, Stephen Jay 15n
grace 74, 30, 88, 107, 111
Gramsci, Antonio 7, 15n, 71, 143
Greenstreet, Sidney 62
Groundhog Day (film) 71–2
guilt 51, 83, 88, 90, 112
Gunning, Tom 90–1
Guys and Dolls (musical and film) 123–5

H is for Hawk 79
Hacking, Ian 9
Hamilton (musical) 10
Hamlet 41, 98
Haneke, Michael 13, 72–3, 138, 140
'hap' 14n, 19–20, 90

hapless people 90–3
happenstance 6–9
happiness 19–20, 24
Hardy, Thomas 12, 14n
Hargreaves, Roger 146
Harry Potter series 147, 150
Hawke, Ethan 66
Heidbrink, Henriette 70
heuristics 9–10
His Wooden Wedding 91
hitchhiking 74n
Hoffman, Dustin 120, 130
Hofman, Gil 102
the Holocaust 8, 13, 73, 93
    survivors of ix, 101–9, 112–13
horseracing 54–5, 120
Howard, Trevor 65
Howitt, Peter 68
Hunger Games trilogy (books and films) 147, 150
Huston, Anjelica 130

I Ching 56n, 151n, 154
iconography 5–6, 8, 10
If (poem) 134n
If ... (film) 134n
'I'm feeling lucky' (Google) 154–6
immunity 79, 82, 90, 94n, 109, 112
Intacto (film) 77–8, 88, 101–2, 107
Internet age 154

Jackson, Shirley 12, 113–14
Jacobs, Harriet 12–13, 100
James, Alison 141
jellyfish metaphor 84–5
Job (Old Testament) 93
Johnson, Celia 65
Joyce, James 93, 129
Julius Caesar 25
Julius Caesar (play) 6, 98
Justice 65, 114–15
juvenilia 138

Kafka, Franz 93
Kahneman, Daniel 9–10, 25, 39, 66
Kander, John 129
Kant, Immanuel 112
Kapuściński, Ryszard 36n
Keaton, Buster 90–2
Kertesz, Imre 13, 93, 105–6, 110
Khadisha 54
Kieślowski, Krzystof 139–40
Kinney, Jeff 146
Kipling, Rudyard 134n
Kluge, Alexander 73
Koppel, Andrés 77

La Chèvre 92
Lady Luck 80, 124–5
Lakoff, George 17
Landau, Martin 130
Landis, John 130
La'Paglia, Anthony 89
The Late Mattia Pascal 127
Latin 25
    providing roots of English language 19

Laurel and Hardy 90–1, 93
Lawrence, D.H. 52
Lean, David 65
Lears, Jackson 30, 88, 148
Lee, Stan 13, 80–1
leggerezza 97
Leibniz, Gottfried Wilhelm 113
Leone, Sergio 44
Lermontov, Mikhail 43
Levi, Primo ix–x, 13, 97, 103–13
'Lillian' (Runyon story) 121–3
Linder, Max 91
Linklater, Richard 66–8
Little Miss Lucky 147
Lloyd, Christopher 81
lockdown 157
Loesser, Frank 123
long twentieth century ix, 9, 12, 33, 153–4
Lopez, Mònica 77
losers 90–3, 130
lottery winners 90
Luce, Henry 29
luck 3–13, 22–3, 26–7, 30–2, 62, 64, 71, 81, 85, 104–5, 110, 112, 116, 121, 124–5
    affinity with early style 138–42
    bad 92–3, 97, 122–3, 128, 144, 147, 157
    calculations and intuition with regard to 157
    and children's literature 142–50
    'conjuncture' in images of 153
    definition of 17–18, 100
    economics of 26–7
    forms of 7, 150
    good 5–6, 19, 29, 48, 55, 64, 77, 82–90, 97, 101–2, 110, 117n, 129, 144, 147–8, 152n, 157
    language of 13, 17–18, 29–31, 153
    and love 156
    and modernity ix
    and morality *see* morality and moral luck
    and narrative *see* luck stories
    nature and meaning of 3–4
    and pandemic 156–7
    recurrence of 146
    sense of 157
    settings for 58, 91, 121
    shadow play of 147
    use of the word 28
Luck (film) 152n
Luck (television series) 120
'luck-ness' 13
'Luck be a lady' (song) 124
The Luck of Barry Lyndon 96n
luck stories ix, 9–12, 17, 21, 24–5, 30–3, 39–41, 50, 58, 64, 68, 71, 82, 89, 103, 120–1, 124, 129–32, 136–42, 145, 148, 150, 153, 156–7
    archaeology and narratology of 8
    emphasis on heaviness 97
    linked to danger 97
    sociology of 120, 130
Lucky (in *Waiting for Godot*) 31
Lucky Jim 96n
Lucky Luciano 31
Lucky Luke 31
Lucky Man (television series) 80–1

Lucky Me (film) 95n
Lucky Strike cigarettes 31
Lucretius 22

Macdonald, Helen 79
MacDowell, Andie 72
MacGuffin 60
Machiavelli, Niccolò 10, 20, 24, 98, 124
magic 5–6, 9, 14n, 28–9, 54, 79–80, 88–9, 137, 146–7, 149–50, 156
Mallarmé, Stéphane xiii, 35n
Manchester by the Sea 118n
The Man in the High Castle 151n
Mankiewicz, Joseph 123
Mann, Michael 120
The Man Who Had All the Luck 82–6, 89, 138–9
Marinetti, Filippo Tommaso 98–9
masculinity 16n, 29, 48–9, 78, 88
The Matrix 53, 67–8
Mayfield, Julian 133n
'mazel' 6, 129
Mediterranean migrations 74
The Memory Thief 101
Mengele, Josef 106
Mercier, Vivian 43
meritocracy 110–11
metaphors 17, 84–5, 98
Middle Low German 19
Milch, David 13, 120
Miller, Arthur 82–9, 138–9
Miranda, Lin-Manuel 10
Mr Bean (franchise) 91
Mister Men series 146
Mnemosyne Atlas 5, 8, 85
Modern High German 20–1
modernism 51–2
  in literature 93, 98, 128–9
modernity ix, 7–12, 24, 32, 39, 64, 78, 121, 137, 153, 157
  darkest corners of 98
Monod, Jacques 15n
Monopoly (board game) 36n
Monte Carlo 127–8
morality and moral luck 5, 10, 51–2, 67, 82, 87–8, 110–13, 125–6, 139, 145
Munro, Alice 13, 101, 117n, 132
Murakami, Haruki 76n
Murdock, George 14n
Murphy, Eddie 130
Murray, Bill 72
Music Box 91
myth and mythology 5–7, 10–11, 31, 63, 72, 78–80, 93, 115, 156

Nagel, Thomas 110–12
New York 11, 58, 91, 121, 132
Newman, Paul 52
Nomadland 134n
Northup, Solomon 100
novels 7, 10, 116, 131
  modern 21
numbers 24–5, 39–40
  centrality of 32
  vocabulary of 26
Nussbaum, Martha 118n

Orbach, Jerry 130
Oulipo group 141
Oxford English Dictionary (OED) 18–23, 26, 29, 124–5

Paltrow, Gwyneth 68
paradigms
  scientific 153
  shifting of 7
paraliterature 136–8, 142, 147
Parrott, James 91
Pascal, Blaise 109, 113
Perec, Georges 15n, 141
personhood 145
Peters, John Durham 154
Phillips, Adam 143
Pichon, Liz 146
Pinker, Steven 14n
Pinocchio 143–5
Pirandello, Luigi 12, 55n, 127–32, 139
Pliny the Elder 20
Polak, Jack 103–4
Popper, Karl 76n
Popwell, Albert 44
positivism 155
Potente, Franka 69
present book, coverage and structure of 12–13, 30, 137, 153
probability 4, 9–10, 24–5, 39–40, 43, 54, 80, 113, 117n, 157
Propp, Vladimir 142
Pure Luck 92

Queneau, Raymond 141

race and racism 12, 47, 99, 111, 121
railways and train stations 64–6, 73–4
Rains, Claude 60
randomness 4, 23, 51, 82, 105, 157
rape and legacies of rape 49–50, 64, 99–100
religion 5
Renaissance 5–6, 8
Rhinehart, Luke 49, 79
Richman, Sophia 104
risk 26–7, 30, 120, 157
Roach, Hal 91
Robinson, Andy 44
Robinson Crusoe 99
Romance languages 19–21
Rosencrantz and Guildenstern Are Dead 41–3, 47, 61, 64, 138–9
Rosencrantz and Guildenstern Meet King Lear 139
Rowling, J.K. 13, 147
Rumkowski, Chaim 113
Run Lola Run 69–71
Runyon, Damon 12, 96n, 121–5, 130, 132
Russian roulette 43–9, 78
Russo, Richard 56n

Said, Edward 140
'saltimbanque' 97, 144
Sandel, Michael 111–13
Sbaraglia, Leonardo 77

Scandinavian languages 19
schlimazel 6, 91
science fiction 114, 138
Sebald, W.G. 76n
Sebold, Alice 99
Second World War 59
'seedcorn' works 138, 141
Segre, Dan Vittorio 118n
Segui, Pierre 47
self, sense of 51, 87, 133
Sellers, Peter 91
semantic associations 18
Seuss, Dr 146–8
Seven Years Bad Luck 91
The Seventh Seal 47, 101
71 Fragments of a Chronology of Chance 72, 138, 140
sexuality 28–9
Shallow Grave 95n
Shakespeare, William 6, 26, 41–2, 146
Sherwood, Ben 104
silent film 90–3
'Silver Blaze' (Conan Doyle) 131
Simon, Raphael 149
Singer, Isaac Bashevis 152n
Six Characters in Search of an Author 55n
slapstick 91
slavery 30, 64–5, 100
Sliding Doors 68–72
slow thinking (Kahneman) 9–10
Smith, Ali 75n
The Smiths 95n
Snicket, Lemony 146–9
Socrates 52
Solar Lottery 114–15, 138
Sontag, Susan 56n, 148
sortition 24–5, 114–15
space and time 66–7
Spock, Mr 9
Stanovsky, Derek 112
Star Trek 9
stochastic events 24
Stoppard Tom 12, 41–3, 138–9
storytelling 7, 10, 21, 23, 29, 71, 131, 138, 143–6
  demotic 33
  spaces for 63
Strangers on a Train 74n, 130
Streep Meryl 48
succession of events 21–2
suicide 83, 127–8
superheroes 80–2
Superman 52, 80, 82
Surdez, Georges 55n
survivor guilt 33, 83, 107, 112
survivors 33, 98–113, 116
Svevo, Italo 93, 129
Sydow, Max von 47, 77–8, 101

The System (television) 53–5
Take the Money and Run 91
Tao 53
Tass, Nadia 92
Taxi Driver 44
teen fiction 149
Tenerife 77
Three Colours film trilogy 140
Tim Tyler's Luck 152n
Titane 99
Tom Gates books 150
Trading Places 130
trains *see* railways and train stations
The Treasure of the Sierra Madre 95n
Tversky, Amos 9–10
29th Street 89
Tykwer, Tom 69
The Tyranny of Merit 111

Ulysses 93
The Underground Railroad 64

Van Druten, John 129
Veber, Francis 92
Veidt, Conrad 61
ventura 23–4
venture capital 27
Verrick 116
Vietnam war 44–8
A View from the Bridge 82
Vinterberg, Thomas 67–8
voices unheard 12
von Clausewitz, Carl 117n

Waiting for Godot 31, 43, 93
Walpole, Horace 27
Wannsee Conference 103
Warburg, Aby 5–8, 26, 64, 85
Warner, Marina 142
Weber, Max 9
Weimar Berlin 129
Weir, Peter 89
White, E.B. 11, 58
Whitehead, Colson 64
Whitman, Walt 51
Willard, Wilbur 121–3
Williams, Bernard 110–12
Wilson, Arthur 'Dooley' 62
Wilson, Thomas F. 81
Withington, Lillian (Runyon) 121–3
Wu, Tim 155

Yiddish 6, 91, 97, 129

Zemeckis, Robert 81
Zeno's Conscience 93, 129
Zsigmond, Vilmos 46
Zuboff, Shoshana 155

The manufacturer's authorised representative in the EU for product safety is Easy Access System Europe, Mustamäe tee 50, 10621 Tallinn, Estonia, (gpsr.requests@easproject.com).